SUPERVISION

A Synthesis of Thought and Action

ADMINISTRATION IN EDUCATION
Harlan Hagman, *Consulting Editor*

SUPERVISION

A Synthesis of
Thought and Action

WILLIAM H. LUCIO–JOHN D. McNEIL
University of California, Los Angeles

New York
San Francisco
Toronto
London
McGRAW-HILL BOOK COMPANY, INC.   1962

SUPERVISION: A Synthesis of Thought and Action

IV

FOREWORD

CONCEPTS of the role of the educational supervisor have
changed as new practices have been introduced into schools
and as the level of professional preparation of teachers has been raised.
However, in many ways understanding and acceptance of new functions
in supervision wait upon clarification and redefinition of objectives and
responsibilities. If the supervisor proceeds with his work, letting his
activities be determined by circumstances and be directed by his desire
to serve educational needs as they become apparent, few would argue
that his pragmatic approach could not result in sizable accomplishments in improvement of the educational service. However, the more
efficient and effective supervisory procedures and the greater gains in
quality of school operation through educational leadership depend upon
the supervisor's ability to apply to his tasks a clear vision of objectives
and a philosophy adequate to new conditions. Behind good practices lies
good theory, and it is to the explication of sound theory that the authors
of this book have labored.

The terms *supervisor* and *supervision* are words which are both appropriate and plain in meaning. Euphemisms have crept into the professional
vocabulary as though the supervisor by using new terms could avoid the
connotations of "snooper-vision" or industrial bossism in the professional
relationships he develops with teachers. But much can be said for the
directness and clarity of long-standing, respected appellations. If unat-
tractive meanings have been attached to honest words, perhaps the fault
can be corrected by the precise and proper use of those words. One

vii

might argue that if supervision connotes snooper-vision to some persons, the term might equally well connote super-vision, the seeing further, more clearly, and to ends of greater significance than in ordinary vision. The plain words say what needs to be said to attach dignity and importance to the position of the supervisor and to the function of supervision he performs.

More than has sometimes been realized, the educational supervisor has been through long years past a teacher educator. Teachers, particularly the beginning teachers, brought to their work a minimum of preservice professional preparation. The task of the supervisor was to teach teachers, to demonstrate, to coach, to direct. The supervisor was expected, because of professional preparation and successful experience in classrooms, to be able to help teachers who were less prepared, less experienced, less qualified to teach. Textbooks in supervision reflected the concept of the supervisor as expert working with the less expert. Because the function of supervision was held to be largely a teacher-training function, supervision in the secondary school, where teachers were thought to be better prepared for professional work, was little in evidence or was of a different kind than that thought proper and necessary in the elementary school.

With extended preservice teacher education now a part of the preparation of elementary school teachers, the concept of supervision as primarily teacher training has become no longer tenable, though the supervisor will still be involved in the improvement of teaching practice. There will be inadequately prepared teachers, those lacking in skills of teaching, those deficient in understanding of psychological and physiological aspects of human development. The supervisor will continue to find it necessary to help teachers realize the objectives of education. He will find a role of importance in helping teachers achieve satisfaction in their work. But in a new generation of teachers, the relationship of expert and nonexpert should be expected to become a relationship between and among experts, with the professionally prepared teacher bringing recognized expertness to a supervisory conference and the supervisor offering expertness to complement and reinforce the professional competence of the teachers with whom he works. The change in relationship is significant of a new day in which educational leadership, though with differences in function, continues to be supportive and stimulative of movements toward the best the educational provision can offer to a free and dynamic society.

Harlan L. Hagman

PREFACE

WHEN the American people grow impatient with flaws in their schools and in their children or their children's teachers, a different emphasis in supervision is required. Because of more and more vigorous demands on pupils' minds, students of supervision must address themselves to the task of shaping the process and content of supervision in accordance with both ideals and reality. This textbook is written on the assumption that students of supervision—superintendents, principals, teachers, coordinators, and curriculum workers, as well as those in preparation for leadership positions in the schools—have responsibility for exploring, surveying, and mapping new terrain in supervision. To grasp and influence the forces which affect our thinking and behaving is a new requirement to which supervision must accommodate its technique.

The reader is reminded that this is a textbook. It is not a monograph dealing in depth with a small corner of the field of supervision nor is it a treatise which attempts to place the facts and principles of supervision into a coherent system. But as a textbook it draws upon a number of treatises and aims at brevity and simplicity of treatment. Our constant target has been to beckon students of supervision into new paths in order to determine why certain procedures are superior to others for given purposes. As a result of reading this book, it is hoped that the supervisor will respond to an environment of uncertainty with better choices because interpretation rather than prescription is featured. The reader is expected to regard all prescriptions for appropriate action in this book as an

ix

invitation to question and adapt. This is not to say that the authors do not seek to evoke a certain kind and quality of response. On the contrary, there is a deliberate attempt to make a case for three beliefs regarding supervision:

1. We believe that supervision requires a super *vision*—a superior perspective attained by special preparation and position. We argue, for example, that a supervisor's education and responsibilities can provide maximum differentiation of conditions and alternatives, bringing a larger view of the instructional mission and process. To the extent that a person is confined to a particular situation and has only a partial or distorted view of teaching and its ends, he is not a supervisor. As a prerequisite to supervision we would require possession of a methodology which respects (*a*) the learner; (*b*) the disciplined approaches to knowledge; and (*c*) social conditions. The features of such a methodology consistent with philosophical and psychological imperatives are presented in detail. We believe that a supervisor must be a statesman, able to give direction beyond merely ministering to the organization's equilibrium. To this end, the notion of the supervising statesman is a recurring theme in this text.

2. We believe that those accepting responsibility for selected behavioral changes in learners must be held accountable. For this and other reasons, nearly every chapter advances the notion of supervision by objectives. We feel that the observation of results of instructional practice for both immediate and long-term consequences is consistent with the premise that supervision is itself a process of discovering what values are worthwhile and proper for instructional objectives. Paralleling our advocacy of supervision by objectives is our concern that data and propositions from a number of disciplines be made available to those accepting responsibility for supervision. However, we offer these data and propositions as instruments for (*a*) defining situations; (*b*) suggesting promising avenues for experimentation; and (*c*) making more intelligent educational decisions. We do not regard theories from organized disciplines as fixed rules for practice in unique situations.

3. We are committed to the supervisory methods of reason and practical intelligence. The method of reason requires the formulation of explicit purposes to be fulfilled by the school and the direction and dedication of the main energies of all concerned in accordance with these purposes. The method of practical intelligence permits all to judge these purposes. It is necessary to ensure that (*a*) these formulated purposes do not become idols which limit freedom; (*b*) the purposes are reinterpreted through judgment of their consequences by those affected in particular situations; and (*c*) those who are expected to invest their

energies can be committed to the purposes and conduct themselves appropriately.

While this book aims at a realistic conception of what constitutes supervision and suggests ways to do better the things that are now necessary, much has been intentionally left to the reader and instructor. Everything that ought to be known about supervision has not been put into the book.

Part One serves as a point of departure by presenting changing views of supervision and the varied roles associated with supervisory positions. It provides requisite descriptive information by which a supervisor can conduct self-appraisal. It sets the stage for a systematic treatment of the human and technical skills associated with successful supervision.

Part Two aims at giving the reader power in observing and interpreting supervisory situations. Research from many sources is used to help the supervisor translate practical supervisory procedures into their theoretical equivalents; to know not merely as a matter of brute fact that certain arrangements work, but to know how and why they work.

Part Three seeks to put the reader in control of the conditions which effect better human relations and increase supervisory effectiveness. These conditions have to do with the elements in human relations, learning, person-to-person communication, and ways of working toward change.

Part Four focuses on those supervisory skills applicable to the assessment of teacher performance and the methods of research. A rationale for curriculum development is presented to help give direction for decisions about *what* and *how* to teach. The supervisor's appropriation of the subject matter in this section should improve his own scholarship and help him to realize more consciously the nature of inquiry and method in supervision.

The planning of this book was a cooperative venture from its inception. Each author contributed suggestions and materials to chapters written by the other. Responsibility for the writing and content of chapters, however, has been placed: J. D. M. for Parts One and Two and Chapter 12; W. H. L. for Parts Three and Four and illustrative figures.

W. H. L.   J. D. M

CONTENTS

xiii

A visual concept of supervision.

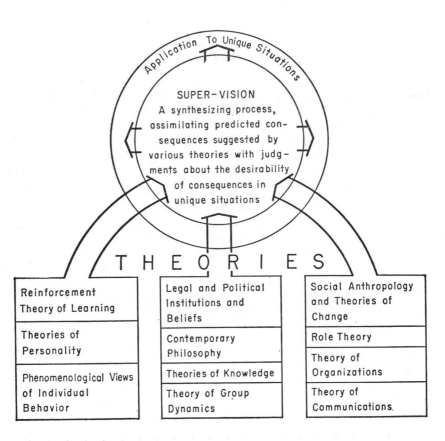

PART ONE

THE NATURE
OF SUPERVISION

1

A HISTORICAL PERSPECTIVE
OF SCHOOL SUPERVISION

HISTORICAL knowledge gives insight into the nature of supervision, for we are wedded in our practice to the thought
of other eras. Such a perspective also focuses attention upon what is
going on today under the name of supervision. Briefly, the history of
modern school supervision shows that in the first quarter of the century
supervision was, in general, dominated by a classical view of man and
institutions. Teachers were regarded as instruments that should be
closely supervised to ensure that they mechanically carried out the
methods of procedure determined by administrative and special supervisors. In the second quarter of the century supervision was conceived
as the practice of human relations. This view endowed teachers with
feelings and motives but often gave less attention to their properties as
reasoning beings. Presently, there are demands for a supplementary
approach which will recognize the importance of both mechanism and
morale, yet stress cognition in its process. By stressing cognition, we
mean helping supervisors and teachers develop the intellectual content
of their tasks, acquiring the theories with which to relate particular consequences to the conditions which produce these consequences.

SUPERVISION BY ADMINISTRATIVE OFFICERS

Supervisory control of American public schools was originally vested
in local civil or religious officers and special committees of laymen with

3

power to visit and inspect schools. In the eighteenth century it was common for official committees not only to become familiar with the methods used in teaching but to "inquire of their proficiency," giving examinations to check on the work. These committees were less interested in improving a deficient teacher than in dismissing him. Early in the nineteenth century the powers and duties of the committees or boards were placed in such positions as "acting visitor," "school clerk," or "superintendent of schools," and upgrading the work of the teacher became a recognized function.[1] Eventually, these positions were filled by professional educators. By 1870, there were twenty-nine superintendents of schools serving as executive officers, with the supervising of instruction as one of their duties in which the improvement of the weak teacher's deficiency was sought more than his rejection. Supervision by administrative officers long remained a primary method for the improvement of teachers, although variations in the method were great. A turn-of-the-century view of supervision was expressed as follows:[2]

In visits for personal inspection and suggestion, I am generous in praise of the good things which I see, and criticize only when I believe my criticism will be received in the right spirit and will probably work improvement. I gave up years ago all criticism for the sake of freeing myself from responsibility. Often I refrain from direct criticism and talk to the principal of the school concerning the teacher's faults. I am reaching the conclusion that I would better always consult the principal before making criticism of any kind. The reason for this will be appreciated by every experienced superintendent.

The best method of helping teachers is, I believe, by example. The superintendent or principal should be always at his post of duty, and always within call of every teacher to assist her in any possible way. Early and late, in season and out of season, school days and holidays, it should be known that he is trying to do all that his time and strength will permit to promote the interests of the schools. He must always say "Come"; must study harder and work more hours than his teachers; must set a pace which his best teachers find impossible to follow. Otherwise, he should resign and let some one who will do more and better work take his place.

The school principalship lagged behind the superintendency in the assumption of a supervisory role, presumably because of the principal's own teaching and clerical duties. Although in 1857 certain principals

---

[1] Fred C. Ayer and A. S. Barr, *The Organization of Supervision,* D. Appleton & Company, Inc., New York, 1928, pp. 7–37.

[2] National Society for the Scientific Study of Education, *The Relation of Superintendents and Principals to the Training and Professional Improvement of Their Teachers,* The Seventh Yearbook, part I, University of Chicago Press, Chicago, 1908, p. 18.

in Boston were released from part of their teaching to assist teachers, the innovation did not spread rapidly. The position of supervising principal did not become well known until the twentieth century.

Supervision of rural schools under the direction of the county superintendent began early in the twentieth century, with supervisors appointed to improve administration as well as instruction. A concrete example of the work of one early rural supervisor is seen in this outline:[3]

1. Installed individual drinking cups in several schools.
2. Had sanitary water jar, or cooler, placed in several schools.
3. Secured the analysis of the drinking water in a large number of schools, with the result that in four cases out of five the water was condemned.
4. In all but one school had window boards installed for ventilating purposes.
5. Had the stoves jacketed in most of the schools.
6. Secured medical inspection of the pupils.
7. Readjusted the seating of the pupils with reference to health and comfort.
8. Emphasized the importance of better hygienic conditions and placed a copy of Dr. Allen's Health Rules in every school.
9. Distributed among the schools four hundred ninety-nine supplementary readers for the individual grades.
10. Enforced the state course of study.
11. Helped the teachers in their efforts to use modern methods and devices of teaching.
12. Encouraged picture study in all the schools.
13. Secured the exchange of pupils' compositions with other school children in Oregon and in other states.
14. Assisted boards of education in securing and retaining capable teachers.
15. Persuaded boards to supply better school equipment.
16. Directed the work of the Teachers' Reading Circle and encouraged many teachers to attend summer schools.
17. Supplied teachers with lists of helpful state and government publications.
18. Held twenty-five public meetings and at ten of these gave stereopticon lectures.
19. Held a district school exhibit or fair.
20. Helped the pupils plan for vocational work during the summer vacation.

[3] L. J. Hanifan, "District Supervision," *The Supervision of Rural Schools,* The Twelfth Yearbook, part II, National Society for the Study of Education, University of Chicago Press, Chicago, 1913, pp. 23–24.

SUPERVISION BY SPECIALISTS

By the turn of the century, a number of new subjects, such as music, drawing, manual training, home economics, and physical education, became part of the curriculum as the result of changing social conditions and the efforts of such pressure groups as organized mothers. Inasmuch as superintendents and teachers were not prepared to teach these new subjects, special teachers and general supervisors were engaged to conduct the classes and to assist regular teachers. Shortly thereafter, a number of cities organized special supervisory departments to provide leadership in connection with language, mathematics, social studies, and science as well as the special subjects.

Problems of authority, function, and procedures arose with the expansion of two kinds of supervisory officers—administrative and specialistic. These questions were commonly asked: "How should school supervision be differentiated from school administration?" "Is supervision the overseeing, inspection, and enforcement of regulations?" "Whose instructions should teachers follow?" In general, supervision was seen as that aspect of administration specifically concerned with raising teachers to a certain standard of performance.

Lowry in 1908 placed responsibility for the policy of instruction upon the principal. "Whether in the regular or in the special subjects [responsibility] should be his and not that of the visiting supervisor, no matter how expert she may be in her particular line." Lowry conceived the principal as releasing the unexpressed talent of the teachers, and the supervisor as working with the principal rather than with teachers directly.[4]

The assumption that teachers were best helped and changed by direction from above was implicit in most of the practice of the day. The way this direction was to be carried out, however, differed according to the qualifications of the individual teacher. Van Sickle's interesting scheme for the treatment of different kinds of teachers by the supervisor not only reflects this differentiation, but also indicates the rising level of professional preparation among teachers:[5]

1. Superior teachers who need no stimulation other than their own ideals of excellence: By the fine standard of work which they maintain and by their

[4] National Society for the Scientific Study of Education, *The Relation of Superintendents and Principals to the Training and Professional Improvement of Their Teachers,* The Seventh Yearbook, part II, University of Chicago Press, Chicago, 1908, p. 19.

[5] *Ibid.,* p. 21.

student-like habits they might, under favorable conditions, set the pace for the entire teaching force. At the present time, this group is a large one. With this group, supervision is chiefly concerned in gaining their cooperation in working out the problems and in bringing their influences to bear on other teachers in tactful ways.

2. Teachers possessing a good degree of executive ability and adequate scholarship of the book-learning variety, who resist change because they honestly believe the old ways are better: They are patriotic defenders of the views and traditions and practices in which they were reared. The greater number of these will as strongly support the new when fully convinced of its advantages; but in the absence of positive orders they resist proposed changes until absolutely conclusive demonstration is furnished in a concrete way. Supervision must confidently accept these conditions and furnish demonstration.

3. Teachers lacking adequate scholarship or practical skill or both, self-conscious and timid, because unacquainted with standards of work and valid guiding principles, desirous of avoiding observation, doing their work in a more or less perfunctory and fortuitous way: Supervision needs to give these teachers courage by an exhibition of standards plainly within their reach and by personal work in their own classrooms.

4. Teachers lacking adequate scholarship or practical skill or both, but not conscious of this lack and therefore unaware of any need of assistance: Some form of positive direction is here necessary in the first stages of supervision.

5. Teachers yet in the early years of their service: Supervision should be able to concern itself chiefly in keeping these teachers in class 1 so far as their personal attitude is concerned. There will, of course, always be differences among them in scholarship and personal power, but all should have guidance in kind and quantity adapted to prevent any of them, even the weakest, from developing the characteristics of class 2, class 3, or class 4. If these new recruits are to be able to lead children to be open-minded, to hold opinions tentatively, to be sure but not too sure, to be willing to give both sides of a question a hearing before reaching a final conclusion, they must keep themselves open-minded. To aid them in doing this, supervision will keep itself free from dogmatism even in dealing with the youngest teachers.

Teachers of class 1, class 2, and class 5 are willing to have their work seen and valued by competent and trusted supervisors. People who know how to do a thing, or who sincerely think they know how, or who sincerely wish to learn how, are neither afraid nor reluctant to have their work seen by any fair-minded person. Supervisors must be both skillful and fair-minded, and their work must prove that supervision means help.

THE SCIENCE OF SUPERVISION

By 1913 the world of material production saw the possibilities of "scientific management," and school leaders were proposing the application of organizational principles to school supervision.[6] These principles called for clear definition of educational ends and coordination of all who work to attain them. The "best" methods of teaching were to be found, and the use of these methods was to be enforced on teachers. The qualifications of teachers were to be specifically defined, and it was the job of supervisors to see that all met these standard qualifications. Supervisors were to keep teachers supplied with detailed instructions and the materials and appliances to be used. They would, of course, place incentives before teachers in order to stimulate desirable efforts.

Scientific management proposed to alter the personal relations between supervisors and teachers. Instead of the supervisors directing the methods of the teachers in a personal and arbitrary manner, as under administrative and specialistic supervision, the primary task of the scientific supervisor was to discover educational "laws" and apply them through the labors of the teacher. The teacher would be expected to find the controlling scientific law through cooperation with the supervisor. Neither was to be personally over the other, for both were under the law of science. The supervisory staff would keep teachers up to standard (1) by involving the labors of the teacher in the social concerns of the community (thereby widening and renewing the teacher's vistas while releasing him from dreary chores at school which dwarf his humanity) and (2) by offering incentives in the form of salary, promotion, social recognition, as well as appealing to his motives for social service.

Scientific supervision was partly a protest movement against the confusion of goals and practices existing at the time.[7]

At present, the chief difficulty is that there are no standards to work to. Schools are simply grinding away without any goal in view. They move in the right direction—they move in the wrong direction. Without a goal their efforts are relatively random, feeble, inefficient. The pupil does not know what to aim at; the teacher does not know how much to require, the principal does not know how high the teacher is aiming; the superintendent has no means of knowing the standards of either teacher or principal. The whole situation represents the jellyfish stage of organization and direction.

[6] Franklin Bobbitt, in *The Supervision of City Schools,* The Twelfth Yearbook, part I, National Society for the Study of Education, University of Chicago Press, Chicago, 1913, pp. 7–96.

[7] *Ibid.,* p. 40.

In place of teachers using every conceivable method and every kind of material in their trial-and-error experimentation with children, the movement anticipated Public Law 531[8] in recommending that the then U.S. Bureau of Education coordinate cooperative efforts of expert staffs in school systems and communities in analyzing the relative efficacy of methods.

It was contended that while the conscientious supervisor earnestly desired to perform his share of the task with teachers, he found himself unable to do so because of the dearth of scientifically formulated information as to what constituted the best control of the various factors of method. The supervisor had his opinions but others of equal ability had neutralizing opinions. When the supervisor turned to the literature of his profession for guidance, he found more conflicting opinions.

To those representing the scientific movement, there was but one avenue of escape from the condition of relative helplessness in the ability to direct and supervise: research and measurement. The earlier assumption that the supervisor could judge the work of teachers by noting the extent to which classroom practices followed general principles was declared false. These so-called educational principles were criticized as being of poor help when one tried to apply them to a concrete task. Their use was of little value in seeking answers to such problems as these: At what age shall addition combinations be taught? What amount of time per week should be devoted to the practice of particular skills? Under what conditions should the teacher make use of concrete problems and abstract examples? What is the relative value of appeal to vocational or civic motives?

It was the supervisory staff which was to have the largest share in the work of determining proper methods. The burden of finding the best methods was too great and too complex to be laid on the shoulders of teachers. The teacher was expected to be a specialist in the practice that would produce "the product"; the supervisor was to specialize in the science relating to the process. Supervisors were to (1) discover best procedures in the performance of particular educational tasks and (2) give these best methods to the teachers for their guidance.

Instruments for measuring outcomes and setting standards were promised. Courtis, for example, tentatively determined measuring scales for arithmetical ability. These scales measured the accuracy and amount of work that could be performed within a given time. Using these measure-

<hr>

[8] Public Law 531 in 1956 authorized the U.S. Office of Education to "enter into contracts or jointly financed cooperative arrangements with universities and colleges and State educational agencies for the conduct of research surveys and demonstrations in the field of education."

ments, Courtis developed norms for setting expectations in mathematical operations for pupils in grades three through eight. It was held that clear expectation would help a teacher judge himself and his methods. Further, the teacher would receive help in proportion to need and recognition in proportion to merit.[9]

Under scientific management the child rather than the machinery of education was to become the center of educational consciousness. The focus was to remain on ends: development of the pupil. Manipulation of process was to be the means. Diverse standards for pupils of varying abilities were recommended. It was assumed that once the pupil knew what was expected of him, the teaching problem was to teach him how to study, and to provide stimulations that would produce the desired effort. The similarity between the educational views of leaders in the early scientific movement and the views of persons currently doing research with autoinstructional materials is striking.[10] Both imply that the effort expended by teachers in carrying the student passively along can be dispensed with; that the pupil can be made to walk and bear his own burdens with his own strength and gain further strength thereby. Both hold that the time saved by pupil and teacher under systematic methods of instruction can be expended more profitably. Then as now the science of education was concerned with the determination of the amount and sequence of presentation in accordance with the individual differences of the learner and a wide variety of social conditions.

SUPERVISION AS DEMOCRATIC HUMAN RELATIONS

The late 1920s saw further protest against imposition of curriculum and method by personal authority of administrative officers. Writers began to conceive of supervision as guidance rather than inspection. Kyte's *How to Supervise* defined supervision as "the maximum development of the teacher into the most professionally efficient person she is capable of becoming." [11] The teacher was presumed professionally efficient when she was competent in self-analysis, self-criticism, and self-improvement. In practice, however, the standards for teaching procedures were still determined at higher levels and transmitted to teachers as supervisors gave commendations and condemnations following visits to classrooms and demonstrations.

[9] S. A. Courtis, "Standard Scores in Arithmetic," *Elementary School Teacher,* vol. 12, pp. 127–137, November, 1911.

[10] B. F. Skinner, "Teaching Machines," *Science,* vol. 128, pp. 969–979, 1958.

[11] George C. Kyte, *How to Supervise,* Houghton Mifflin Company, Boston, 1930, p. 45.

Related to the economic and social transformations of the depression and war years were spirited pleas for a kind of supervision which would embrace the ideals of a democratic order. Instead of emphasis upon tradition, the leader and the led, supervision became associated with precepts respecting human personality and encouraging wide participation in the formulation of policy. Those who opposed the imposition of courses of study and methods planned by upper levels were committed to a philosophy of situational relativism; that is, there were no absolutes, and "correct" procedures depended upon particular circumstances. Gestalt psychology supplied theory and Lewin supplied evidence to support the social supervision desired. Such psychology placed emphasis upon the relation of the concrete individual to the concrete situation, in contrast to former modes of thought which saw the characteristics of the individual as independent of the stimulus. Lewin's work in the study of motivation drew additional attention to the social factors in supervision. His interest and research in such problems as conflict in industry, morale in time of war, and changing of prejudiced groups[12] had much influence on supervisory practice, and stimulated the growth of action research and group dynamics. The latter became useful tools to accompany the growing concept that the supervisor was a cooperating member of a total group studying a particular teaching-learning situation. Special responsibilities of the supervisor (increasingly called consultant at this time) included setting a relaxed atmosphere and obtaining wide participation.[13] The improvement of the entire staff rather than that of teachers alone became a goal to be reached through cooperative attack upon a commonly recognized problem. This view held that leadership for improvement was a shared responsibility. Teacher, supervisor, administrator, pupil, or other could serve as the leader to the extent that he was able to advance the group toward mutually accepted goals. Solution of the instructional problem and personal growth of participants were outcomes to be sought.

A pictorial review of earlier stages of supervision and the current development in this field is presented in Figure 1-1.

DIRECTIONS OF SUPERVISORY THOUGHT

Supervision has no independent thought of its own. As indicated previously, the dynamics of supervision are in constant interrelation with the school and the social whole. However, the main task of supervision

[12] Kurt Lewin, *Resolving Social Conflicts,* Harper & Brothers, New York, 1948.
[13] Kimball Wiles, *Supervision for Better Schools,* Prentice-Hall, Inc., Englewood Cliffs, N.J., 1950.

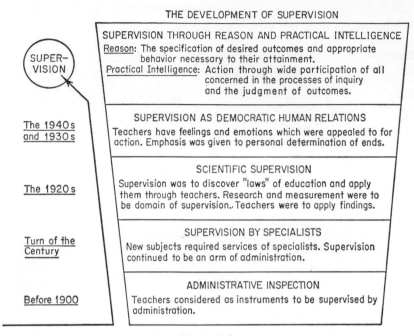

THE DEVELOPMENT OF SUPERVISION

SUPERVISION THROUGH REASON AND PRACTICAL INTELLIGENCE
Reason: The specification of desired outcomes and appropriate behavior necessary to their attainment.
Practical Intelligence: Action through wide participation of all concerned in the processes of inquiry and the judgment of outcomes.

SUPERVISION AS DEMOCRATIC HUMAN RELATIONS
Teachers have feelings and emotions which were appealed to for action. Emphasis was given to personal determination of ends.

SCIENTIFIC SUPERVISION
Supervision was to discover "laws" of education and apply them through teachers. Research and measurement were to be domain of supervision. Teachers were to apply findings.

SUPERVISION BY SPECIALISTS
New subjects required services of specialists. Supervision continued to be an arm of administration.

ADMINISTRATIVE INSPECTION
Teachers considered as instruments to be supervised by administration.

SUPER-VISION

The 1940s and 1930s

The 1920s

Turn of the Century

Before 1900

Figure 1-1

has always been that of the school itself: furtherance of that knowledge or truth by which human beings can comprehend if not control their world.

At different times, societies have viewed this knowledge as (1) existing outside the learner, (2) existing within the learner, or (3) a product of interaction between learner and environment. In any event, knowledge is presumed to be related to harmonious living, satisfaction of physical wants, and propitiation of the supreme power or powers believed to enhance existence. Sometimes knowledge has been conceived as a storehouse of experience which can be transmitted to others or put away for use when needed. At other times knowledge has been seen as the ability to function, to solve problems, and to create new knowledge. These different cultural views of knowledge are associated with two particular kinds of societies—those that are changing, exploring, creating and those that are stable, preserving, conforming. Differences of opinion over the interpretation of the nature of knowledge, as well as over the kind of society that is desirable, have fostered the present conflict in education, with its implications for supervision. Associated with this conflict and of vital importance to the future of supervision is the question of who shall make decisions determining the kind of knowledge to be fostered in schools.

Supervision and Interpretations of Knowledge

The pattern of supervision has been closely associated with reinterpretations of knowledge in response to new situations. When knowledge was thought of as ready-made information and belief, supervisors transmitted traditional practices and disregarded personal discovery. Consequently, supervisors and teachers tended to be obedient and conservative personalities who marveled at the wisdom of the past. Somewhat later, supervisors were captivated by the precise quantitative techniques of the inductive process and concentrated their efforts on measurement and rating, deeming that knowledge was best validated by the measurement of sense perceptions. A subsequent series of social events and a counteracting psychology, focusing on the subjective qualities of the individual, led to a weakened faith in both traditional and empirical pronouncements. Rather, there was a conviction that sense perception was relative to the beholder, to time, and to the situation. Inasmuch as knowledge gained in sense perception appeared to have its source in both physical world and the learner, supervisors sought ways of getting teachers to describe their own situations and to share their individual and partial truths. Staffs were encouraged to define their own goals, collect data on the effects of their efforts, and form their own interpersonal judgments. Validation of knowledge by consensus, in which participants established understanding within their common human association, was recommended.[14] Subjectivity of knowledge also underlined much of the literature read by supervisors, who began to identify growth in knowledge as identical with personal becoming. They believed in an individual's maturity through a knowledge of self as true knowledge. Nothing was really learned unless it was an expression of the whole person, his very action and being. Current practices which are associated with this view invite active participation and personal identification with knowledge rather than objective observation, study, and reflection.

It has been noted, however, that supervisors are not always clear as to what is involved in their helping another person in accordance with the belief that knowledge is personal growth. For example, psychologists

[14] J. Cecil Parker, "Guidance for In-service Education," *In-service Education of Teachers, Supervisors, and Administrators,* Fifty-sixth Yearbook, part I, National Society for the Study of Education, University of Chicago Press, Chicago, 1957, p. 103.

feel that supervisors need to distinguish between requests for help which have their genesis in a professional problem beyond the teacher's experiences and requests for help which stem from a teacher's personal inadequacy and unresolved dependence. If the latter are met by the supervisor, the person's lack of maturity may be reinforced.

Methods of Reason and Practical Intelligence

Two different approaches to supervision currently dominate thought and action. One is the method of reason and the other is the method of practical intelligence. Reason and practical intelligence have become the latest in this series of renewed interpretations of knowledge with implications for supervision. The method of reason rests on the belief that knowledge is best obtained through a theoretical system which serves to guide perceptions and actions. The scheme itself may be discovered by logical thought which goes beyond observed phenomena of "everyday life." Supervisors, teachers, and children are assumed to behave rationally when they act in accord with a given set of theoretical or mental patterns which presumably relate to the characteristics of their own situations. These patterns include assumptions about future events, knowledge of alternatives available for action, consequences attached to alternatives, and a way of ordering consequences or alternatives by preference.

The method of practical intelligence seeks knowledge through experimental procedures and the judgment of participants; its truths must be tested for their adequacy in helping individuals learn how to judge and control their own behavior. In general, this method calls for an interest in desirable consequences as well as respect for the ways in which knowledge is acquired and improved. Supervisors using this method distrust that intellectual authoritarianism which assumes that (1) only a few have the ability to conceive of appropriate ends and (2) any "system" of thought need not be validated in concrete situations.

Rational Supervision. Current demands for purpose, for planning, and for the systematic knowledge believed indispensable to modern life emphasize the method of reason. Davies and Iannaccone, for instance, see conceptualization as the shape of things to come in which encompassing concepts will enable the supervisor to control situations as he achieves "the ability to see the enterprise as a whole." [15] Also, economists have emphasized rationalistic aspects in their studies of the planning process. Psychologists, too, have found theoretical models useful in the study of organizational communication and problem solving. These

[15] Daniel R. Davies and Laurence Iannaccone, "Ferment in the Study of Organization," *Teachers College Record*, vol. 60, no. 2, p. 68, November, 1958.

successes spur the exploration of rational dimensions in supervision. Hypotheses based upon rational models for program-innovating processes, for example, have already been formulated, and they offer suggestions for supervisors to use in effecting change. Cases in point are propositions derived from theory stating that (1) daily routine drives out planning for change, (2) change is fostered by the allocating of resources to new goals, and (3) the judicious use of deadlines is important in speeding the process of change.[16]

Modern theories of rationality[17] assume that members of organizations are limited in their knowledge and their capacities to learn and to solve problems. Because the mind cannot immediately grasp all consequences, the supervisory staff must be able to help teachers toward the coordinated and effective behavior which reflects the broader considerations of the school. In order for the teacher's own decisions to be rational, they must be related to his expectations rather than to his wishes. Supervisory techniques for making teacher behavior more rational, i.e., more consistent with the school's goal, include:

1. Dividing work among teachers, limiting their attention to the immediate task

2. Making school objectives so operational and definite that it is possible to assess the extent to which they are being attained

3. Establishing standardized practices which relieve the individual teacher of minor choices

4. Making it possible for a teacher to receive expert help from more than one source, yet allowing only one authority figure to resolve any conflict among them

5. Establishing systems of influence such as in-service education programs, training conferences, and other arrangements for communicating those attitudes and habits which will lead to the school's objectives

6. Indicating how the school's goals contribute to the teacher's personal goal

7. Building loyalty to the school rather than to the teacher's subject field

Practical Intelligence in Supervision and the Extension of Perception. The use of intelligence in supervision is not altogether unexplored terrain. Most of the present concern for participation and pattern in the problem solving which accompanies the method of practical intelligence goes back

[16] James G. March and Herbert A. Simon, *Organizations,* John Wiley & Sons, Inc., New York, 1958, p. 185.

[17] Herbert A. Simon, *Administrative Behavior: A Study of Decision-making Processes in Administrative Organization,* The Macmillan Company, New York, 1958, p. 39.

to John Dewey's analysis.[18] It is recalled that he presented a certain logic of method by which conceptual frameworks were tested as tools of inquiry rather than accepted as fixed conclusions. To Dewey and those favoring practical intelligence, proposals for action are working hypotheses requiring observation of consequences, interpretation, and revision. Those favoring this method are concerned about the effect of absolutistic logic upon education, "the strengthening of a reign of dogma." [19] Dewey, for instance, warned that the discussion of concepts and their logical relation to one another could substitute for inquiry. One of the most important issues in modern supervision centers at this very point: Should supervisors seek to develop their own vision as well as the vision of others through open-ended modes of thought in which inquiry is pursued and participants attempt to seek new knowledge? Or should supervisors hold a mental picture of some desired end or conclusion, personal or social, which is conceived as fixed and not to be challenged, and use this conception to control the supervising process?

Practical intelligence in supervision cannot be understood without awareness of its relation to a desire for extending vision in education. The method of practical intelligence is a method of inquiry based upon faith in the capacities of ordinary people. The teacher, in dealing with concrete situations and applying his knowledge informally, is often more intelligent than the theorist who observes only a limited sphere because of the restrictions of his science. Fisher[20] and Raup and associates[21] have written extensively on this method which seeks to develop comprehensive perspective as a consequence of the use of the processes of inquiry. Briefly, it requires recognition of varying points of view and accommodation of one's own perspective to others. Under this method, supervisors encourage wide participation in policy-determining functions and seek to have participants see the significance of their emotions as well as facts. The supervisor views himself as one among many involved in the enterprise of learning. The intellectual expert's position in the method of practical intelligence is one of involvement in the process of judgment as he works with others. Predictability of results is not ensured because the method operates within the contingency of any situation. In other words, an ultimate goal and an over-all plan are not absolutes

[18] John Dewey, *How We Think,* D. C. Heath and Company, Boston, 1910.

[19] John Dewey, *The Public and Its Problems,* Henry Holt and Company, Inc., New York, 1927.

[20] Margaret Fisher, *Leadership and Intelligence,* Bureau of Publications, Teachers College, Columbia University, New York, 1954.

[21] R. Bruce Raup et al., *The Improvement of Practical Intelligence,* Harper & Brothers, New York, 1950.

which cannot be changed. Generalizations not only are used by super-visors to guide decisions but are themselves developed along with the problem they are instrumental in solving. It is an implied assumption in the method of intelligence that in attacking particular problems, supervisors and teachers formulate intelligent insight into the interre-lations of events in their given situations. If supervisory action ends in failure, then reflection and abstraction begin.

Because we believe in the method of practical intelligence, later chap-ters of this book will deal with the techniques which are necessary if it is to be effective. Obviously, one-way communication, devastating at-tacks on the personal level, "busy work," urgings for togetherness, and the encouragement of teachers to arrive at decisions whether or not they possess the requisite skill and knowledge to do so will result in a halfway perception. When teachers prefer not to be involved in the method, it might indicate that they have had experiences in fraudulent planning rather than in the process of inquiry.

On the other hand, we recognize merit in the method of reason. We believe with Mannheim[22] that perspective and freedom can best be preserved when capable intellectuals are detached from special interests in society and carry out major roles in social affairs through positions in government and education. Mannheim has proposed that tribunals of experts, aiming at consistency of plans rather than satisfaction of particular interests, should determine the basic planning laws and judge their validity. According to this view, intellectuals having special access to values in the culture should have responsibility for mediating these values to the community. Accordingly, educators as well as others are urging that the services of experts and the resources of social science be incorporated into the educational planning in essential areas.[23] Those supervisors, for instance, who have special knowledge should not hesitate to offer theoretically valid predictions regarding the consequences of alternative instructional procedures. Perhaps, *expertise* through govern-ment is the only way democracy can overcome the breakdown of self-regulative processes of local communities and introduce into school operations the highest possible degree of rationality.[24] If so, supervisors should work to attain higher policy-making boards, utilizing the manipu-

[22] Karl Mannheim, *Ideology and Utopia,* Harcourt, Brace and Company, Inc., New York, 1936.

[23] George S. Counts, *Decision-making and American Values in School Adminis-tration,* Bureau of Publications, Teachers College, Columbia University, New York, 1954, p. 6.

[24] Earl J. McGrath, "Needed: A Balanced Educational Policy," *Journal of the American Association of University Women,* vol. 52, no. 2, p. 85, January, 1959.

lative measures necessary to a plan for freedom. Centralization for the planning of certain basic policies is advanced by the notion that the creative use of government and not just the inventiveness of individuals can support freedom.[25] Our own opinion is that the method of reason should be accompanied with the method of practical intelligence so that the decision makers will not usurp absolute authority but rather will practice distribution of responsibility. Also, in order to keep education from becoming the tool of any one group, supervisors, as individual citizens and as members of professional organizations, must be politically active in local and national affairs, entering into the great debates about both social and educational issues, i.e., exercising their practical intelligence in areas outside the structure of the school.

Current Trends

The approach to supervision for the twenty-first century is paved with both a continuation of progressive developments and new insights which oppose many progressive tendencies.

1. One aspect of the current situation is the relationship of education to national strategy. Preplanned institutes, charged by Congress to upgrade instruction, challenge supervision as carried out by the "workshop way of working." For instance, it is now a common practice for the National Science Foundation alone to offer yearly programs to nearly one-eighth of the high school science teachers of this country. Other Federal programs from mathematics to foreign languages propose alternatives to local study-group procedures. These newer programs are in many ways reminiscent of the teachers' institutes of the nineteenth century, which also were directed at correcting inadequate command of subject matter and deficiency in professional skills.[26]

2. A second feature of the new situation is the concern of professional educators over the hiatus between the school's stated objectives and actual practice. Shaftel,[27] for example, states that classrooms across the country reveal few fundamental changes from those of thirty years ago when teachers used mechanistic theories of learning and standardized routine text materials. She attributes this lack of progress to the failure of supervisors to act upon a systematic theory of action already available

[25] Arthur Schlesinger, Jr., "Perhaps America Has the Answer," *New York Times Book Review,* July 12, Sec. 7, p. 1, 1959.

[26] James H. Smart, *Teachers' Institutes,* Circular of Information of the U.S. Bureau of Education, no. 2, 1885.

[27] Fannie R. Shaftel, "Evaluation—for Today and for the Future," *Educational Leadership,* vol. 14, no. 5, pp. 292–294, February, 1957.

from the social anthropologists. Essentially, this theory would call for (1) study of the particular communities (including the staff of a given school) to be changed, e.g., recognition of their existing personal relationships, values, perspectives, code of behavior; (2) careful delimitations of new changes to be introduced; and (3) a plan for linking the traditional ways of doing things with the new traits desired.[28]

3. The contemporary situation has been affected by an awareness of the numerous conservative strains of thought severely critical of the autonomy of the teacher. Educational objectives and practices are increasingly being defined at legislative and administrative levels and then passed down through courses of study, directives, bulletins, and indoctrination sessions. There is also a protest against the subjectivity of democratic supervision, together with an insistence upon the validity of a hard core of knowledge. Although the mood of recent supervisory thought is one of increased sympathy with traditional modes of thought, it is not simply a return to the past for its own sake. It is a revolutionary movement which has renewed older patterns because it finds in them the elements relevant to the problems of the present.

4. Increasingly, educational planners are making an effort at effecting a synthesis of the most important ideas in the basic discipline so that research and scholarship can be translated into appropriate forms for classroom use. When these efforts are undertaken, individuals specialists and educationists envision how new discoveries can be used to better school personnel. Supervisors and staff members together develop plans for implementing the new knowledge for practice and evaluate their effectiveness in terms of the changed behavior of learners.

5. Many of the above aspects of the current trends in supervision could be summed up as manifestations of the age of planning and the search for perspective. The concern for generalizations as guides for decisions in both the local situation and in the total social undertaking is implicit in most of the controversy over supervision. It remains to be seen whether supervision will be regarded as (1) an instrument for the manipulation of the school in the interest of society as a whole, (2) a process for the facilitation of individual learning experiences, or (3) something more inclusive than either of the preceding alternatives. If supervision is regarded as a tool of society, it will reflect the claims of society. If supervision is conceived at least in some degree as a process for teaching and molding society as well as the individual, it will be fashioned in the light of now unrealized ideals.

[28] Ed. H. Spicer (ed.), *Human Problems in Technological Change,* Russell Sage Foundation, New York, 1952, p 290.

SUMMARY STATEMENT

What has now been said of the apparently contradictory trends in late twentieth-century supervision reflects something of the complexity of the times and the difficulty of making simple generalizations regarding the development of supervision. It does suggest some of the central issues which must be examined in greater detail. Out of the variety of principles and structures of supervision, we shall single out in succeeding chapters those issues which seem most significant for supervisors. Already two may be stated in these questions:

1. How can supervisors justify and make best use of processes which stem from different social philosophies and theories of knowledge, learning, and social change?

2. What should supervisors use as a basis for their decisions regarding the interests of society as a whole and the solution of problems in particular situations?

2

WHO IS A SUPERVISOR?

BIGNESS in education has brought many new positions into the American school system and given rise to new images of the supervisor which conflict with the traditional view of the supervisor as a personal leader. This chapter describes newer supervisory positions and the conflicting roles associated with them. We believe that examination of these positions will reveal that they have a common requirement: a perspective of the instructional tasks and the ability to synthesize data from many sources and to use these data in the formulation of better instructional programs. The common dimension of supervision—found in all positions of leadership—is the ability to perceive desirable objectives, and to help others contribute to this vision and to act in accordance with it.

A SOCIOLOGICAL PORTRAIT OF A SUPERVISOR

As the school system enlarges, more supervisors are required to operate within the organization that selects them for their position and shapes their character. The principal as general supervisor has seen his functions diminish from above by new specialists and the dictates of higher authority; from below his influence has been weakened by the growth of professional organizations and the improved preparation of teachers. At one time, the supervisor was everything to the teacher as he solved problems and overcame obstacles. Further, he was the master teacher, knowing more about the teaching process than others in the school.

21

With specialization and a host of supervisory assistants at both upper and lower levels of the system's hierarchy, the supervisor's sphere of professional competence grows less and his skills become more those of a personnel agent. Embodying the district's approved opinions, the supervisor is chosen for his skill in handling personnel rather than because of his length of service or mastery of a particular field of specialization. "The old functions of the supervisor are no longer found in any one man's experience but in a team." [1]

As a member of a supervisory team which includes principal, counselor, coordinator, consultant, vice-principal, and the like, the supervisor acts only in consultation with other authorities, and the resulting interrelationships are often ill-defined and disturbing. It is in keeping with the changed nature of the supervisor's role that he has been led into the ways of manipulation, developing discipline and loyalty among the teachers by using his own personality as the main tool of persuasion.

All manner of personal traits and behaviors are blandly suggested . . . as indispensable. "The essential quality of friendliness is *sincerity*. . . . They should memorize from the personnel records, the following about [those supervised]: first name, if married . . . approximate ages and school grades of children . . . etc." From local newspapers "he will learn such valuable items as accidents; births; deaths; children's activities; participation in Red Cross, YMCA . . . wedding anniversaries; parties; recitals." "The manner of speech . . . during even a minor conversation is perhaps more important than what he says. . . . Good listening habits are a must. . . . He should fine himself 10 cents for every fall from grace. . . ." He needs a pleasant clear voice (test recordings are recommended). . . . The words "definitely" and "absolutely" are taboo. . . . His own prejudices must be "parked" outside the (school). [2]

THE "GALAHAD" MYTH

Others still hold to their old idealistic conceptions of the supervisor. "Individuals selected to be supervisors should possess moral stamina, a sense for the beauty of the spirit, and an enquiring mind. They should be free of the conventional prejudices and fears. . . . Unless superiors are crucially important they are nothing." [3]

Guidance, encouragement, stimulation, and cooperation mark the supervisor. Naturally, the supervisor is one who accepts and recognizes

[1] C. Wright Mills, *White Collar,* Oxford University Press, New York, 1956, p. 88.

[2] *Ibid.,* p. 90.

[3] Louis E. Armstrong, "Strategy in Supervision," *Educational Leadership,* vol. 4, p. 248, January, 1947.

the dignity and worth of every human being at all times. This means a personal interest in others and participation in activities in which supervisors and teachers learn to understand and respect one another. The supervisor is one who has the virtue of patience, for he recognizes that learning of new patterns of behavior and attitude is a slow process. As a person of integrity, teachers find the supervisor to be a "wailing wall" on whom they can pour out their woes in confidence.

A true supervisor is seen by the idealists as one who promotes harmony and unity as a philosophy of life. The motives or values that guide the supervisor's life are rich indeed if they are based on a deep appreciation of every human being and faith in each person's ability to learn and develop.

Supervisor is a term too cold for the person whom I know that I shall have for my consultant and guide! Teaching is a warm, vital profession and I know that those in higher positions in education will be warm, vital people, to whom I can turn for constructive criticism, counsel and advice of all kinds pertaining to my work as a teacher.

My supervisor will be a *welcome* visitor in my classroom and will add to the light and warmth already present in the atmosphere that is to be found in a classroom full of busy, happy people. She will tell me what she likes about my ways and procedures with children. She will have suggestions as to how I can work more effectively. These suggestions I shall usually honor and follow because her wealth of experience adds value and strength to her suggestions. But, if I should differ with her viewpoint she will listen graciously and we will, together, work out a solution.

On a gray day when Johnny got only one division problem right, when Susie missed every spelling word, when *No* one can tell me why it rains, I hope that on that day my supervisor will come to visit in my classroom and with words of encouragement she will revitalize us all, teacher and children and the whole group; children and teacher will radiate her presence and we shall all feel that we have grown a bit.

My greatest expectation is that this supervisor will have a real interest in me, and confidence in me, too. Through this relationship I will grow as a teacher and my work with children will be oh! so much more effective.

—Marilyn[4]

SUPERVISORY POSITIONS

Reasons for Increased Number of Supervisors

The existence of a variety of titles now borne by supervisors is a consequence both of certain social necessities and of the increasing

[4] Marie Denecke, "Super Vision: Expectations of Beginning Teachers," *Education,* vol. 78, no. 4, December, 1957.

complexity of school organization. Obviously, as the tasks of the school become more numerous and varied, supervisors increase in number and kind. Too, the growth of school organization demands more supervision. An individual or an organization can attend to only a limited number of things at a time. In school systems where various aspects of the whole complex problem associated with effective teaching and learning are being handled by different individuals and groups of individuals, it is a fundamental technique to simplify the problem into a number of nearly independent parts. Each one in a minor supervisory position, such as consultant, vice-principal, and counselor, handles one of the parts but usually omits the others from his definition of the situation. The subgoals held by those in the individual positions must contribute to the objectives of the school system. The greater the specialization by the individual, the greater the need for interdependence among those discharging particular tasks. Therefore, certain supervisory positions have been established to knit the different tasks together, clearing the way for intelligent actions by higher echelons. Through these supervisory positions, decisions of those in higher echelons are made clear to teachers, and those who made these decisions in turn learn how teachers feel, obtaining feedback to guide future decisions. Coordination and communication are central tasks to those occupying supervisory positions.

C. Northcote Parkinson has humorously described another reason for the rising pyramid of official positions:[5]

Politicians and taxpayers have assumed (with occasional phases of doubt) that a rising total in the number of civil servants must reflect a growing volume of work to be done. Cynics, in questioning this belief, have imagined that the multiplication of officials must have left some of them idle or all of them able to work for shorter hours. But this is a matter in which faith and doubt seem equally misplaced. The fact is that the number of the officials and the quantity of the work are not related to each other at all. The rise in the total of those employed is governed by Parkinson's Law and would be much the same whether the volume of the work were to increase, diminish, or even disappear. The importance of Parkinson's Law lies in the fact that it is a law of growth based upon an analysis of the factors by which that growth is controlled.

Parkinson distinguishes two motivating forces responsible for the increased number of supervisors: (1) "an official wants to multiply subordinates, not rivals" and (2) "officials make work for each other."

Applying this law to school supervision, picture a school supervisor

[5] C. Northcote Parkinson, *Parkinson's Law and Other Studies in Administration,* Houghton Mifflin Company, Boston, 1957, pp. 3–4.

who feels overworked. Because of this feeling he may resign, or halve the work with a colleague, or demand the assistance of two subordinates. Rather than lose pension rights or bring in a rival for promotion, Parkinson predicts he will demand the subordinates. Two are necessary for status reasons and to keep them in order by fear of the other's promotion. Parkinson gives a full account of the second force by which several officials do what one did before, making so much work for each other that all are fully occupied and the original supervisor is working harder than ever.

Typical Supervisory Positions and Duties in the Central Office

Supervisory positions in the central offices of urban school districts are those of assistant superintendent, director, supervisor, coordinator, and consultant. The Research Division of the National Education Association has collected evidence of the relative rank of these positions and their duties. Positions, however, are not clear-cut as far as titles are concerned; an administrator in one school system may be called a director, and a person doing the same type of work in another school system may be called a supervisor.[6]

Assistant Superintendent. An assistant superintendent usually has charge of one or more broad areas of school service in the fields of instruction, instructional materials, or other auxiliary services needed by teachers, pupils, or community. Most assistant superintendents have assignments directly or indirectly connected with instruction.

Director. A director is a professionally trained employee attached to the office of the superintendent of schools. His rank is below that of an assistant superintendent. He is in charge of a major level of the school system, a comprehensive area of the curriculum, or an important general function of the superintendent's office. His work is basically instructional leadership (supervision) but includes general administrative functions.

Supervisor. A supervisor is a professionally trained person assigned to the office of the superintendent of schools. His rank is less than that of assistant superintendent and also below that of a director. His work is almost exclusively instructional leadership (supervision). Respondents in the National Education Survey named so many areas of service for which supervisors are responsible that the title is hardly descriptive. Supervisors may contribute to any area of the school program or to any service required to keep the school running.

Coordinator. A coordinator is an employee assigned to promote cooperation between the schools and some phase of community life or among units and individuals within the school system. In rank the coordinator is below

[6] "Certain Positions in the Central Offices of Urban School Districts," National Education Association, Research Division, Washington, September, 1953.

a supervisor. Coordinators are employed for a variety of services. Consultations with teachers, supervision of the testing program, coordination of the public relations program, supervision of pupils on work experience programs, checking attendance, holding conferences with the home, coordination of the work within a subject area, and especially giving help to new teachers are among their tasks.

Consultant. A consultant (resource person) is an instructional specialist assigned to promote the improvement of teaching and the curriculum by advising with teachers, principals, assistant superintendents, and others. He is especially concerned with the discovery and use of instructional aids, materials, teaching guides, methods of teaching, and resource units. He has little or no authority for decision making.

The supervisor is generally responsible for six kinds of duties:

1. *Planning*—individually and in groups; he helps to develop policies and programs in his field.

2. *Administration*—he makes decisions, coordinates the work of others, and issues necessary directions.

3. *Supervision*—through conferences and consultations, he seeks to improve the quality of instruction.

4. *Curriculum development*—he participates directly in the formulation of objectives, selection of school experiences, preparation of teaching guides, and selection of instructional aids.

5. *Demonstration teaching*—he gives and arranges for classroom demonstrations of teaching methods, use of aids, and other *direct* help to classroom teachers.

6. *Research*—through systematic surveys, experiments, and studies, he explores current conditions and recommends changes in practice.

Examination by the National Education Association of the organization of central office staff in 224 urban districts reveals a lack of uniformity. A supervisor may have charge of custodians or of mathematics. Noteworthy is the tendency for directors and assistant superintendents to make decisions, while those in other supervisory positions are restricted to the planning and implementing of these decisions. Table 1 indicates the range of responsibility accompanying each position.

The existence of top-level supervisors (assistant superintendents and directors) in the central office reflects the need for regularity and stability among the wide variety of school interests and activities. Articulation and balance of component parts must be safeguarded if the school is to serve its purpose. These supervisors have particular responsibility to recognize and implement the ordering principles of the instructional scheme. Their specialty is the linking together of the specialties of others.

Supervisors situated between the central office and the teachers serve

TABLE 1. PRIMARY DUTIES ASSOCIATED WITH SUPERVISORY POSITIONS IN CENTRAL
OFFICES OF URBAN SCHOOL DISTRICTS, PER CENT

	Asst. supt.	Director	Supervisor	Coordinator	Consultant
Administrative	31	21	7	16	3
Supervision	22	27	46	19	25
Planning	19	23	15	37	18
Curriculum development	16	18	13	15	24
Research	7	6	4	8	8
Demonstration teaching	5	5	15	5	22
$N = $*	200	338	292	142	67

* $N = $ the total number of times the functions were checked on a questionnaire
by the supervisory personnel who responded.
SOURCE: Based on figures in "Certain Positions in the Central Offices of Urban
School Districts," special memo, National Education Association, Research Division, Washington, September, 1953.

as representatives of the school system. They open a channel of two-way
communication by which policies, decisions, and perhaps problems go
down; and information, problems, and perhaps suggestions come up.
Such supervisors are expected to think, feel, and act in tune with the
decisions made at higher levels. Possibly, the views of these supervisors
and their fellow teachers help frame the decisions. As we have noted,
the knowledge and intelligence required in a complex school system is
so diversified that it exceeds what a single mind can grasp, making necessary the pooling of wisdom at the decision-making level.

We might, at this point, recall an earlier question: Should rationality,
perspective, and harmony in the school's organization occur as supervisors keep each teacher well informed about the work of the entire
organization so that each will know best how to serve the common
cause? Or should the supervisor correlate specialized jobs assigned to
each teacher in accordance with a predetermined scheme?

Other Supervisory Positions

The superintendent, the principal, and the principal's staff, including
vice-principal, counselor, department chairman, teaching assistant, helping and special teacher, and the like, are at times supervisors. So, too,
are cooperating teachers and college staffs when they work with student
teachers. University professors and personnel from professional organ-

izations as well as state and Federal departments play supervisory roles as consultants, influencing others by advisory persuasiveness.

As we shall see, it is the extended distribution of supervisory functions among administrators and teachers and the acceptance of administrative functions by supervisors which have led to much of the confusion as to who is a supervisor.

Supervisors Identified by Staff Functions

The functions of school supervisors have been patterned from those in industry and the military which make a distinction between staff functions and line functions. Line officers are those who have the right to make decisions, to take action in order that things get done, and to exercise necessary control over others assigned to them. Staff officers are those whose main job is helping the line officers decide what to do as well as coordinating the efforts of all and supplying necessary services. It is an administrative principle that those occupying particular positions are either line or staff. School supervisors are likely to be termed staff officers.

Influence versus Authority in the Practice of Supervision

Sometimes one is categorized as a supervisor because he relies upon the use of influence rather than authority in effecting change. Influence occurs when one is able to give another the premises for action, attitudes, state of mind, and habits which will lead to the organizational goal. Communication, in-service education and training, evaluation, and standardized practices are examples of mechanisms for influence. Many hold that it is proper for a staff member to use influence but not to exercise authority or to issue commands. Authority is a power granted by one's superiors to carry out responsibilities; it includes the rights necessary to the discharge of line functions. One accepts authority when he permits his behavior to be guided by the decisions of a supervisor without examining the merits of the decision. The more obedient one is, the less tangible are the evidences of authority.

Although effective action is not possible in an organization in which there are only recognized and accepted channels through which information and authority flow, many school supervisors indicate a desire to be rid of the onus attached to direct command and authority. Ziff's[7] study of supervisors representing all geographical areas of the United States found that they rejected administrative activities and "authority as such." Supervisors often prefer advising and guiding to the initiating of action

[7] Norman Ziff, "Role of the General Secondary School Supervisor," *Educational Leadership,* vol. 16, no. 8, p. 500, May, 1959.

and the making of policy decisions. Popularly, supervisors are seen as "those who justify themselves as they are able to influence fellow executives at all levels by virtue of their factual or technical mastery, consultative skill, advisory persuasiveness—in short by their educational effectiveness. . . . A demand for the exercise of authority is a confession of weakness." [8]

Thus far the assumption has been that within a line-and-staff organization school leaders are administrators when they exercise initiative in movements for the improvement of teaching and learning, making decisions, coordinating the work of others, and issuing directions. When school leaders exert influence rather than authority, bypassing the right to make decisions, to take action, and to exercise control over others, they are acting as supervisors. Conditions in school situations do not always permit, however, the operation of the logic-tight compartments of line and staff or authority and influence.

We believe it is not always desirable to sharply distinguish the supervisor from teacher and administrator on the basis of staff classification and employment of influence. Supervisors are sometimes delegated powers to be exercised authoritatively, and when they themselves are held responsible for results, they must hold others responsible for carrying out instructions. Teachers who are without benefit of title may act like supervisors as they exert unacknowledged influence upon others. Principals, too, may attempt to discharge the supervisory functions of staff officers as they use influence, even though their line responsibilities and authority loom large. The dilemma of one who is expected to use influence but who also is responsible for consequences is well known:

TABLE 2. DILEMMA OF A STATUS LEADER

He can't	*But he must*
Be aggressive	Be alert and eager
Sell ideas	Have many creative ideas
Dominate	Keep things moving
Control	Supply help as needed
Force program	Insure improvement
Question what is being done	Get people to evaluate present program
Threaten	Challenge
Accept mediocre program	Support people who need help

SOURCE: Kimball Wiles, "Dilemma of a Status Leader," *Educational Leadership*, vol. 16, no. 8, p. 492, May, 1959.

[8] Ordway Tead, *The Art of Administration*, McGraw-Hill Book Company, Inc., New York, 1951, p. 104.

EMERGING ROLES OF SUPERVISORY PERSONNEL

Clarification of the supervisory roles of administrators, personnel in teacher education, and consultants from outside the district is a continuous obligation. Indefiniteness and lack of understanding of these roles have led to conflict and disorder.

Role Theory and the Practice of Supervision

Conceptualization of the supervisor may be aided by role theory.[9] Briefly, such theory postulates that a school system is a miniature society in which administrators, supervisors, teachers, and pupils represent positions or offices within the system. Certain rights and duties are associated with each position. The actions appropriate to the positions are defined as roles. It should be emphasized that a role is linked with the position, not with the person who is temporarily occupying the position. A person in a particular position learns to expect certain actions of others, and others expect a given behavior of him. The position of a supervisor can be described in terms of the action expected of him and the action he expects of others. One cannot enact the supervisory role if he lacks the necessary role expectations. These expectations are learned both through intentional instruction and through incidental means. The ability to learn a supervisory role is probably limited by a view of self as well as by previous experiences.

Included in the supervisor's role expectations are certain actions such as organizing abstract material, defining needs of learners, and cooperating with community groups as well as personal qualities such as good-naturedness, cooperativeness, and supportiveness. If the actions and qualities which constitute this role are congruent with the supervisor's own self-concept, then there is a high probability that he will perform according to the role expectations of teachers, administrators, and other members of the community. In the event that the role expectations are incongruent, the supervisor will give priority to some obligations over others. He will, for example, either heed his responsibility to the board of education before meeting demands of the teachers, or he may try to placate both board and teachers by excuses. That is, he may seek others' acceptance of his failure to discharge the obligation of a role by declaring that the competing role had a hierarchical priority. Sometimes the supervisor handles role conflict by enacting subroles separately. Repudi-

[9] Theodore R. Sarbin, "Role Theory," *Handbook of Social Psychology,* Gardner Lindzey (ed.), Addison-Wesley Publishing Company, Reading, Mass., 1954, pp. 223–255.

ating one subrole, "stalling," and "playing one group against the other" are examples of techniques used in resolving role conflicts.

Expectations for Supervisors as Revealed by Research on Existing Practice

A series of studies shed light on the reciprocal role expectations of teachers and supervisors in the improvement of instruction. The satisfaction of teachers with the school system has been found to depend upon the extent to which they perceive that the roles of their supervisors meet their expectations. Conversely, those higher in the school's hierarchy judge teachers in terms of how well they conform to personal expectations of the teacher's role. Respective roles must complement each other if the objectives of the schools are to be accomplished.

When working with others, it sometimes seems to matter little what a supervisor actually does. It matters more that what others think the supervisor does is what they think he should do. Studies show, for instance, that members of a school system tend to evaluate a supervisor's behavior by comparing what they think he does with what they think he should do.

In a study conducted in seventeen school systems, Sweitzer[10] investigated some of the factors influencing the effectiveness of the superintendent in improving the instructional program. For the purpose of the study, five general categories of behavior in improving instruction were listed:

Style A—"Authority-centered." This person sees established authority, absolute principles, expert opinion, and common practice as the "right" answer to problems. He carries out work through official channels and a carefully constructed line organization. The tone of his interaction is formal. He conceives his primary responsibility to be achieving purposes through clarifying and carrying out the official policy adopted by the school board.

Style B—"Inner-directed." He sees the most desirable behavior as that which most closely approximates his own values, opinions, and judgment. He believes he perceives more quickly than others what is good and wise regarding a particular problem and he may ignore official channels and procedures if he thinks it will expedite what needs to be done. He conceives his primary responsibility to be modifying, improving, and interpreting policy and procedures along lines he thinks will best meet the educational needs of the community.

Style C—"Work-group-oriented." This person tries to help the people concerned with or involved in the program to identify their own purposes with those of the school program. He believes that authority should lie in em-

[10] Robert E. Sweitzer, "The Fulfillment of Role-expectations and Teacher Morale," unpublished Ph.D. dissertation, University of Chicago, 1957.

pirical information and in the considered judgment of those who carry out and are affected by the school program. His judgment is made in the context of a specific situation and his tasks are fundamentally determined by the elements of the situation. He takes an active part in groups and he conceives his primary responsibility to be facilitating the cooperative development of group standards and procedures that tend to meet identified local needs.

Style D—"Individual-centered." He sees the most desirable behavior as that which most closely approximates the judgment of those who are or will be performing a particular task. He tends to place emphasis upon fulfilling individual needs and gives priority to decisions that permit individual variation and freedom. He tends to be sensitive to individuals and their problems, and he conceives his primary responsibility to be enabling individuals and groups to carry out their tasks, largely self-appointed and self-defined, with as little interference as possible.

Style E—"Other-directed." This person sees his ability to reflect accurately the wishes of others as the crux of his leadership. He believes that the authority for determining the goals of the school program, and how these goals should be achieved, lies in the will of the people served. He tries to develop friendly relationships with the individuals and groups most influential in the school and in the community. He conceives his primary responsibility to be doing his utmost to know accurately the wishes of the people served, and to see to it that the goals and procedures felt to be most worthwhile are officially adopted and then achieved.

Superintendents, principals, and teachers in Sweitzer's study "viewed the relative desirability (expectations) of each of the five categories in the same way. In order of most to least desirable, these status-group members ranked the role categories in the following order: C (work-group-oriented), E (other-directed), D (individual-centered), A (authority-centered), and B (inner-directed)." School board members, on the other hand, viewed the categories from most to least desirable (expectations) as C, A, B, E, D. There was even less agreement on whether the superintendents actually performed these expected roles. When working on instructional improvement, superintendents tended to fulfill the expectations of teachers to a lesser degree than those of other groups in the school. School board members, principals, and teachers perceived superintendents as employing work-group-oriented behavior less often than they thought superintendents should, while superintendents saw themselves employing each role category as they thought they should.[11]

Four hundred school leaders in California replied to Fielstra's questionnaire, in which they rated their beliefs about supervisory roles. Primarily, they saw their tasks as "service, coordination, and cooperative

[11] *Ibid.*, pp. 2–3.

action" and, secondly, as "direction and guidance." "Inspection and rating" of teachers was rejected as a supervisory role.[12]

Supervising principals from 2,008 elementary schools have reported their roles in interaction with others while developing curriculum and selecting instructional materials:[13]

62 percent responded that classroom teachers, principals, and supervisors develop the curriculum cooperatively for the school system, with adaptation to individual schools up to the principal and teachers; 29 percent, that they follow closely the school system program and have some influence on its development; 6 percent, that they carry out prescriptions of state law and local board policies; and 3 percent, that they follow closely the school system program without trying to influence its development.

59 percent reported that the faculty, working together, makes requests for materials in terms of the school program; 22 percent, that they or their representatives work with a school system committee; 10 percent, that they use materials selected by the central office; and 9 percent, that they have no standard list of materials, but that teachers indicate what they need.

Campbell [14] found evidence in support of the hypothesis that teachers whose wants and needs are in agreement with their supervising principal's expectations express significantly higher job satisfaction than teachers whose wants are in conflict with the principal's definition of the teacher's role. He theorized that maximum goal achievement should result when the principal's expectations for teacher behavior are identical with the wants and needs of the teachers. Campbell also noted a wide disparity between what the principal said he expected his teachers to do and what the teachers said the principal expected of them.

An interesting study of the effect of role expectancy upon the success of consultants was that made by Ferneau.[15] This study attempted to answer why the same consultant giving help on the same problem in two different situations may be successful in one and fail in another. Ferneau used the theory which states that when two or more persons come in contact over a sufficient length of time, each begins to have certain expectations as to how the other and others of the same position will act.

[12] Clarence Fielstra, "Concepts and Purposes of Supervision Held by Educational Leaders in California Public Schools," *California Journal for Instructional Improvement,* vol. 1, no. 1, pp. 16–18, October, 1958.

[13] National Education Association, Research Division, *NEA Research Bulletin,* vol. 36, no. 14, pp. 105–106, December, 1958.

[14] Merton V. Campbell, "Self-role Conflict among Teachers and Its Relationship to Satisfaction, Effectiveness, and Confidence in Leadership," unpublished Ph.D. dissertation, University of Chicago, 1958.

[15] Elmer F. Ferneau, "Role-expectations in Consultation," unpublished Ph.D. dissertation, University of Chicago, 1954.

Ferneau predicted that consultative service would be ineffective if the administrator and the consultant failed to behave according to the manner that each expected of the other. This hypothesis was tested as follows:

1. Three patterns of successful consultative roles were identified:

a. The "expert." He directs his efforts at arriving at the "right" answer for the particular problem in the specific situation. He sees the "right" answers as those based on absolute principles. He believes that when the "right" answer is known by one or more parties, the best use of resources is to make the answer explicit. He then implements action to achieve the desired solution at the earliest possible moment. A person employing this approach may be characterized as an expert contingent upon his knowledge of the right answer in this particular situation at this time.

b. The "resource person." He directs his efforts towards providing an abundance of information so that the persons in the situation can have a choice of a wide range of alternate pragmatic solutions to the problem. He encourages the persons to make whatever selection they wish to make. This necessitates that he possess a wide range of experiences, either vicarious or actual, upon which to draw. He suggests that the persons concerned should consider the available empirical evidence relating to the problem. The person using this approach may be regarded by others as a resource person contingent upon the amount of information he possessses.

c. The "process person." He directs his efforts towards developing a method of working with all persons concerned which will bring about behavioral changes, and these changes will enable persons to solve their own problems. At the same time he hopes to establish the behavioral changes firmly enough so that all persons will be more competent to handle similar situations in the future. A person employing this approach may be characterized as one especially skilled in human relations, contingent upon his knowledge and skill in working with persons.

2. Sixty statements regarding how both administrator and consultant thought each other should act in a given situation were prepared. One hundred and thirty-two administrators and forty-three State Department consultants responded to these statements and also gave evaluations of the consultation help they had received and given. Replies of the consultants were matched with those of the administrators they had attempted to help on curriculum problems. Analysis of the test results validated the prediction leading to these conclusions: (*a*) consultants and administrators must perceive each other functioning in the manner they expect if the consultation is to be effective, (*b*) there is no evidence that any one of the three types of consultants found in the study was any more successful than another, and (*c*) the consultant who operates

as a "process" person is usually destined to fail if he agrees to give assistance to an administrator who conceives the role of the consultant to be that of "expert," or, if he operates as an "expert" when the administrator looks upon consultants as "resource" or "process" persons, he is again limiting very severely the chances of success in the consultation.

This present-day theory of supervision, for instance, modifies the traditional role of the principal in the improvement of instruction by limiting him to the maintenance of over-all balance in the curriculum and over-all quality in classroom teaching. But the *specific* task of improvement of instruction is assigned to a group of teaching specialists within each building unit.

In general, it is reported that the superintendent and the teachers have different expectations of the principal, and that the principal's behavior with his superiors is different from that with his subordinates. "The absence of mutual ratings of effectiveness and confidence is accompanied by confusion, lack of security, general dissatisfaction with the relationship, poorly defined duties, and poor delineation of authority for decision making." [16-17]

*Expectations for the Supervisor as Revealed
in Professional Literature*

There exists a professional ideology which defines the supervisory roles of superintendents, principals, and other personnel with system-wide responsibilities for the improvement of learning experiences. This popular ideology assigns to the administrator the roles of coordinator and facilitator in which he (1) provides inspiration, (2) encourages development of organizations for in-service education, (3) facilitates the work of groups, and (4) creates a climate for growth.[18] Basic assumptions which underlie this professional point of view are these:[19]

1. *Change.* Individuals change as they seek to release tension related to basic needs, interests, and desires. While it is possible for the administrator to induce the required tensions by external pressure, it is better that he do so by helping a person see his needs or interest in a new light. External pressures of command and manipulation are not consistent with the professional view. Instead, the administrator is expected to help an

[16-17] Robert P. Moser, "A Study of the Effects of Superintendent-Principal Interaction upon Principal-Teacher Interaction in Selected Middle-sized School Systems," unpublished Ph.D. dissertation, University of Chicago, 1957.

[18] Arthur J. Lewis et al., "The Role of the Administrator in In-service Education," *In-service Education for Teachers, Supervisors, and Administrators,* Fifty-sixth Yearbook, part I, National Society for the Study of Education, University of Chicago Press, Chicago, 1957, p. 157.

[19] *Ibid.,* p. 153.

individual see things in a new way either by showing how the old way
of doing things no longer suffices or by helping him find new values and
goals. The example is cited of the high school English teacher who gains
a better understanding of youth, thereby developing a new aspiration to
help pupils with their personal problems. With the new goal, the teacher
becomes dissatisfied with his present teaching method and tension for
change is induced.

2. *Group work.* Personal tensions that may arise when emphasis is on
changing the teacher may be avoided when groups focus on ways to improve the instructional program. Further, a group influence can be a
real asset in helping an individual change by generating new problems
and forcing new adaptations. The professional view holds, therefore,
that improvement of the quality of learning experiences should be approached and conducted largely on a group basis, with the whole group
participating in identifying the needs, setting the goals, planning ways of
working, developing materials, putting recommendations into action,
and evaluating results.

The supervising administrator is expected to provide inspiration. He
is responsible for "firing up" the staff and helping it develop a vision of
what the organization might be doing. The professional ideology holds,
however, that the administrator should make it possible for others to
raise aspirations, too.

In his role of coordinator, the supervisor provides opportunities for
activities at system-wide and local building levels. He also tries to provide a means of communication so that the curriculum-improvement activities exert a positive influence on the entire school system and do not
overlay or conflict. He arranges for teachers with similar problems and
special interests to meet; for instance, he sometimes brings together beginning teachers on the assumption that they have particular needs for
belonging and status.

As facilitator, the administrator has sufficient faith in people, and in
the ability of the group to cope with instructional problems, to accept
the group's decision even though it may be at variance with his own
idea. Of course, he has the responsibility for defining at the beginning
of the group's deliberation the limitations within which its members
must operate and for helping them get the facts. Although he needs to
be skilled in the group process, the administrator often finds it difficult
to play various group membership roles other than that of chairman or
director because of expectations held by faculty and higher authorities.
In addition to assisting the group directly in accordance with the principles of group dynamics, he makes available the resources of other indi-

viduals as well as physical facilities, materials, and released time for teacher participation in planning.

As a supervisor of human relations, the administrator tries to "smooth the path of human interaction, ease communication, evoke personal devotion, and allay anxiety. The professional image depicts the administrative supervisor as a humble man who recognizes that every member of the staff excels him in one or more different ways. He consciously looks for strengths in others and knows that teachers are interested in doing a good job and in improving their performance. The growth of "a good-fellow, first-name informality, let's get acquainted pattern" [20] is disapproved. In order that he might understand the individual's problems, the administrator is encouraged to listen with patience and to try to put himself in the position of the speaker, attempting to see the problem through the other person's eyes. He must be approachable and show interest by visiting others in their place of work. He encourages new ideas that are related to practical classroom situations but helps in appraising ideas before action is instituted as well as during and after action.

The Emerging Role of the Supervisor as a Supervisory Statesman

A new emphasis is being given the supervisory role. The professional expectation that supervisors will inspire has been amplified, and responsibility for crucial purpose-setting decisions as opposed to routine housekeeping decisions has been made explicit.[21,22,23]

Differentiation must be made between (1) those whose responsibilities are focused on the development of individual members of the group and their capacity to work together as a group; and (2) those few who are primarily experts in the promotion and protection of the school's values. As we have seen, professional expectations have the supervisor helping members learn from their experience together by thinking clearly about their own problems and evaluating their group efforts. In such a role the supervisor's expertness has little to do with content; he is more concerned with persons than with policies. The new role of the super-

[20] *Ibid.*, p. 170.

[21] Murray G. Ross and Charles E. Hendry, *New Understandings of Leadership,* Association Press, New York, 1957.

[22] E. P. Learned, D. N. Ulrich, and D. R. Booz, *Executive Action,* Harvard University Graduate School of Business Administration, Boston, 1951.

[23] Philip Selznick, *Leadership in Administration,* Row, Peterson & Company, Evanston, Ill., 1957.

visory statesman[24] differs from the human relations specialist's in that
the statesman's inspiration does not derive from the processes of group
interaction and the vision of a harmonious team, whatever its end may
be. On the contrary, the supervisory statesman finds his goal and places
his commitment in the clearly defined purpose and character of the
school itself, not in narrow, practical aims set in haphazard fashion.

There has been too much preoccupation with personal feelings in
supervision. While the interest in human relations has brought a wider
understanding of why and how people work, perceive, and communicate,
it has left the observer with a sense of inadequacy. There is need to
look beyond personal relations to the larger patterns of institutional
development. This is not to say that the school's process can be understood except as it is revealed in the behavior of individuals. The problem is to link the larger view to the more limited one. The school
must be institutionalized, that is, infused with values beyond the technical requirements of the task at hand. An administrative supervisor fails
when the school drifts and is exposed to vagrant pressures, readily influenced both by short-run opportunistic trends and by those who would
commit the school as a whole on the basis of a partial assessment derived from a particular scientific or political perspective.

Essentially, the statesman's role consists in "accepting the obligation
of giving direction instead of merely ministering to organizational equilibrium; in adapting aspiration to the character of the organization, bearing in mind that what the organization has been will affect what it can
be and do; and in transcending bare organizational survival by seeing
that specialized decisions do not weaken or confuse the distinctive iden-
tity of the enterprise." [25]

This proposed role carries the assumption that supervisors have been
led away from their responsibility for making critical decisions, such as
defining the group aims and designing an enterprise directly adapted to
these aims. Critical decisions are those which affect the ultimate development of the school. This is not to say that the supervisor is free to
mold the school system as he wishes, but that he must recognize his potentialities and responsibilities as well as his limitations. Nor does it imply that the school's aims are given once and for all. We know aims are
conditioned by new definitions and adaptations to larger social situations.
The important matter is that the process of change need not be opportunistic; it can be controlled. Accordingly, the supervisor's tasks are
these:

[24] *Ibid.*
[25] *Ibid.*, p. 149.

1. *To define the school's aims.* Aims are defined in accordance with (*a*) the school's long-range commitments, its governing character and ability, and (*b*) the requirements for the school's survival after noting the findings of an assessment of the forces within and without the school. Overgeneralization of purpose is to be avoided, for it is known that when supervisors rely upon vague cardinal principles and all-inclusive imperative needs, more realistic but uncontrolled criteria set the course. In his operation, the supervisor takes care to consider the bearing of an existing or proposed procedure on the distinctive quality of the school.

2. *To transform neutral personnel into those with a sense of the school's mission.* This calls for utilizing the tools for analyzing the school's social structure and techniques for effecting change under a variety of conditions. Such tools and procedures for change will be described in subsequent chapters of this book; it may be mentioned here, however, that the defense of the school's distinctive values and competence may call for special measures in particular local buildings. If, for example, the supervisor in the central office has concern over the school's values, but a principal is under pressure to introduce a practice without taking sufficient account of its long-range consequences, the staff member from the central office must have sufficient autonomy to lay down criteria for acceptance by the principal.

There is a real connection, of course, between the role of the supervisory statesman and the basic question as to whether the school supervisor is without moral choice, a mere minion, or whether he has responsibility for fashioning a distinctive way of thinking and acting and thus help establish the foundation for achieving a particular set of goals. This, in turn, raises the question: Does the school have integrity in itself, or is it without character, merely responsive to immediate pressures?

Other Supervisory Roles

Difficulty in describing particular roles for each supervisory position arises for several reasons. First, distinctive situations make specifically different demands for supervisory behavior. Second, instead of ascribing certain roles to certain statuses, our culture's emphasis upon achievement often makes it legitimate for anyone to play anyone else's role when the usurper has the requisite skill and can help the participants. Third, there is uncertainty concerning the appropriate role for those in the newer supervisory positions associated with preparation of interns and non-professionally trained teachers.

Although the role descriptions which follow can be applied to supervisors at all levels to a greater or less degree, the illustrations are in terms of those who occupy peripheral supervisory positions: consultants and teachers engaged in teacher preparation. The roles of these positions are less clearly identified than are those of official members of the supervisory family.

The fact that these positions are labeled peripheral reveals much about the nature of supervision. Those who are closest to the center of classroom instruction are less likely to be regarded and credentialed as supervisors. Centrality in supervision lies in the ability to see the whole of the school organization, which is required for a clear focus on common goals, i.e., rationality.

Roles of Outside Consultants. What do outside consultants do when they enter a school situation? How can representatives from Federal, state, and local education offices, from colleges and universities, and from professional organizations best promote change and render on-the-job assistance to teachers? What happens to communication, lines of authority, and all the rest when an expert arrives on the scene—a supervisor whose very presence threatens the status quo?

The wide range of consultative services offered by outside consultants cuts across every aspect of instruction. There may be a need for a new developmental program in reading or a special study of anxious children. The variety of tasks means multiple roles. James and Weber, having observed sixteen consultative sessions over a period of thirty-eight days, report that 62 per cent of the consultants assumed at one time or another at least half of the following roles: answer giver, listener, ex officio suggester, interpreter, reassurer, stimulator, adviser, fraternizer, and public-relations representative. Thirty-eight per cent or fewer performed one of the following roles: synthesizer, evaluator, organizer, information gatherer, school sight-seer, demonstrator, or criticizer.[26]

Increased use of consultants by both education and industry is providing knowledge of procedures for guiding interactions of these newer supervisors with school administrator and faculty. Pertinent dangers in the consultative role have been well presented by the industrial consultant William Schwartz.[27] An adaptation of the analysis by Schwartz for school situations follows:

1. *Interference with school policy.* The outside consultant, being unfamiliar with existing policies, must of course be given every opportunity to "bone up" on them. But often schools have certain mores and follow

[26] Edward W. James and Robert A. Weber, *School Consultants: Roles Assumed and Techniques Employed,* Southwestern Co-operative Program in Educational Administration, University of Texas, Austin, Tex., p. 15.

[27] William L. K. Schwartz, "Using the Outside Expert: What to Do till the Doctor Comes," *Management Review,* vol. 47, no. 8, August, 1958.

certain informal policies which, while not spelled out in black and white, have become a tradition. Ignorance or disregard of such informal practices may assume greater proportions than the violation of obscure written policy. This is particularly true of matters affecting personnel, where teachers have come to expect certain practices to be followed because "the school has always done it."

2. *Undermining of authority.* There is a tendency, when a consultant becomes deeply and closely involved in the activities of a school, for him to assume authority for certain actions on his own. A number of conditions can bring this about. The almost constant presence of the consultant may lead teachers to regard him as a sort of "boss" and not only obey his direct instructions but look to him for direction. If the consultant detects weakness or lack of leadership, he may, almost unwittingly, move in and assume authority that is not legitimately his. The more technically competent he is, the more sensitive he will be to a poorly run organization. In such a situation, it takes considerable restraint to avoid interfering with established prerogatives.

A logical extension of the process of undermining the authority of an administrator or a supervisor is a gradual (or perhaps sudden) assumption of duties and authority. This is a particular danger where the program of the consultant is extensive and is scheduled to cover a long period of time. When there is conflict between a principal and a consultant, the attitude of the board or superintendent seems to be, "Since we have invested in the consultant to such an extent, we had best back him to the limit." Thus, duties that properly belong to the principal are surrendered to the consultant. There is an even greater opportunity for the assumption of authority by consultants when an occasional administrator gladly surrenders a portion of his obligations to anyone who will and can carry them out. This is a particular danger in a school that has been subject to difficulty of one sort or another over a long period of time; the consultant who is called in to observe and correct the situation frequently finds himself filling the gap left by the careless or inefficient principal.

3. *Administrative animosity toward the consultant.* Poor handling in this volatile area can well negate the whole value of the consulting program. There are a host of possible causes of animosity toward a consultant, and one of the most prevalent is the fear of implied criticism of an administrator, a supervisor, or an entire school because an "outsider" has been called in. Many people feel that such action is a direct reflection on their efforts.

Another cause of animosity is the feeling that the consultant does not fully understand the problems and difficulties of a particular situation.

He is frequently considered an interloper who enters the school, talks to a few teachers or pupils, and then, from his "objective and detached" position, makes recommendations that are impossible or, at best, impractical to implement. Animosity toward the consulting personnel may also result from an administrator's fear of the danger discussed before, that is, fear that the consultant will undermine or assume his authority. In cases where such usurpation has actually begun to take place, administrators are quick to recognize it and to feel that their position is being abrogated.

There is the danger of too much zeal on the part of the consultant. A "new broom" attitude that suggests "I am here to show you how things should be done" is the consultant's quickest and surest route to failure. A consultant's tasks call, above all, for diplomacy, and all suggestions must be made with tact.

4. *Dissatisfaction of similarly qualified personnel.* It is possible that there are those within the school who could do the job as effectively as the consultant—perhaps, because of their familiarity with the school, even more effectively. To avoid ill-feeling, board and administrators should ascertain who the qualified school personnel are before hiring the consultant. Are there reasons why they cannot do the job as well as a consultant? Are they too close to the job? Are there policy reasons why an objective observer would be more useful or diplomatic? If, after the situation has been thoroughly investigated, it is found that for some reason outside consultants are either necessary or desirable, the reasons should be explained both to the personnel who will work with the consultant and to those with qualifications similar to his. People who see a highly paid consultant doing the same sort of work that they are doing, for no apparent reason, can easily lose confidence in themselves and in the leadership of the school.

There is another aspect of this problem that merits attention—the problem of recognition. When personnel of the school and consultants have worked hand-in-hand to attain a certain result, will the staff be given recognition for their efforts, or will they be ignored when credit is being assigned? This is a special problem when a new idea has come from the consultant but the drudgery of implementation has fallen to the school's personnel.

5. *Jealousy of highly paid consultants.* The consultant is often a highly paid specialist, but his talents may not always be obvious to those with whom he works. When the salary of a consultant or the amount of money that the district is paying for consultant services becomes known throughout the organization, the district must be especially careful to justify its position.

Special privileges enjoyed by the consultant may also be a cause of jealousy. A consultant's obligations to his own organization often make frequent absences from the school necessary. His hours of arrival or departure, the length of time he takes for lunch, and similar apparent privileges may have an adverse effect upon staff morale, particularly among the lower echelons of supervision and among the faculty. By regularizing his privileges and allotting specific times for his outside activities, administrators can often eliminate such criticism.

The Roles of Supervising Teachers. Approximately 75,000 teachers in the United States annually perform major roles in the professional education of student teachers. Many others have responsibility for helping fellow teachers in-service. Known by such titles as critic, cooperating, master, resident, helping, and training teachers, they equip novices with the experience necessary for a beginning proficiency in teaching. These veteran teachers have raised questions about their responsibility, seeking clarification of the behavioral roles they must assume as supervisors. The Association for Student Teaching in its thirty-eighth yearbook[28] gave special attention to an analysis of the work of supervisory teachers, emphasizing that the supervisors stress the development of the teacher-to-be as a "self-directive, creating teacher with ideas of his own."

Systematic study of opinions regarding the desired roles of the supervising teacher has revealed the following:[29]

1. *He helps the beginning teacher find purpose in his teaching.*
In what ways should pupils be different after their experiences in this class? What should they know and be able to do at the end of the semester? Through such questions supervisory and student teachers together formulate a sense of direction and an overall plan. This early planning suggests tentative statements of expected behavioral outcomes for pupils and proposes the kinds of evidence which will indicate the extent to which outcomes are attained. Subsequently, pupils, too, influence the selection of purposes and methods of evaluation. Understandings of goals deepen as they are defined in practice. Purpose is revealed daily as teachers and pupils reflect upon their life in the class and consider what they must do next to attain the skills, knowledge, and satisfactions which they seek.

2. *He furthers the beginning teacher's sensitivity to individual students and the dynamics of the classroom.*
How is the class getting along? Evaluation of the progress of pupils enables the new teacher to focus upon individuals, making him aware of the different rates and different means by which pupils learn.

---

[28] Association for Student Teaching, *The Supervising Teacher,* Thirty-eighth Yearbook, Iowa State Teachers College, Cedar Falls, Iowa, 1959.

[29] John D. McNeil, "What Is the Role of the Teacher of Teachers?" *CTA Journal,* vol. 55, no. 5, May, 1959.

The new teacher is encouraged to take advantage of opportunities for incidental personal conversations with individual pupils and to contribute to
the success of problem-solving groups in order that he might understand
and communicate with all. As he finds himself thinking of children and himself as fellow learners in a common undertaking, the student teacher is freed
from a self-centered view of teaching which calls for indiscriminate dispens-
ing of facts.

No longer does he bluff when he hasn't the answer nor restrict the intellectual curiosity of pupils to the narrow confines of lessons, preserving his
status as authority figure.

3. *He enables the beginning teacher to vitalize instruction.*

What situations will cause the class to feel it necessary to engage in an
important educational venture? What problem areas and sequential activities
are most appropriate? How can we ensure that problems for investigation
are fruitful, calling for valuable content and leading to an understanding of
desirable concepts? What opportunities are there for pupils to participate
in the selection of activities, identifying skills and information necessary for
the success of the undertaking? How might the class generalize, apply and
determine the worth of the results? What instruction must be presented before the class can do these things? What resources and details should be considered? Presenting these and similar questions, the experienced teacher assists the new teacher in thinking through instructional approaches.

Instruction becomes effective through continuous specific attention to
techniques associated with organizing materials, arranging room environment, giving instructions and demonstrations, conducting discussions, con-
structing evaluative measures and the like. It becomes efficient after the two
teachers see and discuss profound and universal questions which are present
in the daily events of the classroom. When a routine task, such as completing
an attendance form, raises questions from pupils as to their obligation to
provide valid information, the student teacher is awakened to the opportunity to increase pupil concern about ultimate values, e.g., the particular worth
of a human being and truth as related to a person.

4. *He gives the student teacher a view of teaching as learning.*

One never arrives in teaching. So complex is the task of working with
unique personalities in ever-changing classes that the teacher must continue
to propose and test new hypotheses. The inexperienced teacher sees that experts develop original plans with each class and that these teachers regard
many of their past procedures and tendencies to action as inappropriate for
the present and future. Sagacity in selecting theoretical content and relating
it to the pupils' lives requires continuing scholarship and intimacy with the
times.

Because he works with a teacher who has faith in himself and in other
people, the student teacher is encouraged to clarify the meaning of his proposals and to try out his own ideas, experiencing the excitement and sense
of growth which accompanies intellectual adventure. Through solitary reflection and joint probing, the two teachers try to extract the full meaning

of the experience in the belief that as they develop their processes for interpreting what has been and is taking place they are best preparing for their futures. The security of the supervising teacher makes possible the acceptance of differences which exist between the two: the supervising teacher knows that good can come from these differences. Warm human relations grow out of the productive conflicts between them since the focus for improvement and resolution of disagreement centers around the progress of pupils and is task-centered rather than personal.

5. *He influences the student teacher to act professionally.* The ethical patterns of the supervising teacher are captured by the one who works with him. Among the behaviors which the new teacher evidences are these: he consults frequently with others in a give-and-take manner, willingly sharing his best teaching practices; he supports his fellow teachers even when they appear eccentric; he lightens the load of custodians; he uses the curriculum guides of the school district, adapting them for his classes and making recommendations for their revision; he is sympathetic toward parents and their problems.

The supervising teacher takes care to point out ways organized teachers are becoming part of the power structure in the school and in the larger social setting, endeavoring to improve education through the establishment of higher standards and participation in all aspects of educational policy making. Frequently, he includes the new teacher in activities of the total staff and professional groups.

What does the teacher of teachers do? It is his responsibility to provide situations where the new teacher can himself discover and appropriate that learning which accustoms to action. In so doing, he seeks understanding of teaching mission and process, trying to identify those matters which have significant influence on his and the student teacher's behavior. Although he invites imitation, the supervising teacher encourages originality and modification of belief and practice in terms of the student teacher's own individuality.

SUMMARY STATEMENT

To ask "Who is a supervisor?" is to invite such responses as these: (1) one who holds a supervisory position, (2) one who actually makes a difference in the operations of the school by exercising authority or influence, and (3) one who spends his time on particular organizational functions. There are kernels of truth, too, in the stereotypes representing the supervisor as a personnel agent intent upon influencing others in group situations and as a central person of virtue and sovereignty in whom the teacher finds emotional support and professional guidance.

We have seen that official responsibilities and honor have been distributed among many supervisory positions. Distinctions have been made, for example, between supervisors who deal with the promotion and protection of the school's values and specialists in human relations who develop individuals and their capacity to work together as a group. Higher status is given those whose duties are to develop policies and to decide upon their implementation as opposed to those who are to spend time on the actual implementation. On the other hand, the supervising teacher who helps the novice find purpose in his work reminds us that in a sense every position in the school carries an obligation to promote values and make critical decisions. We believe that supervision is itself a distributive function, a common dimension in the expected role behavior of those who hold various positions in the school system (Figure 2-1).

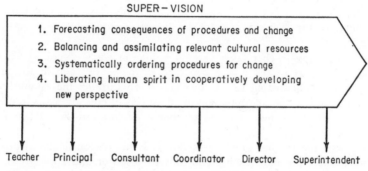

Figure 2-1. Supervision: a dimension of behavior in many positions.

The complexities of the social structure of the school and the requirements for change in curriculum and instruction which demand the exercise of judgment as well as motivation are especially striking. While coordination of effort and a common body of organized knowledge are necessary for the individual teacher to function effectively as a part of the over-all system, it is also essential that the teacher be able to make rational choices without waiting for official approval. *Therefore, it seems fitting to designate the supervisor as a leader who has possession of two properties: one, a clear perspective of the school's goals and awareness of its resources and qualities, and, two, the ability to help others contribute to this vision and to perceive and to act in accordance with it.* This description is not without its consequences and pressing problems:

1. Are perspective and harmony best achieved by correlating specialized assignments in accordance with a system-wide scheme?

2. Are sense of mission and rational behavior attained when supervisors keep each teacher informed about the work of the entire organization?

3. How can the supervisor best resolve the conflict he faces because of differences in the expectations teachers, superintendent, and board hold for his role?

4. Which supervisory position or positions are best fitted for discharging the tasks associated with the supervisory statesman?

5. Can a school have integrity as an institution, or is it without individual character and are its goals subjected to whichever pressures are strongest?

6. Why is the supervisor sometimes considered a mere minion whose human and technical skills are for hire for any purpose?

Procedures for answering these questions and for acquiring the perspective and behavior demanded of the supervisor will be developed in subsequent parts of this book. As the next step, let us see how we can best select and prepare those who are to provide vision to the schools, maintain balance in the curriculum, and offer help with the specifics for the improvement of instruction.

3

SELECTION AND
PREPARATION OF
SUPERVISORS

O RGANIZATIONS with high prestige have long been concerned
with selecting and developing key personnel. They have
learned from experience that they cannot rely on the individual to acquire by independent effort the range of competence that he would need
if he later found himself in a major leadership position. No individual
left to his own devices is likely to acquire the wealth of experience essential to effective performance in a top leadership post. In contrast,
schools have only recently been concerned with systematically recruit-
ing and developing a select supervisory group. Many schools are still
appointing supervisors on the basis of their long service as teachers, their
popularity in the faculty, their success in athletics, or other visible activity. It is noteworthy that a supervisor of an English department in a
large high school could jest that she was nominated for the position because she lost no textbooks the previous year.

Stimulus for more effective programs of selection and preparation is
also generated because of the keen competition among all professions
for top-quality manpower. The disturbing acknowledgment by institutions which prepare educational leaders that education is losing in the
competition for talent has led to (1) proposals for more selective ad-
missions to graduate programs leading to degrees and supervisory cre-

dentials, (2) recruitment efforts revealing the attractions of educational leadership, and (3) higher levels of professional preparation for all certified supervisory personnel. There exists the issue of whether education is best served by encouraging large numbers to undertake the study of supervision or by restricting graduate courses in supervision to a small number of highly qualified students.

Conscious of the need for upgrading the quality of leadership, school systems and institutions offering preparation in educational supervision have begun studying means of developing more effective programs of selection and preparation. In order to understand these developments, we shall (1) survey present policies and procedures in the selection of personnel for supervisory positions; (2) evaluate certification requirements; (3) describe trends in the education of supervisors; and (4) review research on leadership, showing its implications for the selection of supervisors.

POLICIES AND PROCEDURES IN THE SELECTION OF SUPERVISORS

Selection Procedures in School Districts

Appointment and advancement in terms of results obtained is a generally accepted method of filling jobs in higher echelons. "Didn't Miss Smith do a superior job with student teachers? . . . All right—advance her to coordinator for English. Didn't pupils and faculty alike praise Ray Harris for the way he guided the student council? . . . All right—recommend him for vice-principal in charge of instruction." These after-the-fact methods are useful in that those who are good leaders in one situation tend to be good leaders in another. They are wasteful in that it is far from certain that an individual who has been good in one position will succeed in another. While both a cooperating teacher and a coordinator exercise supervision, the supervision required in the two cases is not the same kind or of the same order.

Present procedures for selecting instructional leaders are not encouraging. Extensive studies of the methods used by school boards in selecting superintendents, for example, reveal that seldom are there specific procedures or standards of selection. Interviews held with candidates are usually informal visits during which the board member sizes up the applicant by asking whatever questions occur to him. Members of school boards appear to place more emphasis on the candidate's appearance, ability to get along with others, and previous experience in a similar position than on his vision as an educational leader. Perspective and statesmanlike leadership, including possession of an educational philosophy, are sometimes not considered of consequence by school board members.

The National Education Association Research Division has surveyed statements of policy for selecting supervisory and administrative personnel. Chief among the findings from this survey are these:[1]

1. Most districts require a master's degree for anyone entering a supervisory position, and usually a minimum number of recent postgraduate courses in supervision are required.

2. Only a few systems set any limitation on age, but experience requirements vary a great deal from city to city. Nearly all school systems require several years of "successful" or "outstanding" teaching experience.

3. Persons already in the school system are given preference for promotion in the majority of school systems. Smaller school districts often, however, find it necessary to consider outsiders in order to find qualified personnel.

4. When there is a supervisory position open, most schools advertise as widely as possible. Methods include posting of announcements in all schools, mentioning the job and its requirements in the superintendent's bulletin, sending a letter to all teachers, and notifying placement bureaus and colleges.

5. Those interested in supervisory positions fill out application forms giving their education, experience, and references. These are usually checked for factual information before the applicant is allowed to go further in the procedures. Sometimes a screening committee at this point eliminates those not considered to be good material.

6. In many school districts examinations are required for those who pass the initial screening process. Often the applicant has to take a written test first. If he passes this, he goes on to an oral examination. The oral examination may be an informal interview or a structured interview with the discussion based on specific points on which the applicant is given a numerical rating on the basis of his replies.

7. Essay and interview sections of the examination are usually rated by committees composed chiefly of administrators appointed by the superintendent. Teachers and representatives of professional organizations serve on these committees occasionally.

8. Some districts have elaborate promotional procedures by which all qualifications of the applicant are given numerical ratings. These ratings form the basis of a list of eligible candidates. Sometimes school districts

[1] "Policies and Procedures in the Selection of Personnel for Administrative Positions," *Educational Research Service,* American Association of School Administrators and National Education Association Research Division, Washington, Circular no. 6, 1958.

which have detailed promotional procedures still reserve the right of the superintendent or the board of education to choose *anyone* they feel is best qualified.

9. A number of school districts have instituted training programs for future school leaders. These programs have various names—in-service, leadership training, internship, and apprenticeship.

Certification Requirements for Supervisors

Responsibility for the selection of supervisors rests not only with local school systems, but indirectly with those who set certification requirements for supervisors and with those in college departments of education who establish minimum standards for admission to programs of preparation.

State certification requirements for supervisors represent the minimum standards established by law and reflect the views of official state committees, including representatives from state education department personnel, teacher-education institutions, professional organizations, as well as many persons in various official positions. A status study of certification requirements by Richard [2] reveals that in most states school supervisors must have had specific preparation through college courses in (1) school organization and administration; (2) supervision: its aims, scope, and desirable outcomes, principles and practices; (3) curriculum development and construction; (4) evaluation of instruction; and (5) courses appropriate to the type and level of responsibilities of the particular supervisory position.

A recurrent point of emphasis in statements of requirements is that recency of education and experience are important considerations. Verification of successful public school service which constitutes an adequate basis for the preparation of supervisors often includes such items as these:[3]

1. Leadership in education as demonstrated by superior teaching, participation in activities such as curriculum development, individual counseling, community work, teachers' organizations, supervision of student teachers, and by being selected by teachers and administrators for special responsibilities.

2. Evidence of breadth and variety of experience as an elementary teacher who has served at both the primary and the more advanced grade levels and as a librarian who has also shown competency as a classroom teacher.

[2] Virginia Richard, "Certification Requirements for Supervisors in the United States," *Educational Leadership,* vol. 12, no. 3, December, 1954.

[3] California State Department of Education, Division of Departmental Administration, *The Supervision Credential,* art. 50.1, November, 1956.

PREPARATION OF SUPERVISORS

In general, recommendations for the advanced preparation of supervisors are comprehensive and suggest modifying traditional concepts of scheduling and methods of instruction. The suggested programs usually emphasize the ways teachers can be helped in the specific field to be supervised, including information on materials of instruction, their sources, availability, criteria for selection, and techniques of utilization. Preparation in the techniques of supervision gives attention to the selection, placement, and orientation of teachers, in-service programs, and evaluation of teaching success. Candidates study a variety of ways in which people work together successfully and analyze both individual and group behavior to learn how people may be helped in their professional adjustments and interpersonal relations. Practice in the use of group processes, which includes ways of organizing groups, planning, securing participation, and problem solving, is recommended.

Experiences directed toward improvement of the skills of communication are frequently provided. These include practice in oral and written reporting, speaking to community groups, writing press releases, and preparing supervisory bulletins. With respect to curriculum development, the prospective supervisor becomes familiar with programs in both large and small school systems and identifies the behaviors of the supervisor in encouraging curriculum activity. He studies the roles of professional and lay persons in the establishment of instructional goals. He learns how to use the findings of research and to engage in inquiry himself. He becomes familiar with a number of special answers to the problem of providing for individual differences and evaluating the total learning process.

The candidate for a supervisory position is expected to have a clear understanding of the responsibility and relationship of teachers, administrators, supervisors, and members of governing boards in the organization of school systems and in the profession. This understanding is assumed to come about as he has the opportunity to practice the behavior believed to be most appropriate in meeting the problems of community-school interactions.

The Internship

A popular design for the program of preparation is the internship. This arrangement has been reviewed by Cox, who incorporated in her review the research and promising practices in the education of super-vision:[4]

1. *University recruitment.* The candidate is sought by the university as a prospective supervisor and screened by a committee on the recruitment and selection of supervisors. Noteworthy in the work of this committee is the clear statement of qualifications required and the thoroughness of investigation. Following receipt of the candidate's application, a member of the recruitment and selection committee visits the applicant for a threefold purpose: (*a*) to answer questions about the work of a supervisor, (*b*) to describe the study-work-study program that is to help prepare one for supervision, and (*c*) to secure additional information about the candidate before making a recommendation for his acceptance in the program.

2. *Preparation for supervision while teaching.* The candidate is assisted by leaders in the local school district who make available a variety of experiences. He may accept leadership responsibilities in school and community committees, serve as a resource person to teachers, participate in meeting with supervisors, and help a supervisor in his daily work.

3. *Attendance at a summer workshop for school leaders.* The candidate attends a summer workshop. Members of the workshop are those seeking leadership positions closely related to each other. Each person's position involves him as a member of a leadership team.

a. The team spends about two hours each day considering how the principles of supervision, basic teaching-learning processes, and human development and behavior apply on the job. Often experiences of the team help clarify roles for improving the learning environment and the skills required for these roles.

b. For another block of time, the candidate has opportunities to work with other school leaders in the study of problems of common interest. "For example, an interest group dealing with initiating a system-wide testing program studies the values and limitations of tests, the selection and administration of tests, and the interpretation and use of test data. They then 'spell out' the responsibilities of each school leader in this across-the-board task." The workshop offers much opportunity for seeing how problems might be viewed by those in other leadership positions; for holding conferences, reading and preparing reports; and for considering how principles learned will apply in the particular situation in which each member expects to be working as a supervisor in the fall.

[4] Johnnye V. Cox, "Educating Supervisors in Changing Concepts," *Educational Leadership,* vol. 16, no. 8, May, 1959.

c. Preparation for the fall assignment in a school system is also undertaken during the summer workshop. Candidates visit the school system to secure first-hand knowledge of programs, plans, and problems and to meet many of the principals and teachers as well as parents and children. Visits to community agencies and groups are included at this time.

d. Supervisors at the workshop become familiar with the services provided by the state department of education, meeting consultants who are available to work with them and learning ways the supervisor can assist the department with state-wide activities and service.

4. *Participation in the first year of internship.* The candidate is employed as a full-time supervisor while enrolled at the university for the internship. During the internship, there are monthly meetings with the university adviser for help with personal problems, for evaluation of supervisory activities, and for planning new learning experiences. Records of supervisor's activities are regularly kept, and a copy is given to the adviser weekly. All supervisors participating in the internship meet for several three-day conferences where they share materials and study problems of common concern. Leaders for the conference are the supervisors themselves, although help is given them by resource persons from the university and personnel from the state department of education. Assessment of the intern's understandings and skills in major supervisory functions is determined at this conference, and this evaluation is used for planning work to be undertaken at the university in the summer. The second summer program at the university features development of an action research study in connection with a problem of common concern to the supervisor and other school personnel.

5. *Participation in the second year of internship.* On-the-job study during the second year of internship is concentrated on the action research project formulated during the spring and summer. At the end of the second year and third summer session, the candidate receives a six-year diploma and is designated as a "specialist in supervision."

The number of internships and the number of institutions offering them are increasing. Internships offered in the several training institutions are organized on varying time bases, have no common denominator as to types or extent of experiences provided for the intern, and are characterized by few common standards of supervisory procedure.[5] Using a judgmental procedure with twenty professional experts, Baber was able to list four criteria for evaluating these programs:[6]

[5] Eric R. Baber, "A Critical Appraisal of Internship Theories and Practices Relating to the Professional Preparation of Educational Administrators," unpublished Ed.D. dissertation, Michigan State University, 1953.
    [6] *Ibid.*

1. The internship should consist largely of significant work necessary to the well-being of an on-going educational program—not so-called "made" work.

2. The internship should provide substantial opportunity for creative thought and action on the part of the intern.

3. The internship should make provision for joint planning, action, and evaluation by the intern, his college adviser, and the supervisory administrator in the cooperating school community.

4. The internship should make provision for flexibility in the type of assignment to meet better the needs and interests of the individual intern as determined by himself and his advisers.

Internship programs offer the advantage of improving the relationships between colleges and school communities. Through these arrangements, school systems become acquainted with the philosophy of the institutions preparing supervisors and, in turn, the institutions gain a better understanding of local problems and practices. Theory and practice go hand in hand in raising the level of the profession. It is important, however, that experiences in the program do not become disconnected, repetitive, and divorced from theory. The candidate should be helped to discriminate between desirable and undesirable practices observed in the field situation, and care should be taken that he is not subjected to repetition of routine tasks in which he has previously demonstrated competence.

Other Criteria and Programs for the Preparation of Supervisors

It is emphasized that the internship is only one method by which programs for the preparation of supervisors can be more effective. Attempts to make classroom work, seminars, surveys, and field trips more highly significant are under way. The Commission on Colleges and Universities of the North Central Association, for example, adopted these recommendations for programs preparing supervisors:[7]

1. Attention should be given to specific needs of individual students, yet offer a coherent and organized program—not a collection of miscellaneous courses. Needs of individuals should be based on terms of competence and qualities sought.

2. The institution should clearly define the basic knowledge and competencies requisite for the given specialty, and the students' work should be centered around this basic content.

3. In the interest of maintaining a level of work that is truly of gradu-

[7] *The North Central Association Quarterly,* vol. 33, no. 3, pp. 210–227, January, 1959.

ate caliber, the number of courses open to both graduate and undergraduate students should be limited.

4. A special research project should be required as part of the program. The particular type of project may follow any one of a variety of directions. The project should allow the student to demonstrate his technical skill in the field of specialization and his recognition of the implications of his specialty for the educational enterprises in general.

5. The institution should set a definite time limit within which the program can be completed. When too long a period of time lapses, the impact of the concentrated work required for developing a high level of specialized skill may be lost.

With respect to entering a specialist program, the Commission makes the following recommendations:

1. Possession of a master's degree or the equivalent in academic training.

2. Previous experience appropriate to area of specialization. A curriculum coordinator should probably have had a certain amount of teaching experience at the school level where he intends to pursue his specialty.

Programs for the Continuing Development of Supervisors

Many preparing institutions train for uncertainty and for further inquiry. Typical of the open-ended attitude of some graduate schools is the story of a dean who remarked at commencement, "One-half of what you have learned here is false; unfortunately, we don't know which half."

The answers to the problem of continuity of learning rest upon the habits of learning how to learn, which the supervisor can be led to acquire. Part of this preparation entails saturating the supervisor with the teachings of social, psychological, and ethical philosophy of education as well as equipping him to be a student of the subject matter with which he is to deal. The principles of these fields, however, must be incorporated in his thought processes—in the very way he observes instructional situations and plans courses of action. It is more important for the supervisor to fix his controlling habits in line with the theories of his foundation disciplines than to imitate current practices which he sees succeed in an empirical way. Without theory, his methods will be picked up through blind trial and error. Any immediate supervisory skill acquired only from nonrational observation of experienced and successful supervisors will be at the cost of the power to go on learning. The supervisor who leaves the professional school with immediate proficiency in a number of techniques associated with supervision but who lacks the inquiring qualities of a student of education is not likely to grow as a director of learning. Similar conclusions have been reached regarding the preparation of teachers. "How often do candid instructors in training schools for teachers acknowledge disappointment in the later careers of even their most promising candidates! They seem to strike twelve at the start. There is an unexpected and seemingly unaccountable failure to maintain steady growth. Is this in some part due to the undue premature stress laid in early practice work upon securing immediate capability? . . ." [8]

Instead of criticizing the trainee too specifically, instructors in the university, for instance, should direct their efforts to getting the novice supervisor to judge his own work critically, to find out in what ways he has succeeded or failed, and to discover the probable reasons for both success and failure.

Use of Simulation as an Instructional Method in the Preparation of Supervisors

Simulative materials are being used to relate theoretical concepts to practical problems and to encourage self-learning among those preparing for educational leadership.[9] These materials presently include a variety of both printed and audio-visual aids by which selected representations of supervisory situations are presented to those in training. Participants in simulated situations actually work within the content of an elaborate case study as they assume certain supervisory positions in the study. The procedure calls for each member to act—not merely to tell what action would be desirable. Analysis of consequences of action, study of background materials, role playing, making of decisions, and discussion afforded by the simulative process are generally found to be helpful. A key advantage of this method is that the instructor can get realism in his teaching, yet control this realism so that it results in better understanding of the concepts and theory for attacking and solving educational problems. The specific problems are examined against pertinent background information designed to help one acquire the "ability to see the whole picture—each problem in its broader context." [10] In addition, because simulation provides many opportunities for learner per-

[8] John Dewey, in *The Relation of Theory to Practice in the Education of Teachers,* The Third Yearbook, National Society for the Scientific Study of Education, Charles A. McMurry (ed.), Department of Education, University of Chicago, 1904, pp. 15–16.

[9] Jack A. Culbertson and William H. Coffield (eds.), *Simulation in Administrative Training,* The University Council for Educational Administration, Columbus, Ohio, 1960.

[10] *Professional Administrators for America's Schools,* American Association of School Administrators, Washington, 1960, p. 44.

formance, the novice supervisor has the chance to assess his competencies in relation to a range of supervisory demands.

In-service Education for Supervisors

Because vastly greater numbers of working supervisors need the help
of professional resources than do the smaller number of those who will
be new to the job each year, cooperating programs for supervisors in-
service have been established. Professional organizations, school authorities, and colleges are working together in offering in-service training
programs especially designed to meet needs over and above the traditional degree requirements. These in-service practices include research
undertakings, workshops, clinics, school study councils, informal seminars, and professional conferences—all of which are often carried on
with the cooperation of school systems, state departments of education,
and universities. Organizationally, however, we have seldom arrived at
a program which carries the authority, standards, and conditions of
work in a university and offers an equal partnership to school districts
in meeting their special demands.

Development through Analysis of Performance

Although a long-range objective of a school district's supervisory development program may call for the development of people, an immediate objective is to help every supervisor improve his performance in
his present position. In doing this, the supervisor is, of course, encouraged to prepare for increasing responsibilities. Less emphasis is placed
upon a supervisor's personal and personality qualifications as a potential
for promotion and more on the results he is able to achieve in his
present work. Acceptance of the principle that "all development is self-
development" has led to the supervisor's sharing in the responsibility for
analyzing his performance and setting up a development plan. One illustration is found in the situation where a superintendent of schools and a
director of instruction agree at the start of the year on the objectives the
director is to accomplish. Twelve months later the two review the accomplishments against the objectives and decide what is to be done the
following year, the subordinate taking the lead in determining the developmental action necessary in light of the appraisal. This kind of developmental program promotes better understanding of the performance expected, and enables the supervisor, in this case the superintendent, to
see how certain weaknesses on the part of others (the director) might
be traceable to his own weaknesses in supervision.

Development through the Training Laboratory

Some supervisory development programs try to help supervisors achieve emotional maturity as a leadership variable. The criterion for such maturity is usually "how fully one says what he thinks, holding a conviction, but balancing it with a respect for others." Underlying this goal is the assumption mentioned earlier that one matures only through a knowledge of self. A leader is held to be one who is sure of himself, not threatened by the expressions of others or his own feeling, and secure with his own position. However, ventures into the realm of personal help to supervisors, which have become numerous in education and industry alike,[11] carry with them the need for distinguishing between psychological therapy and education for supervision.

The Research Center for Group Dynamics of the University of Michigan, with the Department of Adult Education, National Education Association, has been responsible for operating a national training laboratory which seeks to help leaders behave in such a way that they solve problems effectively and have individually satisfying experiences. In England, the Tavistock Institute of Human Relations has engaged in research into ways supervisors can develop the ideas, attitudes, and skills of others. Findings from these research centers in group dynamics are tried and transmitted through the various developmental programs for supervisors. Methods taught in the programs are of importance in furthering the leadership skills of supervisors and the continuing growth of the supervisor himself.

Among the problems frequently considered in training programs are those of handling conflict and disagreement. Training procedures lead not only to understanding of the nature of conflict but to recognition of the feeling which accompanies attempts to resolve it. The faith exists that warm human relations grow out of conflict actually experienced by the participants. The following assumptions and practices are often found in supervisory development programs:

[11] Herbert A. Thelen, *Dynamics of Groups at Work,* University of Chicago Press, Chicago, 1954.

Cyril Sofer and Geoffrey Hutton, *New Ways in Management Training,* Tavistock Publications Limited, London, 1958.

Nathaniel Cantor, *The Learning Process for Managers,* Harper & Brothers, New York, 1958.

National Society for the Study of Education, *In-service for Teachers, Supervisors, and Administrators,* Education, The Fifty-sixth Yearbook, University of Chicago Press, Chicago, 1957.

Assumptions

1. Knowledge is important when it carries import for its possessor.
2. Learning is the remaking of experience which makes a difference in the behavior of the learner.
3. Learning occurs only as one can emotionally afford to learn.
4. We seek to dominate others because of our own felt inadequacies.

Practices

1. There are numerous opportunities to diagnose the group's difficulties and feelings, and the member's perception of others.
2. The atmosphere permits expression of unpopular and disagreeable feelings relevant to the problem in order for change to occur.
3. The change sought in an individual's performance is more than an intelligent adaptation; it is a whole new pattern of personality which carries over into other situations.
4. Those seeking to improve their supervisory potential try to acquire an increased sensitivity to social and psychological situations and to the consequences of organizational changes, rather than precise answers and formalities.

The laboratory experience which deals with people's feelings, tension release, and sensitive situations in which participants learn to express themselves and to understand the communications they are making is not necessarily void of reason. There is a connection between intellectual and emotional behavior. MacMurray[12] speaks of a rationality of feeling. A thought is rational when it fits accurately the object or the situation to which it refers; so, too, an emotion is rational when it fits the occasion. Those most concerned with intelligent behavior in organizations have long been interested in finding techniques that may be used to present emotions from blocking rationality. Mannheim, for example, saw the group approaches of psychoanalysis as a means not only to individual self-understanding but for dealing with the maladjustments of groups and institutions.[13] Others who favor the method of practical intelligence deliberately involve emotion in the process of judgment. Practical judgment is said to be "the process in which people are educated to see the significance of emotions and drives, so that they come to use them effectively in securing personal and social satisfaction as part of an

---

[12] John MacMurray, "Developing Emotions," *Saturday Review*, Sept. 13, 1958.
[13] Karl Mannheim, *Man and Society in an Age of Reconstruction,* Harcourt, Brace and Company, Inc., New York, 1941, p. 84.

intelligent method of creating bonds of community." [14] Generally, recognition of our feelings with regard to a problem is the beginning of intelligent behavior.

Obviously, those offering training programs for supervisors are not always successful. Sometimes supervisors grasp the course in the sense of understanding its intellectual content but are not able to achieve greater effectiveness in behavior. The personality differences of some supervisors inhibit them from making appreciable use of training. Also, the requirements of supervisory situations vary so widely that it is difficult to provide all that supervisors may want or need.

QUALITIES SOUGHT IN SUPERVISORS

Admittedly, behavior and qualities identified with successful supervision are not necessarily the same as those behaviors and qualities which facilitate *ascent* to supervisory positions. Nevertheless, clues to supervisory potential can be found through analysis of those leadership characteristics which enable a supervisor to maintain his leadership position.

We have already noted that one objective criterion of leadership in supervision resides in the extent to which the supervisor exercises influence over others. This ability may be treated separately from the power to change the behavior of others because of an official position with its accompanying sanctions, such as ratings and the power of recommendation. A second index of leadership behavior is the degree to which the organization or group for which one is responsible functions as a unit. The achievement of unity is closely associated with the goal setting and communication behavior of the supervisor. Only a limited number of other characteristics of leadership behavior have been identified; among them are technical proficiency, initiating and directing action, consideration for followers, stressing of production, and social awareness.[15]

As indicated previously, leadership is differently evaluated by those above and below. In a school organization those who hold positions superior to that of the supervisor expect him to insist upon rather strict discipline and to follow closely standard operating procedures. Many school boards want a supervisor who has the ability to:

1. Sell, push, pressure, persuade teachers to improvement and loyalty to the system

[14] Margaret Fisher, *Leadership and Intelligence,* Bureau of Publications, Teachers College, Columbia University, New York, 1954, p. 105.

[15] Cecil B. Gibb, "Leadership," *Handbook of Social Psychology,* Gardner Lindzey (ed.), Addison-Wesley Publishing Company, Inc., Reading, Mass., 1954, p. 916.

2. Collect facts, weigh them, and make effective decisions

3. Know the board's policies, objectives, and practices of the district

4. Communicate policies and practices clearly to teachers

5. Evaluate performance according to the board's policies and procedures

On the other hand, the supervisor's subordinates "expect and value his mingling with them, his use of consultation procedures, his showing consideration for them and their needs, and his being socially sensitive." [16]

The expectations of the task and the institutionalization of the group are all factors in the situation to which the leader must adapt. In a steeply hierarchical school organization the most effective leader is one who recognizes the structure and conforms closely to its expectations.[17]

It is generally true that teachers prefer a supervisor who "goes to bat" for them and sides with them in conflicts with higher authorities. However, if a supervisor sides with the teachers but is not capable of influencing the authorities in the teachers' behalf, it is unlikely that the teachers will want him for their supervisor. In one study in an industrial situation, for instance, Pelz found that supportive behavior from the supervisor resulted in employee satisfaction only in the presence of influence upon higher echelons. It was the combination of these two conditions (supportive behavior and influence with authorities) which went with higher satisfaction.[18]

The teacher may not want less consideration behavior but, recognizing the organizational context, he knows he must satisfy himself with less personal attention from his supervisor in order that the supervisor may, in turn, interact more freely with higher authorities and thus exercise greater influence upon them.

Different people want different kinds of leaders. Sanford [19] found that authoritarians prefer status-laden leadership—strong authority and direction on the part of the supervisor. Toward weak leaders they express open hostility. Contrarily, equalitarians are able to accept strong leadership if the situation demands it, but they have no need for powerful authorities. Authoritarians care little for personal warmth in their leader but they do demand that he contribute to their movement toward group and individual goals. "Equalitarians are inclined to evaluate

[16] *Ibid.*, p. 916.

[17] *Ibid.*, p. 896.

[18] D. C. Pelz, "Leadership within a Hierarchical Organization," *Journal of Social Issues*, vol. 7, pp. 49–55, 1951.

[19] F. H. Sanford, "Research on Military Leadership," *Psychology in the World Emergency*, University of Pittsburgh Press, Pittsburgh, 1952, pp. 17–74.

leaders in terms of their 'human relations' behavior and their group process rather than goal orientation. . . . Authoritarians are dissatisfied and uncomfortable under a non-directive leader. A group of equalitarians could be expected to go into a decline under a rigid and directive leader." [20]

There is no doubt that the confusion over supervisory functions is a major factor in the confusion over the qualities sought in the supervisor. If the only function of supervision is to engage in routine decision making, the selection and preparation of supervisors will not be as extensive as it will be if supervisors are expected to serve as supervisory statesmen with important responsibility for making critical decisions affecting the school's development.

Trait Analysis and Personality Assessment

Early analyses of leadership and supervision included lists of the traits and other characteristics which in the opinion of the analyst were important in the performance of the job. Such lists not only suffered from the use of vague terms but appeared almost contradictory: "flexibility," "Catonian strength of conviction," "common sense," "imagination." Further, those who listed traits designated as necessary for a supervisor to possess usually did not suggest which traits were most important and which least, nor did they note how the same trait functions differently in personalities which are organized differently. Height, weight, energy, self-confidence, talkativeness, geniality, originality, and numerous other personality traits do not consistently characterize leaders. Underlying the "trait theory" of leadership is the assumption that leadership resides in an individual, that it is a possession which he is capable of producing in different groups and in different situations. A more supportable contention is that a person does not become a leader because of his pattern of personality traits, but because these traits bear some relevance to the characteristics, activities, and goals of the group of which he is a leader.

Earlier in this chapter the importance of intelligence was stressed in connection with education's competitive race for talent. Even this factor, however, is not the "general leadership trait" which some seek. Investigations of the relationship between leadership and general intelligence lead to the conclusion that while every increment of intelligence means wiser leadership, people prefer to be led—even ill led—by those they can understand. Leaders are, in general, more intelligent than followers, but they must not exceed the followers by too great a margin. Presumably wide discrepancies render improbable the unified purpose of the indi-

---

[20] *Ibid.*, p. 45.

viduals concerned. Hollingworth,[21] for example, stated that a leadership pattern will not form or will break up when a discrepancy of more than 30 points exists between the IQ's of the leader and the led.

Were it not for the hierarchical structure of the school system, a supervisor would not be expected to retain leadership in group activities. Inasmuch as his individual characteristics would be more stable than the goals and interpersonal relations in the group situation, the leadership would be passed among members as they were able to contribute to group achievement.

While personality of the leader makes a difference in group performance, it is the evaluation of that personality by others in the situation which is important. No person can be conceived as an informal leader until he shares a problem, communicates with others about the problem, and gets support for his ideas. Trait analysis obscures the fact that a supervisor's behavior varies with the particular situation. A coordinator may be self-confident with a teacher but lack confidence with the superintendent.

The Institute for Personality Assessment and Research, University of California, Berkeley, has chosen a different emphasis in trying to understand man as a total personality. Growing from the distinctive methods of the Office of Strategic Services during World War II for selecting men for assignments in irregular warfare, the Institute has studied persons by bringing them together with a staff of psychologists for a period of several days at an assessment center. Here, the subjects are studied in a range of situations involving, for example, real life problems, abstract problem solving, projective personality tests, objective attitude and interest inventories, and social interviews.[22] Some of the evidence that is accumulating suggests that effective persons have much in common in their cognitive flexibility, high verbal skills, and interest in as well as accuracy in communication with others.

Personality assessment, as reported by MacKinnon, includes the preparation of a psychological description and analysis of the physical, interpersonal, and group situations in which the candidate will function in the future if selected. Such an analysis requires understanding of the nature of the professional function itself, what it asks of its practitioners, and the rewards it offers. "For until we know these, we do not know what aspects of a person's capacities and needs we should assess." [23]

[21] Leta S. Hollingworth, *Children above 180 IQ,* World Book Company, Yonkers, N.Y., 1942, p. 287.

[22] Donald W. MacKinnon, "Identifying the Effective Teacher," *California Journal for Instructional Improvement,* vol. 1, no. 1, pp. 8–13, October, 1958.

[23] *Ibid.,* p. 10.

Motives for Becoming a Supervisor

Among the factors sometimes looked for in the selection of a supervisor is that of motivation. Granted there must be a willingness to accept the position and the responsibilities involved, it is equally important to develop the organizational structure which will enable those of different motivations to render high-level service regardless of their individual differences.

The hypothesis that people seek supervisory positions and eminence because of economic reward has been proposed. One of the findings of a recruitment study at Long Beach State College, Long Beach, California,[24] was that better than 80 per cent of the teachers in the two southern California counties of Los Angeles and Orange wanted to go into administration, primarily because of higher pay. On the other hand, the wide variability in material rewards among supervisory positions indicates that there are other incentives running through the striving for eminence and leadership. The position of supervisor often admits one into attractive associations that make possible ego-satisfying friendships and memberships. Knowing whose approval is sought by a candidate often enables one to predict his behavior.

Lauterbach[25] declares that financial incentives are part of a complex motivation reflecting needs for self assertion, personal security, and social status. Money is important, but this incentive is likely to be unconsciously neglected when at odds with deeper needs. In Bertrand Russell's words, "What people fear when they engage in the struggle is not that they will fail to get their breakfast next morning, but that they will fail to outshine their neighbors." [26] "It is relative income which measures success." [27] Coordinators have been known to seek aggressively salary increases, admitting their action to be prompted chiefly by a desire to maintain a status differential with other supervisory classifications.

Occasionally a supervisor will go from a well-paying position in one district to another job elsewhere which pays less but promises to give him more voice in the decision-making process or more independence of action. Satisfaction can be built into a position through responsibility

[24] *News, Notes, and Quotes,* Newsletter of Phi Delta Kappa, vol. 3, no. 1, August, 1958.

[25] Albert Lauterbach, *Man, Motives and Money,* Cornell University Press, Ithaca, N.Y., 1954, p. 19.

[26] Bertrand Russell, *The Conquest of Happiness,* George Allen and Unwin, Ltd., London, 1937, p. 30.

[27] Lauterback, *op. cit.,* p. 40.

and a sense of the importance of the work and the value of the enterprise.

It may be that some who seek to be supervisors want to devote themselves to service for others and to gain satisfaction from a feeling of
power over them. This is one way of achieving a sense of worthwhileness.
The will for power and service may be associated with pathological
manipulations: "exaggerated ideas of success, combined with a drive
to overwork; constant inner tension, stemming from inner passivity,
regardless of the importance of the stakes; a propelling impetus toward
more and more success; dissatisfaction and boredom if deprived of new
excitement and resulting opportunities to show off." [28] Without realizing
it, the seeker of position may be trying to prove to himself and to others
that he is a worthy person. Sensing rather than recognizing his inadequacies, he seeks reassurance by winning a position. Obviously, this
success is only temporary, for one cannot be reassured about something
he feels he does not really have. Continuous seeking of other reassurances
is likely to be the pattern.

The search for self-esteem through a leadership position need not be
aggressive or objectionable. Recognition of one's own desire to dominate
and control can lead to freer and closer relations with others and to a
diminished need to exploit others because of an unresolved tension. Further, egoistic motives for self-advancement, just as altruistic motives,
can be harnessed by supervision to the benefit of all. The supervisor is
able to find personal reward while helping to provide good aims, appropriate means, and satisfying outcomes for those who engage with
him in the supervisory enterprise. The important question in the selection of a supervisor is not whether he seeks leadership, service, or opportunity for research, but whether he has the ability to do the job. His
effectiveness is more likely to depend on his relations with others than
on his motives for taking the position. Eventually, he must prove himself and his competencies to others.

Drawbacks of Becoming a Supervisor

Where teaching is a low-status position, many will not accept supervisory positions which exist on a temporary basis because of the severe
loss of status accompanying a return to a teaching assignment. Also,
whether a teacher is willing to vacate his status as a teacher may depend
on the extent to which he anticipates an estrangement from his fellow
teachers and an acceptance by new associates. He may be afraid that he

---

[28] *Ibid.,* p. 52.

will be regarded as a "climber," one suitable for vilification. The effects of promotions have long been noted: [29]

> To dissipate this awkward feeling, I have been fain to go among them once or twice since; to visit my old desk fellows—my co-brethren of the quill—that I had left below in the state militant. Not all the kindness with which they received me could quite restore to me that pleasant familiarity which I had heretofore enjoyed among them. We cracked some of our old jokes, but methought they went off but faintly.

Many teachers do not particularly care to "get ahead." They have found rewards through their interest in a field of knowledge and their ability to work with children. Needing no escape from the classroom, these teachers find freedom in teaching. Many who prefer to work directly with youngsters are resentful of the salary differentials between classroom teachers and supervisors. Unquestionably, the higher salary level of supervisors weakens the attractions of teaching as a career. Professional organizations and schools of education are seriously hunting ways to give greater status to teaching in order that it will not be necessary to take advanced work in supervision and administration solely for a top salary or a professional degree. Granting a doctorate in pedagogy to those who possess unusual understanding and competence in their classroom teaching and making available opportunities for teachers to receive high salaries might keep more master teachers in continuous contact with pupils. It would also be desirable if teachers are not to experience the bitterness and withdrawal that often follow failure to be selected as a supervisor.

Realistically, it appears that the number of conspicuous positions and the chances for attaining them will not correspond to the number of those who are hopeful of securing them. Sociologists have documented the pressure which our society places upon ambition. Carnegie's "Be a king in your dreams," "Say to yourself, 'my place is at the top'," and the idea that "there is no such word as fail" produce frustrations for those who do not make the supervisory or administrative lists. The loss of central goals, resignation from responsibility, cynicism, and indifference are not uncommon following such experiences. The overconformity and overcompliance characteristic of organizational marionettes are found among those who aspire to meet the expectations of those who have the power to promote and are anxious about their capacity to do so.

[29] Charles Lamb, "The Superannuated Man," *The Essays of Elia* and *The Last Essays of Elia,* The Macmillan Company, New York, p. 286.

Predictions regarding Future Selection Procedures

Techniques for finding and evaluating the supervisory potential are both little known and costly. Few systems would undertake a selection program at all if it were not more expensive not to have one. The supervisor who can make the right decision at the right time and stand behind it is difficult to find. Especially rare is the one who can become the educational statesman concerned with goals as opposed to technicians who conceive their role as implementing whatever policies are defined. Procedures in the search for those with decision-making ability and emotional tolerance are likely to follow these directions:

1. *Personality assessment.* Objective instruments will be constructed for the assessment of personality which will minimize subjective aspects of the oral interview. Efforts to predict one's compatibility with others will continue.

2. *Advisory assistance.* Emphasis will be given to a professional advisory committee with wide representation from groups concerned. The committee will be expected to be guided by clear definitions of the position and the requirements necessary for the job. The training of those who sit in judgment will be undertaken.

3. *Definition of the position and its role.* Stereotyped ideas of qualities or talents required will diminish. Firsthand observations of the supervisors actually performing the duties of the position will provide a sharper understanding of the competencies presently in use and those which should be in use. Knowledge of the psychological atmosphere in which the candidate will be working will be considered necessary in making placement.

4. *Classification of prospective candidates.* Classifying a person's potential entirely on the basis of his previous experience will lose favor. Initial "rotating" opportunities in which teachers and supervisors spend some time in many situations will be used to expose talent. There will be more frequent promotion of those who are not fully prepared for the immediate job but can grow into and beyond it, rather than appointment of those whose growth is already at its peak.

5. *Statistical measures.* Numerous statistical measures of the results of the candidate's efforts will be sought. Acceptance of the standards of performance for the classroom as well as identification with purpose will become more important indicators of ability. Assessment of the prospective supervisor's precise knowledge of where and why things occur as they do will be systematically tested.

6. *Present and future requirements.* Assignment of supervisors will

depend upon the life history of the district. A new and expanding district will be sure to count among its supervisory staff those who daringly give direction and are able to build a common point of view among the teachers. Older established districts will want innovators to balance conservative and loyal supervisors who defend the system's traditional values. Selection will be in accordance with the long-range aspirations of the school, making possible the attainment in the future of that which is excluded in the present.

SOCIAL SYSTEMS
AND SUPERVISION

THE term "social system" is conceptual; it is a way of describing the interaction of persons in structured situations. A town or community may be considered a social system in which members relate to each other in a predicted fashion. Organizations within the community, i.e., home, church, school, club, can also be described in terms of predicted relationships and the patterns which maintain these relationships.

It is proposed that concepts which serve to explain the behavior of individuals in complex systems, such as a city or a nation, can be used by supervisors in understanding the miniature social systems which deserve their immediate attention: school district, individual school, and classroom. A primary reason for gaining knowledge about social systems is that it will enable one to understand the behavior of others, to predict how they will behave in given conditions, and to change the behavior of others in desirable directions. Knowledge of social systems should permit the supervisor to mediate between the institutional requirements of the school and the individual attitudes of members of the school community and staff. To understand and control the behavior of individuals within a system, one must

71

recognize the existence of social structures, such as privileges, obligations, and powers which accompany the positions of those within the system. Further, he must be able to predict the consequences of various communication patterns and organizational arrangements.

It is our purpose here to review many of the important social structures which affect the relations of those in social systems and to indicate the consequences of these patterns, factors which if not understood lead to difficulty on the part of the supervisor. Underlying this discussion is the assumption that change in the behavior of the individual rests upon the manipulation of social structures, not upon didactic pronouncements or emotional appeals.

4

POLITICAL, AND BUREAUCRATIC STRUCTURE OF SCHOOLS

THE FALL FROM FAVOR—A CASE STUDY

William McCann is the top supervisor in a mushroomed school district. Instead of the three schools of six years ago, there are now seven. Although Mr. McCann rose in position with this growth, he now awaits dismissal. What went wrong?

The experienced school person knows what an accelerated gain in population means in supervision. Development of common outlooks, articulation of program, and orientation of staff members are problems of no mean size. Especially acute is the danger of shadowboxing with the educational challenge, i.e., busying oneself with the administrative problems of plant construction, school finance, and business management while overlooking responsibility for decisions relative to curriculum.

Poor McCann! He and his supervising colleagues are stunned. They actually believed they had done a good job. Evidence in their behalf included new classrooms with the latest ideas in school architecture, neat schedules for the assignment of teachers and pupils to classes, and a variety of library and audio-visual materials. Faculty meetings, PTA activities, workshops, and other usual trappings of modern schools had

73

been initiated too. The director of instruction had tried to see that procedures used in developing the instructional program were in accordance with what he believed to be the newer practices, practices presumed to reflect the findings of sociopsychological research and humanitarian points of view. Teachers were to be regarded as professional people, independently able to organize learning situations. The supervisory staff was available on a consultative basis. Supervisors were to offer help when asked but were not to intrude. The center for curriculum improvement was the individual school where the principal was vaguely defined as the "instructional leader," and targets for improvement were those noted by the teachers themselves.

Of course, McCann had heard of some dissatisfactions in the fastgrowing system. There were always a few parents who felt that their children were not learning to read as well as they should. Principals knew, although they did not acknowledge the fact to the superintendent, that among the many new teachers hired each year, there were those who were unhappy with existing conditions for teaching. Novices expressed the belief that they would like more direction from the district; others grumbled about the lack of standards and the fact that materials issued by the district and county were not articulated with approved state textbooks. Some new teachers from out of state and returning teachers or "retreads" complained that it was difficult for them to "teach" because of the emphasis upon student activities. Typical official reaction to these protests was that (1) the central office staff had been too busy to develop instructional guides which would indicate anything but very general expected outcomes and suggested areas of study, and (2) teachers were free to teach as they thought best. The director of instruction was not too keen about paper guides anyway. "Hadn't the course of study movement of the 30s proved a failure?"

It is true that occasionally a curriculum worker or principal would voice his concern that teachers and the special supervisors in art and music were not relating these fields to the regular instructional program. Too, principals eagerly commented about the way good ideas spread through their faculties. They mentioned the "creativity" shown by teachers in developing materials for the study of exotic countries. They called attention to the unusual instructional materials being introduced by teachers and praised them for their novel approaches to teaching. Diversity was in fact present. The practice of encouraging the pupils to read through self-selection of books was popular in one building, while science centers had captured the stage in nearly all rooms at another. But uniformity was present, too. In all classrooms pupils routinely filled notebooks with clippings from newspapers and magazines. They also spent more time in making the covers of these notebooks "pretty" than they did in organizing the contents in support of an important generalization. It was common practice for pupils to listen uncritically to committee reports and to ritualize their spelling.

Shortly after the stabilization of growth of the district, attacks began to center around McCann and his staff. During the conduct of a campaign for a school board election, charges of intellectual inadequacy in the school offerings were unusually vigorous. Lack of direction and continuity in the instructional program was singled out as evidence of poor supervision. Teachers were reported as complaining about incoherent planning of the curriculum, and parents spoke of a hodgepodge of methods. Further, when the board demanded that immediate steps be taken "to improve the teaching of arithmetic and reading, to establish programs for talented youngsters, and to develop a philosophy of education for the district," the supervisors responded with platitudes about the importance of "meaningful experiences" and the like which had seemed acceptable in postwar years. Now, however, these generalities and the supervisors' descriptions of present programs were unacceptable. In fact, they were not really heard. With loss of the board's confidence, McCann is seeking another job.

And what went wrong? What theories can a supervisor use as a guide to action? Must the technical competence of the supervisor wait upon the teacher's request for help? Can a supervisor act upon the premises which reflect the human-relations view and are supported by findings from research in group behavior, when the school board exercises its legal authority on the basis of other expectancies and assumptions? Have recommended supervisory practices outdistanced the realities of power and authority? Is there no truth in principles of supervision founded on the assumption that faculty demoralization occurs when the teacher is restricted in his own desire for freedom in the classroom?

Although there does not now exist the single conceptual framework for use by the supervisor in understanding all factors surrounding the "fall from favor," certain variables appear to be relevant. We submit that political theories related to power and decision making as well as sociological concepts of bureaucracy can help supervisors (1) establish boundaries within which they must work and (2) devise methods for dealing with some of their practical and immediate problems. To this end, we shall try in the remaining portions of this chapter to develop three propositions:

1. Tensions exist between (*a*) the formal, legal, and political structures for the control of the school and (*b*) supervisory arrangements for encouraging distributive and informal leadership in school affairs.

The supervisor who emphasizes any one of these structures in his practice to the exclusion of the others will fail.

2. There is likelihood that a supervisor will be associated with low morale (dissatisfaction) if he fosters false expectations regarding the nature of authority and participation in policy making. He should therefore distinguish between (*a*) the process of deliberating policy, a policy which calls for the participation of those who have pertinent data to present (expertness), (*b*) the process of executing the policy, wherein legal responsibility for the act of decision and its implementation rests with designated officers, and (*c*) the process of judging the consequences of the decision which requires the shared wisdom and political action of all affected.

3. The greater the accessibility of the instructional program to persons or agencies external to the school, the more difficult it is to develop a continuous and systematic program required for the furtherance of the learners' intellectual development. Therefore, it is desirable to have a bureaucratic structure which protects the school from opportunistic influences.

A DEFINITION OF POWER

Power is the ability to propose and achieve objectives. In order to exercise power, one must be able to control the means to the ends sought. Such control may come through possession of material resources, general assent and assistance of others, the vision of a variety of future goals, as well as possession of well-tested knowledge and skills. In our society we have asserted that every individual should possess the right to seek power, although we recognize that individuals, groups, and communities differ in their opportunity and ability to attain it.

POLITICAL AND LEGAL REALITIES AFFECTING THE SUPERVISORY POSITION

The supervisor's disregard of power outside the school not only jeopardizes his tenure, but prevents him from participating in critical decisions regarding the character and program of the school. It leaves him and the school in a weakened position. Knowledge of power groups and the bias which underlies their judgment of curriculum gives supervisors the perspective with which to anticipate, assess, and influence demands which can alter the school and its tasks. In general, major policies in the local community are made by a top hierarchy drawn largely from a businessmen's class.[1] While the majority of citizens in most communities have difficulty in initiating and executing changes in the schools, those individuals who comprise the power structure apply their power both directly and indirectly upon the board of education and the superintendency. Decision makers at the national level, too, are increasingly exercising power in the schools by changing the way people perceive education, supplying information and opinion in keeping with national policy. The increased emphasis on science, languages, and use of automated devices in schools is a consequence of positive coercive power, whether expressed through the pronouncements and "academic inventories" of public figures or through the careful allocation of money for particular causes.

The assignment of legal rights and responsibilities to officers at each level of the school hierarchy illustrates the authoritative organization of the school. It is granted, of course, that the nominally supreme authority vested in officials rests ultimately on the political expression of a popular vote.

Ignoring the position of formalized and external authority, some supervisors have concentrated upon procedures in which authority is assumed to reside in particular situations. In their minds, those who work in a situation should determine appropriate outcomes as well as means. There is merit in this belief, as evidenced by the desirable consequences which occur when those affected by decision participate in its making. However, the principle is not sufficient. It must be reconciled with political authority and adapted for dealing with a variety of individuals. An overgeneralized acceptance of the principle of self-determination contributed to McCann's predicament. He was not able to relate the demands of traditional power with the newer principles which minister to the individual staff member.

Three outcomes usually follow when equalitarian assumptions and exclusive attention to internal processes of organization overshadow the realities of the external and nonequalitarian structure. First, goals set by individual faculties which are inconsistent with the goals of the district organization and the larger community are certain to be repudiated after much conflict and considerable cost to the persons involved, as in the case of McCann. In addition, supervisors cannot well afford to ignore the school's hierarchical structure in which special privileges and status differentials predominate. Certainly, supervisors should not give the impression that individual teachers determine school policy. If each

[1] Floyd Hunter, *Community Power Structure,* University of North Carolina Press, Chapel Hill, N.C., 1953, p. 113.

teacher goes his way, there is no policy and disorder results. This is not
to say that supervisors must not encourage wide participation in the determination of purpose and procedure. Nor is it meant that teachers and
faculties should not be supported as they try new ideas and engage in
self-regulation. Rather it is facing the fact that no school group is autonomous in the setting of expected outcomes of instruction and that the
process of directing and overseeing the execution of public policy with
respect to the school presently rests within hierarchical and formal
structures. These structures are not necessarily operating in accordance
with theories of good human relations.

Second, there is often resentment when supervisors deny the existence
of authoritative structure. It has become popular to play down authoritative supervision and to denounce the exercising of authority over others. Frequently supervisors try to decrease the power visibility of their
positions. This may reflect either (1) a sincere interest in persons as
ends in themselves, (2) a belief in the superiority of all men and the
desire to fulfill presumed equalitarian norms, or (3) a calculated device
to influence teachers by a more effective means, emotional blackmail.
In these latter instances, supervisors try to obligate teachers to them by
requesting cooperation even though they have the power to issue orders,
tolerating prohibited practices, and showing an excessively considerate
manner. The validity of these procedures has been questioned:[2]

In their eagerness to be known as democratic administrators, some school
principals deny that there is such a thing as a school hierarchy. But the de-
nial does not alter the fact. Even though the superintendent prides himself
on being a democratic administrator, even though he has decision-making
groups within his school system and within his community, even though he
has teacher-representation on many important committees and teacher-in-
volvement in all phases of school administration and policy-making, not-
withstanding all this democratic procedure, he is still the "head man" and is
so considered by his teachers, supervisors, and custodians and by the people
of the community. The hierarchy cannot be denied. Even if it were possible
for such a superintendent or principal to throw off and to distribute all
power and authority, he would continue to be looked upon as a power figure, and, therefore, as something of a threat.

Most teachers feel that it is important for school administrators to recognize the existence of the school hierarchy, to look at it, to talk about it, and
to be aware of its faults and values. Surely it is helpful to teachers to be able

---

[2] B. J. Kinnick et al., "The Teachers and the In-service Education Program,"
In-service Education for Teachers, Supervisors, and Administrators, The Fifty-
sixth Yearbook, part I, National Society for the Study of Education, University of
Chicago Press, Chicago, 1957, p. 141.

to discuss the hierarchy with those persons at all steps in it, and to give them some thought to what it means for the work we do in in-service groups as well as in our classrooms.

Third, the effectiveness of schools and the morale of teachers are weakened when supervisors are not encouraged to examine the authority of their experience and knowledge. Some supervisors take for granted that all teachers have the ability to perceive objectives and arrange appropriate learning situations independently. This is a mistake. Many new teachers demand guidance when the novelty of the situation precludes their ego involvement in particular procedures. For them, direction is not interpreted as a criticism of ability. One of the findings concerning leadership techniques is that morale is sometimes higher when supervisors are less permissive. It is necessary to admit the superior and technical wisdom of the supervisor. Recognition of varying degrees of expertness calling for the exercise of more power and authority is found in all professions.

It has been forcefully contended that educators are hypocritical when they say that all teachers are a community of equals in which the competence of the supervisor must wait upon the teacher's request for help.

The power structure of education should have an open and straightforward recognition of supervisors' technical competence where there are genuine differences in this respect; however, this does not mean that school administrators should have the power to tell teachers what and how to teach if and when the administrator has more formal training than the teachers. The school administrator with a doctor's degree may very well have had less training in mathematics and the teaching of mathematics than the mathematics teacher with only a few years of formal education. It does not make sense to give the administrator power to control content and methods even if his total training exceeds that of the teacher. The additional training must be functionally related to the behavior which is controlled. This is why the analysis has repeatedly insisted on the *inadvisability* of administrator control over instruction. Such control represents a splitting, not a fusion, of power and technical competence. The administrator cannot know more about each and every subject and how to teach it than the teachers of the various subjects.

Indeed, from a professional point of view, prevailing theories of administration and supervision should be reversed. The dominant trend is for the administrator (who tends to lack superior technical competence in instructional matters) to be vested with power and responsibility for the outcomes of instruction, whereas the supervisor (who presumably has superior technical competence in instruction) is being divested of power over teachers.[3]

[3] Myron Lieberman, *Education as a Profession,* Prentice-Hall, Inc., Englewood Cliffs, N.J., 1956, p. 505.

DECISION MAKING

Questions about the supervisor's power, authority, and responsibility center in decision making. We have already raised the issue as to whether a supervisor, by virtue of his position, should make decisions regarding instructional practice without the participation of those teachers who must carry out the practice, and whether he should himself participate in decisions regarding instructional policy.

It is impossible for one to participate in the formulation of all decisions which affect him. Whenever decisions are being made, those who have the greatest degree of expertness relative to the question at hand should be given an opportunity to contribute their knowledge. This does not mean that the expert makes the decision, although his data should influence it. We recognize that legal authorities or agents have responsibility for the actual decisions of policy and the execution of measures ensuring obedience. Wide participation should take place not in formulating or deciding policy but in judging the consequences of that policy; the registering of approval or disapproval of the consequences may occur through political channels. Too often supervisors and teachers have taken flight from political responsibility by conceiving their role as merely that of implementing whichever policies are defined. "The policy maker supplies the goals (ends, objectives) and we technicians, on the basis of our expert knowledge, indicate alternative means for reaching these ends." All teachers and supervisors have the obligation as citizens to influence policy through their political instruments, such as professional and political organizations. At the point of deliberating policy, however, the supervisor has special responsibility for helping authorities of the school system (1) bring policy into line with public laws and (2) make decisions on the basis of knowledge of instructional alternatives and their predicted consequences.

The supervisor shows whether he is a statesman or a technician by his initiative in providing relevant data to the policy makers and by his activity in politics. The former is in keeping with his role of expert to predict consequences; the latter is part of his duty as a citizen to express his feelings about consequences. When an area of inquiry is opened by officials, the supervisor can exert leadership by focusing attention on certain alternative lines of action and by ascribing greater weight to certain types of evidence. A director of instruction, for example, who, in an early planning conference with a school board, points out the relative long-term cost of a remedial reading program as opposed to a developmental reading program is initiating influence over a top-level decision.

When the supervisor finds himself called upon to implement a policy already formulated with respect to the teaching of reading, he is likely to act largely as a technician. When problems reach him at a late stage in the continuum of decision, he must carry out the prevailing decision even if it is ill-formed. Figure 4-1 depicts this rationale for decision making.

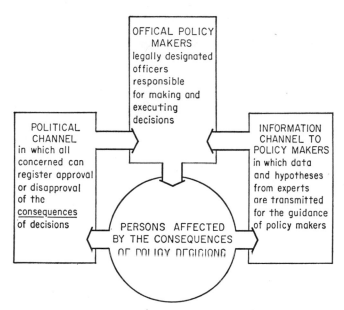

Figure 4-1. A decision-making framework.

Admittedly, the locus of actual decision-making power is not always appropriately placed. Sharma found that teachers wanted to accept responsibility for decision making, especially when the decisions related to instruction and curriculum, and that more teachers desired participation than actually participated. These same teachers felt that superintendents and boards of education assumed more responsibility for deciding instructional matters than was desirable.[4] Too, many teachers as well as supervisors are concerned about indiscriminate decision making by both lay "advisory groups" and official status leaders who are making judgments without the requisite competence. It is necessary that our society admit the indispensability of expert judgment and that a degree of professional autonomy, a scope of independent judgment, be reserved

[4] Chiranji Lal Sharma, "Practices in Decision-making as Related to Satisfaction in Teaching," unpublished Ph.D. dissertation, University of Chicago, 1955.

to professional workers because of their expert skill and knowledge. If the decisions to be made require highly specialized intellectual training, the persons making the decisions should be professional experts. If the decision is primarily an ethical one which does not require expertness, then it will be a matter for a lay individual or agency to decide. Unfortunately, the supervisors are not so likely to be considered such experts as other specialists are. The far greater contingencies with which their problems deal make it very difficult to predict the consequences of the alternatives proposed. Because the school does not control all variables necessary to guide performance by pupils, school men find it difficult to speak with the authority of a science. Unfortunately, supervisors have accepted assumptions about process without really testing validity in terms of consequences, and, therefore, they are unable to defend their judgments with real evidence. Further, they are likely to be dealing with problems about which others are convinced they too have considerable knowledge.

Usually, however, those in the top hierarchy have control over such a range of interrelated matters that the complex can be dealt with only in aggregative form. For instance, the school board may decide to emphasize reading, leaving specific programs to be developed at lower levels of the organization. Staff participation in decision making generally takes place in connection with the development of these specific programs. Numerous considerations originally not taken into account by policy makers require decisions by teachers and others when policy is translated into action in the classroom.

Under certain conditions, staff participation in decision making at the action level helps the teacher identify with the program and its purposes, ensuring that the proposal gets a fair trial and increasing the quality of the decision. A key advantage to shared decision making is that through his participation with the staff and coming face to face with the individual problems of the teacher, the supervisor may extend his own perspective. Ideally, wide participation in decision making may result in a better decision because of (1) the increased range of alternatives likely to result, (2) the inclusion of factors which contribute to the workability of the decision, and (3) the increased attractiveness of the idea to those who will be expected to carry out the decision. In reality, the conditions which make these propositions valid are difficult for the supervisor to arrange even when hierarchical factors are not considered. The topic of procedures for effective and efficient group decision making is itself so important that we shall treat it at length in Chapter 6. For the time being, our point is that decision making by a group of teachers and supervisors takes place in the context of a political system which in turn must develop its strategy with awareness of the rules and government of a larger society and in response to the demands of an unseen public. Procedures for shared decision making should be encouraged only after recognition of the limits of authority available to participants. Teachers and supervisors are governed by official leaders and these leaders are in turn controlled by law.

THE SCHOOL'S BUREAUCRATIC STRUCTURE

Functions of the School

The school has responsibility to provide a systematic program of instruction to ensure that pupils acquire certain types of learning not likely to be found anywhere except in school. Tyler lists the following:[5-6]

1. Learning that requires organization of experience and distribution of practice over considerable periods of time.

2. Learning in which the central factors are not obvious to one observing the phenomenon, and where basic principles, concepts, and meanings must be brought especially to the attention of the learner.

3. Learning . . . where the experiences cannot be provided directly.

4. Learning which requires experiences of higher quality than are commonly available in the environment of the student.

5. Learning where examination and interpretation of experiences are essential, where it is not enough simply to have had more contact with, but where periodically there is need for reflection upon, and examination of, experience and an effort to interpret it to have it become more meaningful.

Accountability and Autonomy

Where these kinds of learnings are made explicit and are accepted as consistent with the concept of the school as a unique institution, they can serve as criteria for determining content and procedures. Previously we have indicated that the school is not autonomous, separate from the political structures which permit its existence. Once political and professional leaders recognize that schools have a unique function, arrangements must be made by which schools (1) are held accountable for attainment of the specified goals and (2) are given the autonomy and the resources necessary for the accomplishment of the task. The achievement of favorable long-term results requires an organizational structure which ensures consistency in its operations and protects the school from both external and internal opportunism.

One way of ordering such a structure is through the development of

[5-6] Ralph W. Tyler, "The Education of Teachers: A Major Responsibility of Colleges and Universities," *Educational Record*, vol. 39, pp. 253–261, July, 1958.

a bureaucratic mechanism which induces an impersonal and rational orientation to the instructional task. If the school can develop an inner life of its own, it will be better able to guarantee the permanence and impartiality of thought and organization necessary for the logical progression of educational experiences leading to desired educational objectives. Pressure groups and self-oriented teachers who enthusiastically promote their favored ideas at the expense of planned educational experiences must be regulated by bureaucratic aspects in the school. A bureaucracy can also protect those teachers who are legitimately serving their function as vicars of the community by offering experiences and ideas of higher quality than are commonly available and by aiding students in the formation of concepts with which to interpret critically events around them. Without this protection, the community might lack the self-criticism necessary for survival.

Supervisors who work with teachers in extending purposes and developing a cooperating organization are part of the bureaucracy and have a responsibility for its continuance. In this connection, a supervisor has the duty of (1) providing those incentives which lead the teacher to attach himself to the organization as a career and (2) securing the teacher's compliance with the task as defined by the system.

A Bureaucracy Protects against External Forces

Sayre has noted [7] that the school defends itself within the political envelope of a bureaucracy against external forces as it attempts to separate itself from other governmental institutions. It seeks to maintain separate elections, separate budgets and taxes. It isolates itself from other administrative agencies such as police and welfare. Supervisors and teachers try to neutralize and limit the board of education in its powers to intervene, using the board as a buffer between the school and other community forces. A school is less vulnerable to others when it meets the specifications of a bureaucracy.

TABLE 3. CONTRAST BETWEEN STRONG AND WEAK STRUCTURE

Protective features of bureaucracy	*Status of organization inviting attack*
1. "The regular activities required for the purposes of the bureaucratically governed structure are distributed in a fixed way as official duties." *	Supervisory staff members are unclear in their duties for instructional improvement and are not assigned on the basis of expertness. Principals who are limited in their knowledge of curriculum are designated instructional leaders. Curriculum experts are

[7] Wallace Stanley Sayre, "Additional Observations on the Study of Administration," *Teachers College Record,* no. 60, p. 73, November, 1958.

TABLE 3. CONTRAST BETWEEN STRONG AND WEAK STRUCTURE (*continued*)

Protective features of bureaucracy	*Status of organization inviting attack*
	not playing roles in keeping with their knowledge.
2. "A specified sphere of competence . . . has been marked off as part of a systematic division of labor. . . ." †	Responsibility for the selection and organization of curriculum is not defined in precise terms. Teachers, principals, consultants, directors of instruction, and superintendents do not test the assumption that the staff is composed of professional equals by noting consequences of individual performances.
3. The official "is subject to strict and systematic discipline and control in the conduct of his office."	Mechanics for rendering systematic accountability of instructional practice and for directing attention are missing.
4. "The organization of offices follows the principle of hierarchy; that is, each lower office is under the control and supervision of a higher one."	The assistant superintendent of instruction has no control over principals; the supervisor is "on call" to teachers.
5. Officials are "subject to authority only with respect to their impersonal official obligations."	Some attempts at controlling personal matters of teachers are made by principals. Although these attempts are rationalized as important to the effectiveness of instruction, there is no evidence that these general variables are related to the learning of pupils.
6. "Candidates (for bureaucratic positions) are selected on the basis of technical qualifications. In the most rational case, this is tested by examinations, or guaranteed by diplomas certifying technical training, or both. They are *appointed,* not elected."	Personnel officers make efforts to do this, but shortage of teachers affects the standard of the minimum level of competence a teacher should have. Substandard licenses for teachers are accepted and ambiguous criteria are used for the selection of supervisors.
7. Being a bureaucratic official "constitutes a career. There is a system of 'promotions' according to seniority or to achievement, or both."	High turnover in staff evidences that the positions are not regarded as permanent. Criteria for achievement are not defined.

* Max Weber, *Essays in Sociology,* translated and edited by Hans Gerth and C. Wright Mills, Oxford University Press, New York, 1946, p. 196.

† This quotation and all others following it in this table are taken from Talcott Parsons (ed.), *Max Weber: The Theory of Social and Economic Organization,* translated by A. M. Henderson and Talcott Parsons, Oxford University Press, New York, 1947, pp. 330–334.

Weber has specified that all operations should be governed by a consistent system of abstract rules. But teaching cannot be circumscribed by rules that do away with the need for exercising judgment. Rationality in the school program will occur by specifying results rather than techniques. We might also add that it is easier to specify outcomes than procedures when teachers have more skills and understandings relevant to the instructional task than do supervisors.

Pathologies of Bureaucracy

Thus far we have indicated that the bureaucratic structure is advantageous to the school and to the achievement of educational goals. Opposition to this kind of structure comes from those who have been frustrated by the bureaucracy in their attempt to capture the system in furtherance of their particular interests. Disadvantages of bureaucratic structure have also been noted by specialists in organizational theory who have examined the consequences to individuals within the bureaucratic structure.

Excesses of bureaucratic behavior are said to prevent schools from being responsive to need and change. Charges are heard that schools and staff are characterized by routinism imposed by a seedy tradition, complacency, and inertia following a long period of success. Supervisors and teachers are accused of heel-dragging after feigned acquiescence because of their desire to keep the old ways.

There are other "unanticipated" responses within the school bureaucracy, such as these:

1. Evaluation and promotion are made more often on the basis of seniority than of achievement, inasmuch as the supervisor reacts to the teacher as a representative of a position, i.e., the teacher is characterized by such classifications as first year, probationary, permanent, physical education, English, or mathematics teacher. The teacher has certain rights and duties, not as an individual or a superior teacher, but by virtue of his classification.

2. Procedures originally desired to achieve educational goals assume a positive value independent of these goals. Means become ends; routine becomes a passion. A particular way of grouping pupils for instruction, for instance, is validated by habit and opinion rather than by consequences.

3. "The trouble with education is hardening of its categories." Although categorizing is a basic part of thinking, school men tend to restrict the categories they use to a small number rather than search for other categories that might be applied. Reliance upon the single concept of IQ as a measure of intellectual development is an illustration.

4. Interorganizational conflicts occur as departments and special service branches try to make their subgoals a part of the official doctrine

for the system and to legitimize their demands. Also, special supervisors can be so intent on their own specialty that they are oblivious of the total task. Upon occasion, a "tail" activity wags the school.

Imbalance between the concerns of the school organization and the individual has been a chief cause of pathological behavior in the school and an area of inquiry as to what "teaching does to the teacher." When self-expression of the teacher or supervisor is artificially limited by the work environment, and superior effort receives no recognition, the teacher or supervisor tends to disintegrate, becoming recessive and insecure while showing aggression toward others. When there is excessive institutional concern for rules and ritual, prolonged occupancy of a teaching position results in depersonalization and rigidity.

IMPLICATIONS FOR SUPERVISION

The supervisor must encourage intelligent activity; not activity as an end. The potentiality of the school has been weakened by those who have assumed that the organization for instruction can be improvised. Supervisors must take responsibility for establishing patterns for an expanding development of educational content. They must not permit individual teachers and schools to engage in activity without observing where it is leading, checking by precise methods to insure that it leads to intellectual ends, to the clarification and expansion of ideas.

In order that pupils may become skilled and mature persons who are able to control their environment, attention must be given to the orderly development and organization of experiences and subject matter. There must be a scheme of organization that can achieve a cumulative effect in learning. The significant questions to ask concerning any school system are: Who has responsibility to identify the behavior to be acquired and the concepts to be learned? Who is best qualified to select particular instructional contacts, experiences, opportunities, and the like? Who is responsible for seeing that learners will meet a program designed to provide instructional continuities and relationships? Who will make the evaluations necessary for determining the next steps? *Who will take the long look ahead?*

Supervisors must not pass lightly over the need for assuming these responsibilities. When these tasks are delegated to teachers and pupils, it is the supervisor's business to guide the teacher in the exercise of this responsibility. The supervisor should not be afraid to make suggestions as to what others should do. If the supervisor does not share his larger experience and his wider horizon, he is negligent. He does not have to abuse his office, but he can use his ideas as a starting point for a better plan that evolves from a reciprocal give-and-take with others. He can be aware of and can use the capacities and past experiences of those with whom he works.

Autonomy within each school building should be permitted only to the extent that the principal and staff are in accord with the curricular objectives of the system and the pathways others are taking to achieve these objectives. Closeness of supervision should vary from individual to individual, depending upon one's ability to frame purposes and arrange means to put the school's ends into operation.

The supervisor must be a realist with respect to authority and influence. One is said to accept authority whenever he permits his behavior to be guided by a decision without independently examining the merits of that decision. When exercising authority, one need not try to convince but only obtain acquiescence.[8] Authority is sometimes defined as the power to make decisions which guide the action of another. Usually the exercise of authority is accompanied by attempts at persuasion and suggestion. However, since persuasion and suggestion permit examination of the merits of the proposal, they can be categorized as attempts at influence rather than as acts of authority. There is no authority unless it is accepted. Three important advantages of authority are: (1) it permits a decision to be made and carried out even when agreement cannot be reached; (2) it secures rational decisions, holding the staff team to account; and (3) it permits coordination of activity.

Authority is useful in prescribing certain types of action and can be employed to enforce responsibility. For example, authority is present when teachers follow prescribed procedures for selecting instructional materials, resource persons, and field trips. It serves also to prevent teachers from getting conflicting commands from a principal and a curriculum coordinator.

When specialized and expert consideration is necessary, responsibility for decision should be allocated to those with certain competencies, and they should have the opportunity to be effective. The director of instruction, for instance, should be located in a strategic position in the formal hierarchy of authority so that premises drawn from his professional expertness will be accepted by principals and others.

Teachers and principals must do more than share common goals; their behavior must be coordinated. Their individual plans must be combined or at least be mutually consistent. Authority secures the centralization necessary for the development of those plans which (1) define appro-

[8] Chester I. Barnard, *The Functions of the Executive,* Harvard University Press, Cambridge, Mass, 1938, p. 163.

priate roles for school personnel and (2) establish premises for the se-lection of content and activity.

Sources of hypotheses for dealing with problems which arise because teachers are unwilling to cooperate in the attainment of system goals, and problems associated with decline in staff morale (such as rapid turnover) are sought in sociopsychological theory. Essentially, such theory suggests that the supervisor must offer an outlet for personal capability within the formal structure by diffusing leadership responsi-bility and authority. Consequently, teachers are encouraged to share in decisions regarding operational procedures. Valuable as this new ap-proach to supervision has been, it has not removed the necessity for a hierarchical authority. Legal limitations upon the school and the cen-tralized requirement of accountability for performance still make neces-sary an authoritative structure. Decisions made by individual faculties must often be modified so that they become part of an over-all gen-eral plan. "To achieve integration of individual and enterprise end-means hierarchies, the enforcing agent must be committed to the latter hierarchy; he must be in a position to obtain accurate information about the behavior of staff members and he must be able to apply this sanction of authority in the light of his commitment and information." [9] Under these conditions, the supervisor cannot be an equal with teachers in all problem-solving situations. When, for instance, faculty groups present conflicting value premises, the supervisor must have the requisite au-thority to resolve the conflict.

Let there be no mistake about it. Sociopsychological concepts of struc-ture and process which have fostered shared leadership in supervision are important tools to be used either for the furtherance of freedom or for the manipulation of others. They should, however, be used only after consideration of other aspects of the social system, especially its political and legal realities.

[9] Charles E. Bidwell, "A New Dilemma in Administration," *Harvard Educa-tional Review*, vol. 26, no. 4, p. 400, Fall, 1956.

5

STRATEGIES AND TACTICS
FOR PROGRAM
IMPROVEMENT

S TRATEGY and tactics are terms representing the act of employing certain procedures adroitly for the accomplishment of ends. Strategy involves the development of objectives and a plan of action for a large-scale operation; tactics call for skillful direction of specific tasks and arrangement of particular conditions which contribute to the fulfillment of the plan.

There are various levels of strategic planning. At the classroom and individual school level there are strategic estimates of educational requirements and tactics necessary to implement decisions made in the strategic planning of local systems and state bodies. State and local systems in turn are influenced in their planning by the policies of national strategists, who view the school as an additional instrument for tactical use in the attainment of the American objective of preservation of society against disintegration from within and against assault from without.

Throughout the nation changes in schools occur when, for example, (1) congressional committees are advised that America is linguistically unprepared either to defend itself in the case of war or to exercise the full force of its leadership in building a peaceful world; and (2) manpower studies indicate that x number of persons will be needed for research posts before a given year. Moneys are made available for the development of new media which will make possible the extension and alteration of language instruction, and organized groups are encouraged to plan the nationwide reform of curricula in mathematics and science. But local supervision must provide leadership in interpreting these new proposals, appraising them in light of desired goals, and selecting the recommendations for the school system. Supervisors also have responsibility for initiating the systematically planned programs of in-service education for the teachers who will carry out the proposals. Although the government has entered the field of teacher preparation through such enterprises as summer institutes sponsored by the National Science Foundation, there is no assurance that a specialty-trained teacher will either be given the opportunity for carrying out the new procedures in his own teaching or be able to change the local program. Valuable as the newer developments may be, the school supervisor must articulate them with the local situation. In the last analysis, there is need for a local strategy for program improvement.

It is not our purpose to imply that curriculum change is dependent upon a national strategy. As a matter of fact, there is much argument whether there is or should be a national strategy for curriculum change. Some hold that we are entering a period in which our survival requires that the Federal government influence the direction and policies of schools.[1] Others believe that the ends of teaching are sufficient unto themselves, that schools must not become instruments for a national policy.[2] Obviously, national projects are altering the course of schooling in the United States, but these changes are more the result of partial adaptation to immediate pressures than responses made in accordance with a comprehensive Federal strategy for education.

Change without strategy is common. Schools have often drifted, responding to the strongest pressure from state and Federal agencies, private foundations, accreditation agencies, and citizen groups. Locally, the increasing weight of conflicting ideas from these forces is encouraging schools to assume institutional responsibility, to establish controlling functions to guide their decisions, and to resist many of the immediate pressures. Nationally, the case for the development of a national policy for education is being strengthened. Hanna,[3] for instance, has proposed

[1] Harold W. Stoke, "National Necessity and Educational Policy," *Phi Delta Kappan,* vol. 40, no. 7, pp. 266–269, April, 1959.

[2] Philip H. Phenix, "National Necessity and Educational Policy—Reconsidered," *Phi Delta Kappan,* vol. 40, no. 7, pp. 269–271, April, 1959.

[3] Paul R. Hanna, "Design for a National Curriculum," *Nation's Schools,* vol. 62, p. 43, September, 1958.

a national curriculum laboratory with a team of representative specialists and lay people to develop a comprehensive rational design. McGrath[4] has effectively argued for a stable educational policy which would serve as a guide to government and require pressure groups to defend their requests in terms of large national policies rather than their own special concerns.

To a large extent there is a trend in the schools toward long-range planning and clear statement of objectives. This trend reflects the universal demand for a blueprint of national goals and the effort to fit democratic government for prolonged competition with totalitarianism. At all levels, there is a shift from the overgeneralization of purpose and the practice of working out compromises among conflicting groups. Instead we are witnessing the establishment of sharply defined choices of policy to guide decision making.

Reservations about the establishment of national goals have been expressed. Such reservations are also voiced wherever there is discussion of procedures for planning and innovation in school settings: In a free nation should we attempt to confine men with plans made by others? How can there be planning when there are so many imponderables in life? Isn't it better to let many virile minds plan in their own way, inventing and adapting? Doesn't the inbuilding of purpose challenge creativity? Is it possible to translate the goal values of American life into institutional terms? These questions must be kept in mind as we assess the strategic factors involved in the process of directed change.

ELEMENTS OF STRATEGY FOR CURRICULUM CHANGE

Strategy is a convenient way of talking about the objectives of the school and the basic factors to consider in effecting curriculum change. Before giving special attention to the procedures available to the supervisor in his work for instructional improvement, it is necessary to consider two requirements of a sound strategy: valid objectives and a basis for courses of action.

Valid Objectives of Strategy

Objectives must be operational and consistent with the functions of the school. There can be no strategy without objectives. Schools have frequently been charged with failure to determine, proclaim, and pursue consistently basic objectives. The habit of sanctimoniously protecting classroom practice by appeal to abstract goals such as "worthy home

[4] Earl J. McGrath, "Needed: A Balanced Educational Policy," part I, *Journal of the American Association of University Women,* vol. 52, no. 2, p. 87.

membership," "citizenship," and "understanding of the environment" has led to misconception and misdirection. There are signs that we have passed the time when schools can get by with pious hopes and high-sounding shibboleths. Supervisors are beginning (1) to state what schools should strive for, (2) to determine the capabilities needed for attaining these objectives, and (3) to lay concrete plans for their implementation.

The school must devote its major energies to what it can do best. Therapeutic and custodial functions are not automatically the responsibility of the school. The fundamental purpose of education is to see that children do not grow up "naturally." It is rather to see that they are systematically conducted through carefully planned series of experiences which will develop their desirable potentials. The major purpose of schooling should be kept clear. In the hierarchy of values fostered in schools, distinguished intellectual attainment should occupy a leading position.

Such statements of purpose as that above are still not adequate to develop strategy at lower levels but must be refined in the district, school, and classroom until there are agreed-upon criteria for determining the extent to which the objectives are being reached. The objective "developing critical thinking," for example, might be considered appropriate in accordance with the previous statement of purpose. However, this objective is nonoperational in its present form, i.e., it has not been made clear how it will be possible to observe and test how well pupils are thinking critically. In order to determine what steps to take in achieving this end, it would be necessary to specify the subject matter or areas of life in which one is to think critically and the skill, method, or other action which is indicative of critical behavior. As a general goal, a system might decide that critical thinking in science will be shown by ability of pupils (1) to identify scientific problems; (2) to isolate a problem from a mass of given scientific material; (3) to suggest hypotheses; (4) to design experiments; (5) to draw generalizations from scientific data known or given; or (6) to reason quantitatively and significantly. This general type of goal is operational enough for undertaking a concrete problem of action, for it permits measurement of the contribution of particular instructional programs; but it is inadequate for individual classroom planning. At this level, the teacher has to ask, "What must the pupil know and be able to do if he is to identify a scientific problem?" The answer will suggest specific operational objectives—concepts and behavior stated as expectations for the learner—which will become new subgoals for the teacher in planning and guiding the arrangement of the teaching-learning situations. Note that these definitions of purpose are open-ended enough to avoid placing ceilings on human endeavors, yet sharply enough focused to establish areas of institutional responsibility.

Simple and related objectives must substitute for complex objectives. In the present context we are stressing the importance of stating objectives which permit teachers and supervisors to handle programs of limited complexity. The teacher is not expected to set broad educational goals which depend upon study of the enterprise as a whole, including (1) its inner impulses (the many informal groups and personal interactions which affect the system) and (2) external demands from the larger society. Nor is the superintendent as the top-level supervisor responsible for analyzing the complexities of instruction in a particular classroom. He need not select the tactics necessary for working with pupils, whose behavior cannot be predicted in advance. The teacher and the superintendent have primary responsibility for a restricted range of situations and a restricted range of consequences.

In-service programs must be related to objectives. In order that overall and individual classroom goals may be consistent, the in-service programs should focus upon (1) securing agreement on the objectives and principles that will be used as the basis for action and (2) acquainting participants with relevant activities of others in the system. Problems encountered at the classroom and district levels must be communicated if objectives are to be realistic. Teachers must be aware of the pressures upon supervisors, just as the latter must appreciate the difficulties of classroom instruction.

Unless in-service education is related to the school's educational objectives appropriately defined at all levels, the selection of activities by participants will be inconsistent and will preclude intelligent action and the development of organized educational experiences. Once these objectives are made explicit, freedom of action is increased. When objectives are operational and accepted, a staff can center on a variety of problems of special concern to the immediate members: study of children, preparation of materials of instruction, promotion policies, and the implications of community changes. These activities must follow the statement of objectives, for they are not ends but means. A group program-improvement activity dealing with the problem of classroom control, for example, is relevant only as control is necessary to the attainment of behavior change in pupils specified in the objective. Concomitant results from the group's program, of course, should be considered in subsequent planning.

Parenthetically, those who plan the in-service program are responsible for a knowledge of the participants and the subject matter which will enable the activities to lend themselves to school objectives. Participants should be able to state precisely how the supervisory activity will improve instruction, indicating the evidence of effectiveness in terms of pupil behavior. Requisite advanced planning should be firm in its direction, but flexible enough to permit free play of individuality; it should invite those contributions and expressions of interest which are related to the common outcomes sought. An overlapping group form of organization is particularly useful in performing the processes necessary to develop an integrated set of system objectives and corresponding objectives for subunits and individuals in the school organization.

The point of view expressed so far is a departure from current practice. In our opinion, the popular notion that the primary objective of programs for instructional improvement is that of "teacher stimulation and growth" is misplaced. The logic of present practice goes as follows: The teacher makes the actual curriculum through the learning activities of pupils. Hence any improvement in instruction must come through the teacher. This popular view also assumes that stimulation and growth are best furthered when teacher activity is emphasized, and that nearly any study undertaken by teachers will contribute to instructional improvement. We regard this position to be a half-truth. Instead of extolling the importance of the teachers' growth and activity, supervisors must give priority to the objectives of instruction. A number of studies conducted in school systems have revealed that participants have often merely become more facile in discussing child growth and development without altering their classroom practice in accordance with the new knowledge.[5] Without focus upon classroom objectives and accompanying indicators of pupil progress, there is no assurance that the in-service program is relevant to instruction. Nor is there a valid way a teacher can appraise his growth as an instructor. Once a teacher is able to evaluate the results he is obtaining with his present procedures, he is in a position to offer innovations for improvement, bringing contrariety to uniformity and the status quo.

In advocating instructional improvement through supervision by objectives, it should be clear that neither the objectives of the school nor the goals of individual teachers are stable and unchanging. Both must change in response to evaluation of subsequent effects of the objectives and to altering conditions. There is, consequently, at all levels of the school hierarchy, a continuous process of examining and modifying (1)

[5] Ronald C. Doll, "Teachers' Attitudes toward the Initial Steps in a Curriculum Improvement Program," unpublished doctoral study, Teachers College, Columbia University, 1951.

Stanley Dropkin, "Attitudes of West Orange Teachers by Types of Participation," unpublished doctoral study, Teachers College, Columbia University, 1954.

objectives, (2) methods for achieving them, and (3) indicators of attainment and other consequences.

Objectives in school are more limited than are educational objectives. Education consists of three processes: (1) instruction necessary to satisfy physical wants; (2) instruction in the customs, rules, manners, and morals necessary for harmonious living; and (3) instruction in the theories necessary for the explanation and prediction of natural events, i.e., theories or ceremonies by which man seeks to control his present or future life. Many agencies other than the school have responsibility for these instructional tasks. The church provides theory and practice for propitiating man and spirit. The home furthers manners and morals. Vocational institutions offer training in the specialized skills and understandings necessary to holding a particular job. Political parties as well as primary groups equip members with the rights, duties, and "knowhow" of political competency in society.

Failure to distinguish between education and schooling places an impossible burden upon the school, an institution deliberately charged with the specialized task of simplifying the environment. A school must be a place where pupils can pursue intensively a restricted number of studies without the distraction of competing demands, and where they can abstract the key ideas or theories of nature with which to interpret the complex events of life. One criterion of a valid objective is that it grants access to facts and ideas upon the basis of which rational judgments can be made. Supervisors can also use this criterion before accepting those tasks which call for teaching children to brush their teeth, serving as custodial agents for working parents, writing essays of indoctrination, acting as the date bureau for the teenage set, and selling physics, welding, or some other going interest of the government.

Objectives are related to contemporary life. The immediate demands of contemporary life can be helpful in the selection of objectives. Crucial problems of society call for interpretation of the basic principles, concepts, and meanings taught in the school, and offer opportunity for validating them. But to say that the school should be closely associated with life does not imply that it shall duplicate thought and practice of a particular community. Occupying a central position in the social structure, the school can serve as a mirror to society by indicating conflicting pressures, ideals, and practices. It is obligatory that supervisors make known demonstrated consequences upon classroom learning which arise from changing social structures and conditions. They should be in a position to make clear what the school can accomplish in light of these changes and the means at its disposal. While cooperating through community councils and the like in the planning of action programs for improving community relations and education in general, supervisors must not permit the school to assume the total responsibility merely because it is the only institution which reaches all youth. The school alone cannot undertake the solution of major social problems for at least two reasons:

1. It does not control the variables necessary for resolving cultural difficulties. It has not the authority, organization, or staff to alter economic, political, and other social forces which underlie the situation.

2. Preoccupation with social problems and the constraint of immediate practicality would get in the way of the school's responsibility for systematically arranging central ideas which are not obvious nor necessarily present in problems of the moment.

A realistic perspective of objectives demands that curriculum planners be continuously aware of cultural change. This is shown in the following illustration which features the lag in curriculum planning and the likelihood of acting upon assumptions about conditions which no longer exist.

Early in this century great educational prophets protested the gap between an academic curriculum for an intellectual elite and the dynamic content of American life. At that time the school was seen by men of vision as the only organized agency competent to educate young Americans in all aspects of life.

Neither the home, the church, nor the press can be expected to do it. Certainly, the home, which in an ideal democracy would serve as the most potent educational agency, is not now equipped to attack the problem. . . . American home life gives little promise of being able to lift itself above the dead level of humdrum monotony which now characterizes it. It is the product itself of an eighth grade education; it is still too often supported physically by an income insufficient to maintain even a minimal comfort standard of living; hence its attention is still centered on the struggle for physical existence.[6]

By mid-century schools had responded to the conditions of 1900. Most schools were launching programs of education for family living, health, vocational training, and were trying to attack the social problems resulting from industrialization and urbanization. Paradoxically, appropriate schooling for the sixties was more like the narrower intellectualistic and academic programs of 1890. Facetiously, one could say, "Resist all changes for fifty years, and you will find yourself on the forefront of progress."

America has moved with headlong speed into a new era, as shown by

[6] Harold Rugg, "The School Curriculum and the Drama of American Life," *Curriculum-making: Past and Present,* The Twenty-sixth Yearbook, part I, National Society for the Study of Education, University of Chicago Press, Chicago, 1926, p. 5.

a very different kind of home from that of 1900. The home today has become the seat of much learning through the influence of television and increased use of family libraries and autoinstructional materials. Motivation for academic study is high because parents are both generally more affluent and possessed of a high school or college education; they weary not from the struggle for physical subsistence but from hunger for the pursuit of intellectual meaning or at least the status with which it is associated. Lessened are the pressures for the introduction of directly functional courses and the reconstruction of the community. In their place are articulate demands from regional publics in different types of communities that the school give its major attention to teaching the three R's. At the end of twelve years of schooling, the knowledge that students have acquired of reading, writing, arithmetic, and science is seen as of immediate importance, and other facets of the school's program must proceed from it.[7] "The three R's" is, of course, a verbalism requiring critical reexamination by the professional staff. What, for instance, are the intellectual techniques associated with reading? To what kinds of problems do we expect this intellectual tool to apply? What current situations in the everyday life of the child can we use to effect linkage with the discipline of reading itself? Reflection upon these critical questions will immediately demonstrate that the dimensions of reading or any other intellectual discipline must be different in current times. "Time maketh ancient good uncouth."

Subject-matter specialists aid in validating objectives. We have seen that valid objectives show clearly the kind of behavior expected as well as the specific content to which the behavior applies, such as pupils' use of principles of molecular motion in predicting and controlling problems of evaporation and condensation. Content specialists help validate these objectives by indicating the basic concepts, generalizations, principles, and techniques of particular disciplines which can uniquely serve to explain and control the world about us. We look to the subject-matter specialist to indicate the set of processes and standards of performance which enable man to analyze certain kinds of situations and to test solutions. Those who have a special competence for tackling completely strange problems in a specific field should share the intellectual techniques and systematic view which constitute their competence.

Studies of the learner are sources for valid objectives. As Dewey indicated: "There is no such thing as educational value in the abstract."[8]

---

[7] Lawrence W. Downey, "The Task of the Public School as Perceived by Regional Sub-publics," unpublished Ph.D. dissertation, University of Chicago, 1959.

[8] John Dewey, *Experience and Education,* The Macmillan Company, New York, 1938, p. 46.

The capacities and current level of performance of the particular set of individuals with whom the school is dealing certainly should be a guide in the selection of objectives. Objectives should include ideas which the pupil does not now hold but should hold. To be valid, an objective must also be within the pupil's range of capacity. "That the immature cannot study facts and principles in the way in which the mature experts study them goes without saying. But this fact, instead of exempting the educator from responsibility for using present experiences so that learners may gradually be led, through extraction of facts and laws, to experience of a scientific order, sets one of his main problems." [9]

Objectives are consistent with ideology. Finally, the objectives should be consistent with the image of the fundamental values of the society the school serves. Where concrete plans for action are formulated, there is opportunity for continual debate regarding the interpretation of these values.

While the ideal of educational opportunity has been implemented in the practice of granting to all the right to schooling at public expense, interpretation of the concepts of equality and individual freedom in school has only begun. American ideology which emphasizes respect for the worth and dignity of each person and asserts that "all men are created equal" will be interpreted anew in these kinds of decisions:

1. To what extent should we differentiate between pupils with respect to both educational outcomes and experiences? Can we avoid giving to those who have and taking away from those who have not as we plan, for instance, programs for the talented and the culturally deprived? More specifically, which pupils will be assigned the best prepared teachers?

2. Will objectives based upon pupil preferences and individual potential in a variety of areas endure in light of the manpower needs of the nation? How can the school best further individuality by which one rises above his self and thinks in terms of the good of all?

In all our talk of the good of society it is agreed that the individual shall not be sacrificed for that good. Indeed, it is believed that real social progress will come only when opportunity is given to the individual to develop, provided the individual is not selected because he represents a particular group or level of intelligence.

The Process of Change as Basis for Courses of Action

Thus far we have emphasized the importance of developing a strategy for curriculum improvement based upon the behavioral objectives sought for pupils. This focus is essential if curriculum planners are to undertake

[9] *Ibid.,* pp. 98–99.

the intensive study of teaching and learning in what are peculiarly school problems. This means that the first priority is not the search for more fields of knowledge which are becoming more intimately related to strategic decisions. That can be left to the researchers. Nor is it the strengthening of the process skills and attitudes of town-hall democracy, the pursuing of the "search of self," or the "releasing of creativity," although all these may be by-products of curriculum improvement. The formulation of objectives is a prerequisite to the supervisor's immediate concern: the intelligent, imaginative, and comprehensive application of the knowledge we have about curriculum and instruction. A second requirement for a sound strategy is the selection of a plan of action to attain the objectives. Pursuant to the latter task, it is necessary to consider the factors involved in the development of an organizational plan of change.

There is as yet no single set of principles for effecting curriculum change. It is true that many of the behavioral sciences have studied one or another aspect of change. By setting out in broad outline some of the systematic knowledge about the process of change now available and suggesting its application, the supervisor may select courses of action which are preferable to that based solely on intuition, experience, or certain currently exalted slogans.

THE PSYCHOLOGICAL APPROACH
TO ORGANIZATIONAL CHANGE

Two studies of the psychology of change within an institution have shown that the concepts of the psychology of learning can be relevant to programs of curriculum improvement. Coffey and Golden[10] and Ginzberg and Reilley[11] have garnered psychological generalizations useful in controlling the process of change in large organizations. Using these sources as well as the pertinent psychological principles for effectiveness, we present the following factors as important in effecting change.

1. *There is clear evidence that the leadership is strongly supporting the new proposals for change.* People are responsive to what their leaders want. No one should remain in doubt about how the principal feels about a change in the case of an individual school or about the attitude of the

[10] Hubert S. Coffey and William P. Golden, Jr., "Psychology of Change within an Institution," *In-service Education of Teachers, Supervisors, and Administrators,* The Fifty-sixth Yearbook, part I, National Society for the Study of Education, University of Chicago Press, Chicago, 1957.

[11] Eli Ginzberg and Ewing W. Reilley, *Effecting Change in Large Organizations,* Columbia University Press, New York, 1957.

superintendent in decisions of a system-wide nature. By way of example, a curriculum worker in a large secondary school was successful in getting initial approval for a series of curriculum-planning conferences. The fact that the principal did not participate in the sessions nor inquire about them when they were over led the teachers to believe that the proposed changes were unimportant or not desired. Consequently, changes were not effected and the curriculum worker was discouraged by his loss of influence with the teachers. It is also recalled that if the supervisor is recognized as influential with authorities in the system the better satisfied subordinates will be. Attempts to help others when one is perceived as noninfluential do not increase anyone's satisfaction.

2. *Individuals realize that their own future is intimately linked with the fortune of the schools and the proposed change.* The more the system strengthens its position, the greater the advantage (prestige, security, etc.) there will be for those who serve it well. Pervasive identification is of great help to supervisors seeking wholehearted acceptance of a plan. Through consultation, both status leaders and teachers will have a better perception of the need for change. When supervisors and teachers share each other's demands and pressures as part of a problem-solving situation, their different perspectives can become channels for facilitating change rather than barriers.

3. *There is institutional resistance to forces which endeavor to change the character of the school.* Supervisors and teachers have a loyalty to the way they see the school and their role in it. This resistance is itself desirable, for without it there would be no stability or integrity. Resistance may mean that the change is taken seriously enough to endure once it is accepted. When new conditions put present practices to strain and modification is necessary, the process should save as much of the old as is relevant. The prospect of the new is likely to arouse anxiety in some teachers. The more confidence teachers have in the integrity of supervisors, the more such feelings will be under control. Consultation and factual announcement during initial stages of the change, so that rumors of impending change do not have free run, lessen disturbance.

4. *The behavior of individuals is affected by the actions of the group to which they belong.* Teachers are likely to be more positively oriented to a plan of change when it is approved by an informal group to which they are attracted. The influence of the group stems from the desire to be identified with the group which serves as a frame of reference against which opinions, attitudes, and behavior can be evaluated. If each person is a member of a small supportive group in which he can express his feelings of doubt, hostility, and excitement, he can better strike out into the unknown.

5. *The success of any plan for change requires that individuals have opportunity to master new skills.* Once objectives at which changes are aimed are illuminated, the learning of new skills becomes paramount before teachers can alter their behavior patterns. The fostering of aspirations without providing means produces behavior which is withdrawn, aggressive, or ritualistic.

Teachers should have the chance to practice with the kind of behavior and content necessary to the attainment of the new objective. If, for instance, a proposed curriculum change calls for pupils in the elementary school to recognize the difference between numbers and the symbolism of numbers, it might be necessary to ask teachers to illustrate ways in which the same number can be represented by different number systems and to suggest how these ideas can be used in their own classrooms. Incidentally, the setting of the informal group is an excellent place for a teacher to practice his new performance, making observations and getting reactions for improvement. Teachers, like children, must know whether their new responses are correct if they are to acquire the new skills.

Briefly, four common principles of learning can be applied in helping teachers acquire the specific knowledge and skill necessary for change:

a. The teacher wants to learn. He is propelled by his own standards of accomplishment, and he can gain prestige and approval to the extent that he can further the learning of pupils in the direction of the objectives for the classroom.

b. The teacher has been given the necessary cues which indicate those elements in the situation which lead to the correct response, i.e., the supervisor has spelled out the response which the change requires.

c. The teacher has been given time and support for sufficient practice of the new response. Work loads have been relocated when necessary.

d. Rewards for the new response occur through indicators of improved instructional effectiveness and the reinforcements which are related to progress toward the objective.

6. *The process of change is expedited if effective measuring devices are developed.* As indicated above, teachers gain a clearer understanding of the objectives and principles which should guide their actions when appropriate measuring instruments are designed and perfected. Feedback of the results of the change being introduced as well as a periodic audit facilitates the plan of action by informing supervisors where further action or revision of objectives is indicated.

OBSOLETE MAXIMS FOR CURRICULUM PLANNING AND IN-SERVICE EDUCATION WHICH RESULT IN RIGIDITY RATHER THAN CHANGE

Rules or slogans for effecting curriculum change have appeared so frequently in professional journals during the last thirty-year period that it is sometimes supposed that the sayings are unchanged despite the most unbelievable changes in everything else. This is not to say that they are wrong or useless, but that our respect for them should not be so extreme that we enshrine them as dogmas or that they become a bias which prevents a view of the obvious. The following are examples of such statements which bear analysis.

1. "Discussion leads to change and action." Coch and French[12] studied the effectiveness of different methods of introducing changes. They found that informal group resistance to change could best be overcome and efficiency and effectiveness obtained by involving all group members in planning the change, arranging for them to learn the required new operation and to give suggestions. They also found that a method by which a few representatives chosen by their group participated in the planning and then trained their associates was superior to the customary method where the supervisor did the planning for the subordinates and told them about it at a meeting. The method of partial participation was somewhat less effective than where all participated.

A number of similar studies followed the work of Coch and French, leading to the conclusion that new standards are more readily accepted when the individual participates in setting them than when they are introduced by fiat or with exhortations and assurances. We have already discussed the necessity for considering the conditions which must accompany participation before such a conclusion is warranted. It will be recalled that there is danger in asking faculty members to discuss problems with which they have had very little experience and do not have the background out of which to formulate recommendations for desirable change. We have also previously established that participation of the faculty in decision making results in higher morale, and greater willingness to change, but does not guarantee that changes will be more intelligent or will improve the program. The point which is now to be made is that many supervisors base their plan of action upon the assumption that discussion itself is the critical factor influencing change and action. Many programs for curriculum improvement have used the idea that

[12] Lester Coch and John R. P. French, "Overcoming Resistance to Change," *Human Relations,* vol. 1, no. 4, pp. 512–532, 1948.

group discussion, as an influence technique, is a more effective inducement to action than a lecture method or no persuasive attempt at all. This is not a valid idea. More recent studies have discounted it. While decision is essential in effecting change, discussion is not.

In her studies, Bennett[13] found that desired behavior occurred more frequently when (1) members were asked to make a decision and (2) when they perceived near-unanimity. Whether a lecture or group discussion preceded the decisions and whether individual decisions were made public or not had no effect on the outcome. Increasingly, the implication is drawn that in effecting change it is most important both to work for decisions and to arrange conditions where the wisest decisions can be made. Discussion alone is not enough. If a wise decision requires the drawing of conclusions by one whose superior knowledge or ability is in the area under consideration, it should be part of the plan of action. The informational influence of an authority who points out the reason for change to the teacher without discussion may lead to more stable change than that which stems from the social influence of a group discussion.

2. "One cannot use force in effecting change." Professional literature seldom recognizes that change can be produced by force. This position may seem unrealistic when viewed against a world setting which at times appears to reverse the moral order and proclaim "might makes right." Force is a dominant method in schools, too. To the extent that the supervisor controls values important to teachers he can apply force. Coercive influence comes from the ability to reward and punish through the threat of poor ratings, nonpromotion, or other form of personal approval or disapproval. The use of force is usually unintentional. At times, supervisors think they are gaining acceptance of a plan because of its merits, but teachers are thinking of the retaliatory power which can be applied (real or imaginary) if they do not go along with the change. In fact, force is probably most effective when it is not necessary to use it actively. We believe that force should be acknowledged as an instrument for the attainment of strategic objectives and that its use can be minimized. Supervisors should be alerted to its presence if they are to avoid its harmful effects. In the long run, its values are transient. Social psychologists[14] have found that coercive power becomes ineffective as soon as the subjects' behavior no longer is observable. A comparison of a supervisor's situation in which there was full support of the

    [13] Edith B. Bennett, "Discussion, Decision, Commitment, and Consensus in 'Group Decision'," *Human Relations,* vol. 8, no. 3, pp. 251–273, 1955.
    [14] Bertram H. Raven, "The Dynamics of Groups," *Review of Educational Research,* vol. 29, no. 4, pp. 332–339, October, 1959.

group and no threatening behavior by the supervisor with a situation in which the supervisor had, without clear justification, threatened subjects showed that both groups displayed conformity in their public behavior but the noncoercive supervisor exerted more influence in private attitudes. Coercion also resulted in greater hostility and tension.

The use of force closes the normal lines of communication and leads to the introduction of synthetic formalities. Its direction is always negative. While it might sometimes be necessary to use force in order to arrive at the place where reason can take over, force itself contributes nothing to reasonableness.

3. "The dynamics of the learner coming to know is a movement out of self into externality multidimensionally." Although vague but emotionally satisfying expressions like this have been used to explain the change process of children and frequently appear as guidelines for supervisors in such form as: "The supervisor does not attempt to develop programs for change; he creates a climate for growth," or "Experience is the best teacher," these phrases usually represent a point of view which holds that change requires primarily a climate or "garden" for growth and removal of restrictions hampering to the evolution of the individual. They represent an invalid application of a biological analogy and belong to the doctrines of "naturalism" and "developmentalism" which appeared in the eighteenth and nineteenth centuries. These prevalent expressions agree with Froebel's[15] assumption that all that one can become lies within and that the purpose of an agent of change is to bring more out of man, not put more into him. There have been many desirable supervisory practices in accordance with this belief: supervisors have attempted to build programs of improvement by giving words of encouragement to discouraged teachers, recognizing minor contributions as a spur to greater achievement, considering individual differences in the staff, respecting the right of people to be different, taking the time to find out how a proposed change looks to teachers, being willing to listen, working on problems of concern to the individual, and other actions to provide the security necessary for teacher growth.

Our criticism of the "climate of growth" approach to change is that it assists those changes of behavior which would arise as a consequence of maturation or chance factors in the larger society rather than those which are tied to classroom learning. Just as children are not likely to acquire through random experiences the concepts required for reading in mathematics, so teachers require a limited range of alternatives if they are to concentrate upon their instructional task. The supervisor,

[15] Friedrich Froebel, *The Education of Man,* D. Appleton and Company, New York, 1887.

therefore, must consider as he develops programs for curriculum improvement only those aspects in the life of "the whole teacher" which are known to be related to classroom performance. The environment for the in-service program must be arranged to result in changes consistent with the objectives of the school. When he tries to consider all variables in the life of a teacher, the supervisor is likely to treat those which are insignificant to curriculum and instruction, and because of the complexity of this inappropriate undertaking, overlook items central to the primary changes sought. Further, in order to help the teacher himself recognize essential factors in the classroom which are not obvious to him, certain meanings must be brought especially to his attention. Rather than let the teacher "learn by experience" in the natural way, programs of in-service education should deliberately structure artificial situations in which teachers can be rewarded with words of approval and other reinforcements for making appropriate responses to specific problems. The use of simulation devices and materials in which teachers face standardized situations demanding action and are immediately rewarded for their correct responses is one way this can be achieved.

THE SEARCH FOR INNOVATION

It is the belief among strategists that the big difference between schools that are just sort of getting along and those that are out in front lies chiefly in the promptness with which the latter detect relevant challenges in the environment and new opportunities for innovation in response to these challenges. Instead of being "pinned down" by urgent problems which are handed to them, these schools give attention to problems which are not immediate. The supervisor who wants to improve a school on this score develops the habit of asking, "What new things or events are happening in the world right now that this school ought to look at?" More than this, he develops a number of prods and rewards that set others looking for problems. The staff is alerted to developments in other fields which throw light upon (1) the new ways of teaching by which intellect becomes a product rather than a prerequisite and (2) techniques for un-learning inappropriate conceptions. Implications for the school from the spreading of a political doctrine and the latest technical achievement are topics for speculation by all.

In helping teachers shift to new programs of action, the supervisor tries to alter levels of aspiration and satisfaction. This occurs as the outcomes of instruction are periodically reviewed and when exchange visits, demonstrations, and other activities make the staff aware that there are courses of action that yield substantially better results than the present program. Evaluation on the basis of results rather than techniques fosters an orientation to search and a sensitivity to the environment.

The practice of changing a condition so that older methods are no longer appropriate is another way of increasing innovation. A "textbook-bound teacher" sometimes becomes "creative" when he tries to fulfill the new responsibility of student adviser. Such private adaptations are to be encouraged when the teacher is clear about objectives and the effect of the innovation upon others. We have already pointed out that the path to new adjustments is paved with the security found in the social support of peer group and supervisor. One of the real contributions a supervisor can make is to aid teachers in their search for innovations by indicating likely sources of information. The teacher who is dissatisfied with his present approach will welcome knowledge as to what he can get from others, for without it he must find an answer in a more painful fashion.

Organizational theory suggests that most innovations in a school are borrowed rather than invented. Borrowing takes the form of either direct imitation or the importing of new personnel.[16] The former is exemplified by supervisors who visit a reading clinic in another district and subsequently start a similar one in their own system, avoiding many of the errors and costs associated with the initial development. The importing occurs when "avoidance of inbreeding" is a factor in the selection of personnel and when a group of new persons from a sub-culture not previously represented become members of the staff. Perhaps it is unrealistic to expect that schools or individuals will engage in vigorous search for innovations while they have responsibilities in existing programs and are caught in daily routine. But most are willing to go out to meet new events when they have a clear sense of objectives, secure conditions, a favorable work load, and the knowledge that the system expects innovation.

PATTERNS OF DIRECTED PROGRAMS FOR CURRICULUM IMPROVEMENT

Many proposals have been offered for modification of the curriculum. Some of these require surface changes, such as the listing of additional offerings or the introduction of the latest instructional materials. Other proposals entail a fundamental redefinition of the school's purpose and require a shifting of values. It is expected that teachers and the public

[16] James G. March and Herbert A. Simon, *Organizations,* John Wiley & Sons, Inc., New York, 1958, p. 188.

in general will bring countervailing pressures for continuance of the established and familiar and that there will be resistance to what appears to be another educational epidemic. In the past, this opposition to change has been quite successful. Ross,[17] for instance, reports that fifty years are required from the first introduction of an adaptation in the first school of a state until 100 per cent of the schools are using the adaptation.

Organized programs in response to curriculum demands are likely to increase in importance. Understanding of the patterns for directed programs which have been followed may be helpful to the supervisor in devising better ways of developing programs for curriculum improvement.

Programs for curriculum improvement have tended to follow four patterns:[18] (1) bargaining, (2) persuasion, (3) politics, and (4) problem solving. Where bargaining has been used, disagreement over the objectives is seen as fixed. *Bargaining,* therefore, acknowledges and legitimizes heterogeneity of practice, permitting modification on a piecemeal basis. *Persuasion* assumes that everyone is in favor of certain broad objectives and that if there is disagreement over the way individual schools are moving, these differences can be mediated by reference to the common goal. *Politics* also assumes a conflict of interests but uses the basic strategy of including potential allies (community groups and teachers) in getting support for the plan. In *problem solving,* it is assumed that objectives are shared and that all must identify a solution that satisfies the shared criteria. Action research, where the staff assembles information and seeks new solutions, is consistent with this problem-solving pattern. Trends and points of emphasis in these patterns are shown in the descriptions which follow.

Bargaining Long the Pattern

Benjamin Franklin in 1749 presented revolutionary ideas for the curriculum. His *Proposals Relating to the Education of the Youth of Pennsylvania* could well be used, with minor changes, as a prospectus for schools today. Advocating, for example, student experimentation in science and a functional approach to the teaching of English, Franklin recognized important demands for living successfully in a current world. It was his desire to make a clean break with the traditional program and

[17] Donald Ross (ed.), *Administration for Adaptability,* rev. ed., Metropolitan School Study Council, Teachers College, Columbia University, 1957.

[18] This differentiation of patterns follows March and Simon's analysis of organizational reaction to conflict. James G. March and Herbert A. Simon, *Organizations,* John Wiley & Sons, Inc., New York, 1958, p. 129.

methods of the Latin Grammar School, but in order to obtain the wealth
and influence necessary for the institution which could carry out the
change, he resorted to bargaining, deferring to those with different educational values. The Latin classics were included as an essential part of
the curriculum even though Franklin himself wanted the priority placed
on other studies. Instead of education leaping ahead one hundred years,
there was a compromise with tradition and Franklin's program failed
to exemplify itself completely.

In his Sachs Foundation Lectures of 1951, Professor Briggs commented upon the story of Franklin's failure which has been repeated
time after time in the later development of the curriculum:[19]

> The first cause of failure was the necessity of compromise with tradition.
> Both an influential part of the public and the available teachers respected
> the conventional program so strongly that they forced an organization of
> three departments—a Latin, an English and a Mathematical—each with its
> own master. Before his death Franklin felt called on to protest the treatment
> of the English school, the master of which, he said, had been reduced by
> discrimination in favor of the classical studies to a position subservient to
> the Latin master.
>
> A second cause of failure . . . to achieve the ideals that Franklin had
> proposed was that the teachers, however much they might have sympa-
> thized with the proposed program, had only a general plan, with no text-
> books, detailed syllabi, or knowledge of suitable methods. They had vested
> interests in what they themselves had been taught and, being humanly
> selfish, were doubtless reluctant to give up the impartation of the acquired
> knowledge that had given them prestige. Even if they had wholeheartedly
> accepted Franklin's program, they would have been supermen had they
> been able in their full schedules to invent or organize the details of courses
> that would have made their novel instruction successful. Likewise, they
> knew in a way how to teach what they had been taught, but the new sub-
> jects did not lend themselves to memoriter work, and the masters could not
> devise suitable new methods that were convincingly effective with those who
> were accustomed to assigned lessons that would be recited verbatim the next
> day.

Curriculum Change by National Committees Using Persuasion

At the end of the nineteenth century, planned programs for curriculum
change came largely to be the prerogative of national committees and
commissions. Prior to that time, governing boards, administrators, and
textbook writers were responsible for additions to the curriculum, and
curriculum change was characterized by the piecemeal adding of new

---

[19] Thomas H. Briggs, "The Secondary School Curriculum: Yesterday, Today,
and Tomorrow," *Teachers College Record*, vol. 52, no. 7, p. 403, April, 1951.

courses. National groups, including the Committees of Ten and Fifteen[20] and the Commissions on the Reorganization of Secondary Education and Life Adjustment Education for Youth,[21] have issued pronouncements utilizing a persuasive approach. That is, an appeal is made by the committee for broad general goals to which all adhere, i.e., "preparing for life," "unifying the people," and "achieving self-realization."

Specific recommendations from these national bodies have reflected, however, the perspective and interest of the academicians and school administrators comprising the particular committees. Usually, the recommendations have been formulated by a priori methods without scientific investigation. National strategists have frequently shaped the curriculum by their opinionative recommendations through appeal to high-level goals, to the prestige of the organization, and to the status of the specialists designing the recommended program.

Even more important in effecting the recommendation, perhaps, have been other pressures evoked by those implementing the strategy. Instructional materials, including textbooks and courses of study, have been prepared in accordance with the committees' reports. Policies regarding college entrance examinations have altered from time to time in order to conform to the recommended changes. Testing services have been asked to develop instruments for evaluating proposed outcomes which resulted from deliberations by national groups. Also, the policy statements themselves are made available as a framework for discussion and as an outline for the various action programs conducted in state and local systems. These action programs include provision for the training and assistance of those who must carry out the program.

National campaigns for change are advanced by pinpointing responsibility to designated individuals for translating the program into effective action. In this connection, leaders in education effect a close liaison with school administrative organizations and leaders in teacher-education centers. Procedures at the level of action rely upon political strategy, an approach which differs from both (1) the persuasive appeal to common ideals and (2) the acknowledgment under bargaining that disagree-

---

[20] U.S. Bureau of Education, *Report of the Committee on Secondary School Studies Appointed at the Meeting of the National Educational Association,* July 9, 1892 (hereinafter cited as Committee of Ten Report), Washington, 1893.

Report of the Committee of Fifteen on Elementary Education, published for the National Education Association by the American Book Company, 1895.

[21] U.S. Bureau of Education, *Cardinal Principles of Secondary Education: A Report of the Commission on the Reorganization of Secondary Education Appointed by the National Education Association,* Washington, 1918.

U.S. Office of Education, *A Look Ahead in Secondary Education—Education for Life Adjustment,* Washington, Bulletin no. 4, 1954.

ments about curriculum are permanent and that those who differ must be outbid rather than converted.

Politics as an Approach to Organized Programs for Change

Curriculum planners employing a political strategy try to manipulate factors crucial to change. Their procedures follow some such pattern as this:

1. *Selection of a leadership team.* A professional steering group is chosen in which each member is selected because he has a particular role to play in the proposed change and because the superintendent respects his judgment and objectivity. In the typical school system, the basic composition of the group would be the superintendent, curriculum director, principal, and two teachers. The team may have more members but generally it is better to have the smallest number that will embrace the requirements for initiating the program. In large districts there may be a central office team with representatives from all the schools in the district. This central coordinating team is formed in conjunction with leadership teams in each school who are responsible for the program in their own buildings. A leadership team is composed only of professional persons; there are no advisory or lay members, for this elite alone must make policy decisions to guide the course of events.

The key person in developing an effective program is the superintendent. He must recognize the importance of the change and be willing to devote time and effort to planning the change with the team. The superintendent usually takes responsibility for seeing that the school board, staff, and community understand the change. The principal is also needed for supporting teachers as they endeavor to change in accordance with the plan. His enthusiasm or opposition can determine the success or failure of the program. Further, he has special responsibility (1) for interpreting the program to faculty, student body, and patrons and (2) for scheduling and coordinating events in the building. The curriculum director is essential because of his (1) comprehensive understanding of the total curriculum, (2) ability to select and organize content, (3) familiarity with resource materials, and (4) competence in evaluation. The classroom teachers are expected to reflect the perspective of their fellows in the planning phase. Later they will demonstrate and interpret the program. For this reason, they should be known to supervisors and fellow teachers as influence figures of ability. It is important that all team members have enthusiasm for the ideas underlying the program.

2. *Considerations and tactics of the leadership team.* How much time should be allowed for change? Should the change occur on a broken front, in which those most ready are approached first, or on a uniform

front, in which the plan is put into operation at one time throughout the system? When should the proposed change be announced? How can the results of the change be noted and accountability be maintained? Such questions are faced by the leadership team once it has been decided to effect the plan.

Through interviews and informal discussion with a representative sample of those in the system, team members seek cooperation, alternative proposals, and relevant information about the readiness of the staff for change. The development of the plan of action takes time, for it cannot be borrowed from other systems. It must be forged by the team in light of the district's unique history as well as its present and likely future conditions. The plan will flounder unless the team is sensitive to such factors as memories of former plans which were introduced and failed, forces of tradition, outside pressures, as well as the anticipated effect upon the position and power of those to be involved. But calculated risks must be taken if the plan is to get off the ground.

In some situations it may be better to move on a broken front and to effect initially only part of the program. This is not only because schools and teachers differ in their readiness for change but also because the strategists do not control enough of the forces for change and must gain support by small successes. On the other hand, evidence from other institutions which are bureaucratically organized as opposed to the open society indicates that a total change on a uniform front can be more effective. The elimination of segregation in the Armed Forces is given as an illustration of how a bureaucratic organization can effect rapid change by clarifying through specific directions what is expected and moving with such authority, certainty, and speed that those who would otherwise organize for resistance never have the chance. It is customary in schools, however, to take the course of gradual diffusion of practice in effecting change.

The strategy of "starting small and spreading" has been used in attempts at mass curriculum change in the nation's schools by school groups such as the Citizenship Education Project.[22] Usually, in these instances, change is introduced among a few teachers who feel that the new proposal is an answer to a problem. Some teachers will adopt it and try to make it work in spite of those who say it is a poor idea. When the change is to begin on a small scale, it is generally believed best to include only those teachers who want to participate and who are among the most skilled and respected leaders on the teaching staff. Caution must

[22] William S. Vincent et al., *Building Better Programs in Citizenship*, Citizenship Education Project, Teachers College, Columbia University, New York, 1958.

be taken that the program does not become tagged as belonging to a particular school or teacher. If it becomes "the Valley School's program," adoption is delayed. This need not occur if it can be made clear that the initial teachers are serving as representatives of all, and steps are taken to involve others in the progress of the plan. After pioneers demonstrate the effectiveness of the innovation and show that no one need fear it, others will try it. It is at this point that change can be introduced to all schools and teachers who should make use of it.

It is important that everyone understand the immediate change as well as the model toward which the system is moving. Uneasiness created by rumors resulting from initial inquiries during the preplanning phase can be lessened at special meetings where final decisions are announced and the main outline of the plan is clearly delineated. The formal announcement includes (1) the reasons for the plan and the care taken in developing it, (2) a realistic assessment of the difficulties expected in implementation, and (3) positive emphasis upon the long-range advantages. The announcement cannot include all details, but it should make explicit the responsibilities that are attached to supervisors and teachers. The staff should know the extent to which authority and responsibility for detailed planning have been delegated to them. Before too long, it might be advisable for each individual to prepare a personal responsibility chart in which he notes his understanding of the proposal and his conception of the specific role it demands of him. Opportunity for acquiring the understanding of new principles and the proficiency required by the change must, of course, be provided.

Appropriate measurement and control devices are necessary if the leadership team is to judge whether schools and teachers are making sound progress and to adapt the plan as experience dictates. A few basic performance yardsticks and scheduled reports are included in the original plan, but others are fashioned after the plan is implemented. Supervisors and teachers develop new measures and refine existing ones in light of particular conditions. Indicators of change must be related, however, to the objectives of the plan. Active participation in the development of these devices aids individuals in understanding more fully the directions in which change is desired. In those instances where individual schools and teachers have been given major responsibility for deciding upon the appropriate manner of reaching the objective, it is necessary that there be an increased number of adequate measures of performance. Only in this way can supervisors and teachers be held accountable and improvement be assured. Results help the professional staff to test the significance of their judgment in the classroom and suggest further action by the leadership team. Ordinarily, the results call attention to other requisites of the planned change and to the inadequacy of in-service education.

Problem Solving as a Pattern in Curriculum Improvement

Problem solving represents an attempt to secure private as well as public agreement to a change. It is used as a means of getting teachers, for instance, to accept objectives not because of the promise of a pay check, but because of a belief in the worthwhileness of the objective itself. When curriculum does not change because individual teachers do not change, there are efforts by curriculum planners to involve the faculty in the search for additional information on the alternatives available to them and the consequences attached to these alternatives.

The involvement of teachers in problem-solving activity as an approach to curriculum improvement was introduced through organized group program-improvement activities which generally followed the prevailing educational interest by studying "the developmental needs of pupils" and reflected social conditions by undertaking surveys on "the current needs in our community." Workshops and conferences in which participants attacked problems of concern to themselves were frequent.

From the vantage point of the present, with its emphasis on academic excellence, there is a tendency to criticize these early problem-solving efforts to improve the curriculum. The implications for the classroom of the studies undertaken were seldom drawn or acted upon. Individual effort did not lead to over-all curriculum plans which had consistency in the experiences offered pupils. Most serious of all, there were almost no investigations of the effect of these problem-solving activities on pupil accomplishment. To be fair, one has to consider the needs and purposes which existed at the time these activities were initiated.

Recent studies of similar in-service programs stressing problem solving reveal many of the same weaknesses. There is little effort to relate curriculum-improvement activity to the educational behavior of children and youth. The few findings we have from research report that when individual school groups determine their own plans of action, they are likely to stress child study, guidance, and human relations more than subject-matter areas.[23] Teacher participation in child study programs does not seem to affect pupils' reading and arithmetic achievement, but may result in more positive ways of working with children and more

[23] Marvin L. Berge, Russell E. Harris, and Charles B. Walden, "In-service Education Programs of Local School Systems," *In-service Education of Teachers, Supervisors, and Administrators,* Fifty-sixth Yearbook, part I, National Society for the Study of Education, University of Chicago Press, 1957, pp. 197–223.

"democratic" classroom organization.[24] There is a paucity of precise evidence that workshop experience produces significant change in the behavior of teachers. The participation of teachers in cooperative programs of curriculum planning does not seem to result in greater student achievement than that which occurs when the curriculum is planned either by supervisors alone or by teachers working individually.[25–26]

One should not assume from this that the problem-solving approach to curriculum improvement is ineffective. On the contrary, it can produce more of an effect than any other pattern, provided steps are taken to see that (1) the problems selected by teachers are related directly to the objectives of classroom instruction; (2) the activity is not dispersed without a guiding plan for the school curriculum as a whole; and (3) attention is given to factors associated with efficiency and effectiveness in the problem-solving process.

Taba and Noel [27] describe instances of the problem-solving approach in the Yolo County (California) School Curriculum Department which show its great potential. One example features the efforts of a third-grade teacher in a group program-improvement activity who sought to further the progress of "slow" readers. This teacher was clear about the behavior she was seeking from her pupils but had evidence that she was failing to help them attain it. Together supervisor and teacher searched for those factors which are known to be associated with nonreading and which were present in the particular classroom. Further diagnosis revealed that pupils were missing many basic sight words, and were not able to attack unknown words. The teacher was helped to devise procedures by which the pupils could develop the use of context clues and have concrete experiences in making the words meaningful. The teacher was guided through additional steps of problem solving to find out what words the pupils did not know in the material she planned to use. Diagnosis was followed by experiment in which there were sequential presentation of the material, careful formulation of questions which would call for use of the desired vocabulary, and other events, all of which were planned as simple increments of instruction. Events offered immediate reward to the pupils and were cumulative in the direction of the reading skills sought. There was continual measurement of changed behavior,

[24] Richard M. Brandt and Hugh V. Perkins, Jr., "Teachers Change as They Study Children," *Childhood Education,* vol. 34, no. 5, pp. 218–222, January, 1958.

[25–26] George K. McGuire, "The Effect on Student Achievement of Teacher Participation in Curriculum Planning," unpublished Ph.D. dissertation, University of Chicago, 1959.

[27] Hilda Taba and Elizabeth Noel, *Action Research: A Case Study,* Association for Supervision and Curriculum Development, Washington, 1957, pp. 27–58.

and five months after the experiment started results on an alternate form of the reading achievement test revealed gains ranging from one month to one year three months. The significance of this account for our purposes is that it points up the importance of helping a teacher (1) think about her problem in a more fundamental way, considering factual evidence and causal factors, and (2) relate problem-solving activity directly to those objectives of the individual classroom which are consistent with the functions of the school.

AN ISSUE IN THE DEVELOPMENT OF STRATEGY FOR CURRICULUM IMPROVEMENT

The main effort of this chapter has been to provide a picture of existing strategy and tactics for curriculum improvement and to indicate factors which are associated with sound strategy. Further comment on one of the salient issues raised in the discussion is warranted.

There exists the concern that an intellectual elite will select the strategy for curriculum development and that the rights and welfare of an unwary public will be violated. This concern is part of a larger social issue: Is society best served by the method of practical intelligence, whereby all learn how to participate in the processes of planning—a method which seeks to develop common purposes for life? Or is it best served by the method of reason, whereby men of expertness and democratic intent are given the authority for planning strategy so that social affairs are conducted in the most fair and efficient manner—a method which aims at consistency of plans rather than satisfaction of particular interests?

Supervisory acceptance of the first alternative carries with it the obligation to generate leadership among all citizens and to improve methods and conditions for discussion and problem solving. Cases in point are those situations where supervisors endeavor to make the school a center for social reconstruction by involving adults and pupils alike in the attack upon local problems and engage in goal-setting discussion, posing such questions as "What do we want our community to be like in 19—?" and "How can the school best cooperate?"

Reaction against the "grass roots" approach has increased of late. The college subject-matter specialist is once more serving as an expert in curriculum planning at lower levels of schooling. The trend toward national projects which define content and method promises to replace "one of the most pathetic sights on the current educational horizon—myriads of local school communities, whose members have had little or no scientific training, trying to produce a modern science curriculum." [28] Supervisors are urged to "shape public opinion concerning the curriculum" and to tell, not ask, what should be taught.[29]

Instead of holding meetings and presenting questionnaires to determine what the schools should teach, supervisors should adopt a sounder approach of spending time in the "study of conditions and trends in contemporary society and . . . requirements for living in the second half of this century. Their findings may reveal definite implications for changes in educational objectives, curriculum, and instructional methods of the schools." [30]

Curriculum and instruction are held to require the leadership and participation of persons who possess certain professional competencies, i.e., those who can claim (1) specialized knowledge of the subject field or academic discipline and (2) the knowledge of instruction, curriculum designing and organizing.

We sympathize with those who want to see lay participation in curriculum planning. The school has been one of the few institutions where a scattered public could recognize itself and express its interest. Inasmuch as citizens feel even more remote from civic, national, and international affairs, it is desirable to preserve those neighborly vehicles by which the individual is able to feel the effect of his voice in crucial public matters. Further, such participation makes possible the innovations and new creations which are essential in the execution of an adequate plan. Is there not a way in which the school can enlist the community in the process of curriculum change without jeopardizing its primary responsibility for helping pupils acquire and use those thought processes associated with the systematic organized subject matter? There are several propositions which lead to an affirmative answer:

1. No one person or group arrogates the last word on objectives of the curriculum—and gets away with it. Professional authority is granted to individuals demonstrating superior knowledge, but the privilege is revocable by decisions of the people through their elected representatives.

2. The public relies on supervisors who possess certain professional competencies to present to the elected representative body definite recommendations for improving the curriculum for children and youth.

[28] Alexander Calandra, "Some Observations of the Work of the PSSC," *Harvard Educational Review,* vol. 29, no. 1, p. 22, Winter, 1957.

[29] Myron Lieberman, *The Future of Public Education,* University of Chicago Press, Chicago, 1960, p. 60.

[30] E. T. McSwain, "Who Should Guide the Public Schools?" *Educational Leadership,* vol. 14, no. 7, pp. 424–425.

Supervisors are not primarily arbitrators or facilitators and must not keep silent on recommendations for the public and teachers.

3. The public may have opportunity to react to the recommendations before the elected body makes its decision. The development of practical intelligence among adults in the community could occur at this time as they engage in the process of judgment.

4. Groups and individuals in the community can aid in devising supplementary learning situations and in attacking those conditions which are shown to be detrimental to the instructional program. But in their collaboration with the community, supervisors must guard against making incidental functions dominant and responding to pressures which attenuate the systematic organization of learning. It is proper for the professional staff to cooperate in community undertakings for the purposes of gaining information related to the conditions of formal learning, i.e., (1) relevant aspects of pupils' out-of-school experiences and (2) situations for the application of the intellectual techniques being taught. The school's contribution to the community, however, must be within its own field of action. It must not put the immediate concern of the community before the pursuit of intellectual truth.

5. The adaptation of the fact finding and fact interpreting described in a later chapter will provide the knowledge of consequences by which both citizen and expert can judge the effectiveness of the curriculum and can effect improvement. Until there is systematic evaluation, communities will either do "what has always been done, or adopt and discard innovations with each spin of fashion."

6

FACTORS DETERMINING EFFECTIVENESS AND EFFICIENCY IN SCHOOLS

CONFLICT between the organization of the school and the wishes of the instructional staff has resulted in undesirable consequences, such as personal disintegration of the teacher, resistance to change, and departmental arguments. This chapter discusses aspects of the social structure of the school which are related to both efficiency and effectiveness. Efficiency refers to the extent to which the school provides satisfaction to its members; effectiveness means the degree to which the school achieves its purposes.

MORALE AND SOCIAL STRUCTURE OF THE SCHOOL

World War II and postwar years saw the introduction of concepts like morale and satisfaction into the school setting. Morale was regarded as the attitude and behavior which denoted a willingness to be involved in the school and its work. A concern about motivating the teacher and the human relations approach to supervision found paramount expression in educational literature until recently, when the concern for academic achievement and pursuit of excellence began to crowd affective and equalitarian considerations. Parenthetically, we can say that at-

119

tempts to relate high morale to achievement have failed to reveal consistent relationships. High morale is not a sufficient condition for excellence in achievement. Nevertheless, because morale is valuable as an end in itself, supervisors try to structure for it.

Watson's five factors in morale[1] identify targets and imply assumptions about practice which direct the behavior of supervisors:

1. *A sense of positive goal.* Without a sense of purpose, activity seems unclear, and teachers do not become involved. There must be a magnetic pole for drawing the aspirations of teachers. Definition of goals is a task to which all should contribute.

2. *Mutual support.* If several teachers are engaged in a purposeful and common task, they probably will feel a greater sense of support than if they work on unrelated activities.

3. *A sense of commitment.* Complacency about the schools and the values schools represent is a liability. Currently, there is an implied attack upon the idea of a strong public school and the promise that all should be educated. Teachers should be helped to feel a personal commitment to these theoretical ideals and be ready to defend them at cost.

4. *A sense of contribution.* The supervisor must find ways to help individuals contribute to group tasks and reward them for their efforts. Eventual achievement of a task which is not a sure thing brings the greatest reward.

5. *Advance.* The supervisor must emphasize the amount of progress, thus providing an awareness of results. Progress is measured by determining how much distance has been covered and must yet be covered to reach the goals. A supervisor is qualified to evaluate progress because of his perspective and position. It is not enough to have a goal and know that there are techniques for reaching it, one must feel himself advancing toward it. Morale is much stronger when the teacher can see that he has the competency to improve existing conditions.

EMPHASIS UPON PARTICIPATION IN DECISION MAKING

The success of industrial experimentation which provided for group members to participate in decisions quickly led to similar practice in school supervision. It is recalled that one of the most talked-about experimental examples of action by participation supported the hypothesis that participation in the decision to effect change would overcome group

[1] Goodwin Watson, "Five Factors in Morale," *Civilian Morale,* Second Yearbook, Society for the Psychological Study of Social Issues, Goodwin Watson (ed.), Holt, Rinehart and Winston, Inc., New York, 1942, pp. 30–47.

resistance to the change and lead to higher productivity.[2] Perhaps the findings from studies of small group behavior were applied too readily to school situations. We have already mentioned the difficulties involved when a school system disregards the authority-possessing power which lies outside the enterprise. At the system-wide level, at least, supervisors should heed the traditional hierarchical forms necessary for economic and political reasons. Also at the school level, the principal who attempts to act as a spontaneous group leader and to encourage equal participation faces the fact that equality does not exist within the framework of the school hierarchy.

Nevertheless, there is much evidence that participation in decision making is a powerful force for modifying the behavior of a group. It is far from clear why participation is so effective. The motivation and the change brought about by participation are explained in these general ways: the teacher sees himself and his teaching in a new light; participating groups themselves improve communication within the school organization; and teachers get a more realistic picture of the importance of problems and practices within the system.

Explanation of the basic factors which underlie the relation between participation procedure and goal acceptance is only beginning. Although participation increases the likelihood that a goal will be set which is congruent with individual goals, sometimes individual preferences are set as one engages in group participation. Kelley and Thibault[3] suggest the possibility that discussion leads to more adequate knowledge of the goal and its value to participants as well as a more realistic view of its attainability. Perhaps, too, a positive evaluation of the goal is derived from hearing that other members value it.

Logically, we might expect that when supervisors directly communicate decisions without prior consultation, there would be more consistent behavior, fewer alternative ends and means, than when free and equal discussion is stimulated. The fact that this does not occur and that participation does not lead to any departure from a system's goals and means has been explained in two ways.[4] First, there is often a cultural attitude which makes at least token participation in decisions a condition

[2] Lester Coch and John R. P. French, "Overcoming Resistance to Change," *Human Relations,* vol. 1, no. 4, pp. 512–532, 1948.

[3] Harold H. Kelley and John W. Thibault, "Experimental Studies of Group Problem Solving and Process," *Handbook of Social Psychology,* Gardner Lindzey (ed.), vol. II, Addison-Wesley Publishing Company, Inc., Reading, Mass., 1954, p. 757.

[4] James G. March and Herbert A. Simon, *Organizations,* John Wiley & Sons, Inc., New York, 1958, p. 54.

for their acceptance. The less the visibility of power differences, the less the resistance. Second, where there is participation, the setting permits the organizational hierarchy to control in part what is proposed. There is a kind of human relations which is manipulative rather than affective. Inasmuch as teachers will plan anyway, better to have a supervisor present to influence this planning.

Acceptance of goals is heightened by a goal-setting procedure involving participation or at least the feeling that one has the opportunity to participate if he wants. Marquis, Guetzkow, and Heyns[5] have provided data suggesting that *the possibility of participation is more important than the actual participation.* Actual influence over a decision being made is of less importance to the individual than acknowledging his influential position.

INFORMAL STRUCTURE IN THE SCHOOL

Informal structure is represented by those interpersonal relations in the school that affect both its effectiveness and its efficiency. It includes the personal relations that develop among teachers and supervisors, such as cliques and friendship groups. Informal groups are the source of much social control. They are able to exercise power or set expectations which may or may not be at variance with the formal organization of the school.

The "bungalow boys," a group of teachers located in temporary buildings at an expanding school plant, were able to develop their own pattern of behavior, resisting the goals and processes being furthered by official leaders of the school. These rebelling teachers expressed their indifference by ignoring topics of general school interest and instead focused on subjects which were irrelevant to the organization. Even little requests, like asking for the prompt return of audio-visual equipment, were met with grumblings by those in this informal group.

On the other hand, a group of primary teachers who lunched together and shared ideas and instructional materials set expectations that called for each member to work in school after three-thirty, to participate in school-community activities, and to perform other tasks peripheral to the instructional task but held as desirable by the school hierarchy.

Sometimes these influential informal groups are formed along subject-matter lines, e.g., cliques of teachers of English or teachers of physical education. Again, the individual school or teachers' club within a district comprises the informal structure. The traditions, status system, rou-

---

[5] D. G. Marquis, H. Guetzkow, and R. W. Heyns, "A Social Psychological Study of the Decision-making Conference," *Groups, Leadership, and Men,* H. Guetzkow (ed.), Carnegie Press, Pittsburgh, Pa., 1951, pp. 55–67.

tines, and communication patterns of informal groups are seldom spelled out like those which appear in the handbooks issued by the district and school. But the unofficial leaders within these groups frequently exercise more power than supervisors in summoning teachers to action, either negatively or positively. Facetious comments by informal leaders belittling a suggested curriculum change can destroy official plans; support by these leaders can create a climate of acceptance. An important implication for the supervisor is that he should learn as much as possible about the informal structure of his own situation.

Conflict between Individual and Organizational Demands

Perhaps the most helpful way of interpreting informal groups, suggesting appropriate ways of working with them, is to regard them as reaction to a conflict between the individual's personal desires and the demands of the school organization. Whenever teachers join a system, they give up some individual freedom concerning the values and objectives that guide their individual decisions. The teacher must acquire an organizational personality which ensures that his actions will be consistent with the decisions of the system. Efforts of different persons must be coordinated if instructional consequences are to be maximized. Organizational restrictions upon individual teachers are entirely proper when the consequences of teaching extend beyond the immediate classroom situation. Those entering teaching must abide by a set of ground rules regulating their behavior as teachers. For example, the individual teacher may believe that only those who can profit from an education should receive it; but in his institutional role he must carry out the practices which show the most promise for making education profitable to all. But whenever the school system attempts to impose pressures for action which are seen as exceeding those necessary for the institutional task, teachers should not be expected to behave as organization men.

Conflict between individuals and the framework of the school may be most productive. If there were no protest by teachers against the organizational pattern, the institution would lose one of its strongest safeguards—self-correction.

Acting upon the assumption that human beings are always striving for "self-actualization," a tendency to maintain themselves and to guarantee the constancy of personality, Argyris[6] sees a basic incongruency between the needs of a mature personality and the requirements of formal organization. Healthy teachers will experience frustration, conflict, and failure when they (1) have minimized control over instruction,

[6] Chris Argyris, *Personality and Organization*, Harper & Brothers, New York, 1957.

(2) are expected to be passive and subordinate, (3) deal predominately with decisional situations of short-time perspective, and (4) are induced to perfect and use a few shallow abilities. Argyris proposes that informal structures serve as a partial remedy for these conditions, mitigating feelings of dependence. Informal relationships mark the attempt on the part of the individual teachers to salvage their own directions, a means by which one can take an active role in influencing the formal organization. Without informal organization the teacher may become indifferent to the quality of his teaching. "Given no responsibility, he showed none; treated as an automaton, he behaved as such." [7]

Supervisory Reaction to Resistance by Informal Groups

There is always danger that in rejecting what appears to be antagonistic behavior of informal groups, supervisors will develop programs negatively rather than positively. When this happens, of course, supervisors are being guided by that which is rejected instead of constructively developing a sound program. How should a supervisor react to informal groups who resist improvement by showing apathy, disloyalty, lack of enthusiasm, or who give their attention to ways of battering personal status instead of giving time to the welfare of students? Three common responses and their predicted consequences are these:

1. *Restrictive reaction.* This reaction is a crackdown. There is a reduction in personalized relationships and an increase in the use of trappings of authority. Rule making is more common, and supervision is more close. Supervisors communicate the system's policies and practices clearly to teachers and make it known that evaluation of teachers will be strictly and honestly in accordance with these policies and practices.

The impact of the crackdown upon teachers does not always bring the results desired. While teachers tend to become more passive and centered upon the organizational goal, they are also likely to be anxious about the future and rigid in their behavior. [8] Rules, for example, provide cues for teachers beyond those intended by the supervisor. By defining unacceptable behavior, supervisors may also increase knowledge about minimum acceptable behavior. It is hypothesized that the disparity between the ideal goals of the school and the minimum acceptable effort being made by teachers is about as disconcerting as the original condition, leading to even closer supervision and a higher tension level in the informal group. That is, in setting a minimum performance level, the supervisor does not really want teachers to conform only to the specified

---

[7] *Ibid.,* p. 34.

[8] Clyde M. Campbell, *Practical Applications of Democratic Administration,* Harper & Brothers, New York, 1952, pp. 107–108.

level; he wants the individual teacher to achieve in keeping with his potential. The able teacher who does just what is required and no more is still seen as resisting a behavior which often invites further negative restriction on the part of the supervisor.

There are some grounds, however, for the belief that imposed structure and direction aid the faculty in solving problems of complex patterns which require decisions in early phases, inasmuch as the supervisor is able to induce all teachers to proceed from a single initial conception.

2. *Persuasive reaction.* Persuasion is that approach to informal group adaptation which tries to sell teachers on the value of official leadership and its goals through "human relations" by (1) giving teachers confidence in themselves and a feeling of belonging, (2) giving teachers a proper understanding of their task and accentuating positive aspects of the work, and (3) keeping teachers informed of progress being made in improving their working conditions.

Under this approach, programs which stress "communication" and "participation" are exemplified in workshops, conferences, social activities, and joint projects such as beautification of the school grounds. Channels for keeping teachers informed of the supervisor's action on teachers' problems are maintained because "it pays good dividends in building a feeling that someone is concerned about how staff members feel and is spending effort to help them." Teachers are told that they are important and that the supervisors are truly interested in them. Participation by teachers is encouraged in noncritical meetings. This participation usually lacks give-and-take expression and offers no rejection of the district's plans. Teachers do not openly challenge official leadership.

Group spirit is "built" by increasing the number of social occasions in which the staff gets together and by keeping the faculty informed about special contributions that individuals are making. The worth and importance of each individual is stressed, but derogatory remarks and hostile feelings are not vocalized. In his bulletins or talks to teachers, the supervisor makes sure the content of his communication deals with the school's interests and specifies the response he seeks.

An interesting variation in the process by which formal authorities react to a hiatus between consent and control is *cooptation.*[9] Cooptation occurs when those teachers who reflect the sentiments of the informal group or have the confidence of relevant dissenters are brought into a leadership position within the formal organization as a means of

[9] Philip Selznick, "Strengthening Leadership in Cooptation," in Robert Dubin (ed.), *Human Relations in Administration,* Prentice-Hall, Inc., Englewood Cliffs, New Jersey, 1951, pp. 238–340.

winning consent. Respect for those in control and the establishment of stability are, of course, expected to follow. The practice of appointing key figures in teacher groups to school administrative committees is a case in point. Individuals coopted share in the responsibility for power but ordinarily do not hold power themselves.

There are three criticisms of this persuasive approach. First, a faulty assumption underlies each procedure, namely, that teachers are at fault, not the formal organization or leadership. The fact that the school bureaucratic structure might need changing rather than the teachers' attitudes is not considered. Second, the procedure assumes that it is good to reward those who do as the district wants and that teachers should feel dependent, passive, and grateful to official leaders. Third, the approach has many unanticipated consequences. Teachers do not express their true feelings because they might not be "pretty" or "nice." This makes it difficult for supervisors to know about concerns which are vital to the success of the school system. Critical discontent, which could serve to strengthen the school organization if overtly recognized and valued, often comes out in covert expressions of disloyal and destructive attack upon the schools and their operations. Fourth, appeals to one's "professional attitude" in connection with projects which are not seen by the teacher as important lead to a corruption of the term *professionalization,* and it becomes *exploitation.* As one teacher said, "When the principal prefaces his request with the comment, 'You are a professional person,' I know I'd better watch out." Telling teachers they are important when they see that they have little responsibility may only increase their dissatisfaction and the antagonistic behavior within the informal group.

3. *Nondirective reaction.* Supervisors who react to teachers' withdrawal or other forms of protest by advocating equal participation in decision making are likely to hold the belief that individuals are more important than the institution and that the development of teachers is the chief end of supervision. From this viewpoint they develop principles stressing nondirective and group-centered approaches which call for

a. Listening, helping others clarify thoughts and arrive at their own decisions

b. Understanding individuals rather than conquering them

c. Noting the growth and self-insight achieved by individuals, instead of trying to achieve predetermined goals quickly

d. Encouraging individuals to determine their own goals and the means they intend to use to achieve these goals

e. Recognizing conflict and tensions, knowing that when feelings are expressed and discussed better understanding can result

Acting upon these principles, the supervisor believes that responsibility for change and development rests with the teacher himself. The supervisor is concerned with developing the potentialities of teachers so that they may become more capable of constructive self-direction, freeing them from overdependence on the skills and insight of the supervisor. Therefore, the supervisor is careful not to usurp initiative, self-confidence, and interest in a particular solution to the group task because he knows that teachers will then show less of this behavior than they otherwise would. In casting aside his official role, the supervisor frees himself from teachers' need for dependence and reduces his own anxiety about the outcomes of the action.

In meeting with the faculty group, the supervisor accepts the group at its existing developmental stage and places responsibility upon the members for planning its future life. Since he suspends his own ideas, the supervisor has no need to get them across and is free to "be the other person." Meanings are made clear as the supervisor reflects contributions and relates them to previous ones. This supervisory process brings a reduced threat of devaluation; teachers achieve a clearer expression of ideas and open their minds to new understandings, thinking more flexibly. In listening, the supervisor neither agrees nor disagrees. He avoids expressions that convey intent to influence, such as "You might try this," "That is a good idea." He recognizes that approving statements may threaten and embarrass, as well as further the teacher's dependency. In answering factual questions, the supervisor responds in a manner that demonstrates his interest in helping teachers reach good solutions rather than in protecting his own prestige.

As noted in Chapter 4, it is unrealistic to give exclusive attention to the point of view that supervisors should focus upon the development of teachers through informal leadership. The principles for working with individual teachers in informal group settings are different from those to be used in working within the formal organization. The pattern of action centering about individuals and the informal group constitutes only a part of the school's social system. Group-centered leadership must be weighed against the political structure of the school. But perhaps the chief objection to the nondirective approach is that the school is not primarily a psyche organization in which the interaction of teachers is itself the object of membership. There is also some evidence that when groups are permitted to focus on purely personal goals rather than on the common task, there is less satisfaction with each other, with the leader, and with the decisions reached.[10] For some groups, the designated

---

[10] N. T. Fouriezos, M. L. Hutt, and H. Guetzkow, "Measurement of Self-oriented Needs in Discussion Groups," *Journal of Abnormal and Social Psychology*, vol. 45, no. 4, pp. 682–690, 1950.

leader's control over procedures and the extent to which he alone performs leadership functions is directly related to satisfaction of members.[11] When there is an opportunity to become more autonomous, many become confused and anxious perhaps because of the increased responsibility. The consequences of any style of supervision are affected by the expectations of members and outsiders concerning how the supervisor's role should be performed.

4. *The inclusive reaction.* The supervisor who views his task as inclusive makes every effort to link individual, small group, and bureaucratic structure. He combines the authority of his office with persuasion and personal influence. His principle of operation is best represented by an adaptation of "the law of marginal antisepsis":[12] Whatever is undertaken in order to attain the objectives of the school must at least be harmless to the individual teacher: Whatever is done for the good of the individual or the informal group is at least harmless to the school and its tasks. Since school life is multidimensional, the supervisor varies his behavior. He offers warm acceptance to the individual but makes it known that the teacher is accountable for achievement of the system's goals. Emphasis upon maintaining a friendly atmosphere is not pushed beyond the point where it reduces effectiveness. Innovation is encouraged along with the demands for attainment of prescribed ends. The supervisor does not hesitate to use "buddy-buddy" groups, coffee-drinking groups, faculty cliques, and standing committees in furthering his task; nor is he indifferent to weakness in the bureaucratic structure which shows itself in faculty indifference, buck-passing, laziness, and other forms of resistance.

The inclusive supervisor recognizes that the school by its very nature will have conflicts but he hopes to reduce these conflicts by understanding what they are. The supervisor comes to an understanding with teachers about the areas of authority which he retains to himself and the limits of decision making delegated to them. Within the latter limits, teachers must accept consequences of their actions.

Obviously, inclusive behavior requires that a supervisor be highly adaptable, keenly sensitive to varied situations. His ability to diagnose the dynamics of the organization, groups, and individuals is necessary for combining the imposed structure for supervision and the voluntary motivation of the teacher. Assessment of the school situation is enhanced

[11] L. Berkowitz, "Sharing Leadership in Small Decision-making Groups," *Journal of Abnormal and Social Psychology,* vol. 48, pp. 231–238, 1953.

[12] George V. Sheviakov and Fritz Redl, *Discipline for Today's Children and Youth,* Association for Supervision and Curriculum Development, Washington, 1956, p. 25.

by understanding of specific factors which affect effectiveness and efficiency.

SPECIFIC FACTORS DETERMINING EFFECTIVE AND EFFICIENT OPERATIONS

A variety of factors may determine the degree to which a staff working together fulfills its purpose and at the same time provides individual satisfaction. In the paragraphs which follow we shall indicate the manner in which such factors as clarity of goals, types of task, size of group, and friendship relations affect the quality of the work accomplished. Throughout the discussion, however, one should remember the distinctions already made between the two kinds of groups: (1) the informal group in which any person may be the leader during the time he is able to direct and control others in the pursuit of a cause and in which there is also a shared feeling or concern, and (2) the formal group in which the position of leadership is maintained by the organization and in which the objectives of the group are arbitrarily set rather than internally determined by the teachers themselves.

A supervisor must also keep in mind the dangers of generalizing findings from research on small-group behavior to problem-solving groups in school settings. The tasks performed by groups which exist for experimental purposes of the researcher are often less complex than those presented to teachers. Word puzzles, for instance, need not require the same attack as inquiry upon the nature of intellectual development of children. Just because research in small groups leads to the conclusion that effectiveness and efficiency are maximized when members take an active part in choosing the goals and devising their own solutions to problems, supervisors should not encourage such participation in sponsored workshops and formal study groups. The findings of studies made of small groups in isolation from formal organization are suggestive but not directly applicable to school situations. Too, a small group of teachers may effectively and efficiently attain their goal and still not contribute to the effectiveness of the school system.

Clarity of Objectives and Paths to Goals Necessary

Studies of the effect of unclear objectives on both individual and group adjustment and organizational strength have particular implications for schools where there is often a gap between institutional functions and classroom practice.

In a carefully designed investigation of the consequences of varied clarity of group goals and paths to these goals Raven and Rietsema[13] demonstrated that it is not enough for individuals to know "exactly what to do." One also needs to be told how an immediate assignment contributes to a long-range goal and how his part links with that of others in the attainment of the ultimate aim. Where the latter conditions prevail, it has been shown that participants are more interested in their personal task and less hostile. Those who have a clear picture of the group's goal and paths to this goal experience greater feeling of commitment and sympathy with emotions expressed in the group. They also are more willing to accept influence from the group than are those who are unclear about the goals and paths.

The inference is that supervisors should keep teachers completely informed of the objectives and procedures of the organization. It is not enough that the teacher believe the system has a general goal, namely, the education of children and youth. He must know what to do and how his action fits into an over-all plan. An unstructured group situation has adverse implications both for a teacher's individual adjustment and for his relationship with others.

Necessity for Linking Three Kinds of Goals

In one sense an objective or goal is that which directs and maintains individual and group behavior. The supervisor has major responsibility for arranging those conditions which will link system goals, individual goals, and group goals. The public goal of the school may be to further intellectual development or to develop citizenship. It is the job of the supervisor to clarify for the teacher these abstract public objectives. He also hopes the objectives will gradually become "internalized" to the point that teachers will acquire an attachment to them and the procedures that will lead to their attainment. The supervisor must in addition concern himself with action designed to make particular goals found in individual classrooms and schools consistent with the broad objectives of the system as a whole.

Teachers may be more or less aware of the meaning of goals that are publicly formulated by the system. However, they are certain to have personal goals, such as the desire to be recognized as intelligent persons and to be secure. They are also likely to hold group goals in common with other teachers where the progress of one constitutes progress for all. Effectiveness and efficiency are dependent upon the degree to which these three kinds of goals are integrated.

[13] Bertram H. Raven and Jan Rietsema, "The Effects of Varied Clarity of Group Goal and Group Path upon the Individual and His Relation to His Group," *Human Relations,* vol. 10, no. 1, pp. 29–45, 1957.

Ineffectiveness of Abstract Goals

The supervisor experiences serious difficulty in linking system goals when the statements of objectives are vague. Overabstracted goals, such as "citizenship," "academic excellence," "critical thinking," are not sufficiently concrete to provide direction to activity. It has been fashionable in school organizations to state objectives or goals which mean all things to all people and which serve as a compromise to the various interests which sustain the institutions. This tendency, of course, is not reserved to schools. The lack of accountability which accompanies general goals is well illustrated by an incident at a meeting of a political party's platform committee. An opponent of a certain plank drew much laughter over his remarks: "You can put into it what you want—in generalities— but don't be so specific." Although general statements may be necessary to influence public opinion or protect an organization, they must be made specific in order that the individual teacher and his group can be a willing and effective partner in the task. This is not to say that the absence of clearly formulated goals precludes a teacher or group from becoming identified with the organization and its procedures. It is all too easy for a staff to become enamored with the process of their daily operations and in a ritualistic manner place values upon certain activities without knowing whether the consequences are relevant to the unique functions of the school. Regularized faculty meetings, workshops, or a tradition of orientation days can become important to supervisors, just as the selection of classroom officers or the writing of a set number of compositions can become the ineffective stock in trade of a teacher.

Supervision by Objectives

The primary need in school systems is the operationality of organizational objectives. There must be a way to observe and tell how well objectives are being achieved. There is some indication that improved measures of educational progress will support a movement toward supervision by objectives. Dimock[14] has drawn attention to this new approach in business and industry, pointing out that if the objectives of the enterprise can be made clear to the individual, he may find that his own ambitions coincide with the institutional goals of his employment. Dimock believes that one can have more responsibility and latitude in working out appropriate means to the ends inasmuch as the goal of the program is jointly agreed upon. It would be a mistake, however, to assume that given common goals participants in a school plan will auto-

[14] Marshall E. Dimock, *Administrative Vitality*, Harper & Brothers, New York, 1959, p. 189.

matically select for themselves their own most effective roles. We have already shown that in a cooperative system, the selection of an appropriate means also involves a knowledge of the actions of others.

There are at least two ideas in the plan for supervision by objectives which hold much promise: First, the school will be forced to analyze and operationally state the aims from which all teachers receive their mandate. Teachers will, of course, have a chance to offer facts and points of view, but they will also be held responsible for the adequate attainment of the objectives finally agreed upon. Once it is clear that teachers are to be held accountable for pupil acquisition of certain ideas important in analyzing situations and in testing solutions related to fields of knowledge, there will be less evaluation of teacher effectiveness on the basis of process and more attention to pupil performance. Already supervisors and teachers are beginning to focus upon operational ends of instruction, specifying both the concepts and the skills the learner should acquire and the area of life in which these are expected to be used. There is emphasis upon examination in connection with college entrance and the use of instruments which measure understanding of selected key concepts rather than rote memorization of information. Instead of condemning the practice of "teaching to the test" which often obscures the results desired, there is likely to be concentrated effort to make clear the behavior expected and to provide opportunities to practice it throughout the instructional period. It will be necessary, of course, to gear tests to the instructional objectives.

Second, a school district will have to allocate a larger share of its budget to evaluation of instruction in terms of pupil gain. This procedure should place in demand those supervisors who can help the teacher improve his instruction. Currently, many teachers acquiesce to institutional demands from an authority figure because they fear his power or are reduced to compliance by the emotional appeal of a consultant. A principal, for example, often carries a sanction or threat in the form of a rating. The limitations of a sanction are (1) that it causes teachers to "cover up" their earnest desires for assistance with a weakness or difficulty and (2) that unless the wielder of the sanction continues his surveillance, the teacher selects another pattern. On the other hand, supervision is also unsatisfactory when supervisors feel that they must lose the taint of authority and exercise influence by waiting in the faculty lounge or library until they can meet the teacher in an "unthreatening" situation, hoping for an opportunity to win the teacher's confidence before "selling" their advice. The plan for supervision by objectives promises to change this. Once teachers know that their evaluation does not rest upon the opinion of an administrator but upon the extent to which they achieve the institutional objectives which they themselves agree upon, it is predicted that they will voluntarily make more fundamental improvements in instruction. Further, the consultative service of supervisors will no longer be regarded as something which can be ignored without cost. Supervisory help will be eagerly sought and used because it will be directly related to the attainment of the goals upon which the teacher's own success depends.

Identification with the Objectives of the School

A person will work for a common objective if he feels a direct personal gain will follow or if an indirect reward will be derived from its completion. It has also been noted that in addition to personal interest in a task, he develops an "organization personality" [15] in which his behavior is determined not by personal motives but by the demands of the institutional objectives. One identifies with an objective when he makes his decisions in terms of consequences for the objective. We have previously mentioned the fact that many persons also identify with the organization itself rather than with the functions it is to fulfill. It often happens that administrators and teachers alike give their allegiance to a particular school, grade level, field of knowledge, or department instead of to the over-all objectives of the system. The problem of narrow organizational identification with its resultant rivalries, jealousies, and limited perspective is a special responsibility of supervisors. It is up to the supervisor to weaken those narrow identifications which may prevent, say, a teacher from pointing out something in his own school situation which is against the interest of the objectives of the system. To counteract the teacher's fear of prejudicing his local popularity, the supervisor must develop in him a loyalty to a larger system. So far, the best we have to offer in helping the supervisor develop such loyalty are suggestions from the theories of Simon[16] and Thelen:[17]

1. The individual's salary, prestige, friendship, and other personal incentives must be tied to the success of total organizational objectives, not only to certain procedures, a given school, or an informal group.

2. A narrow span of attention must be extended so that those in the system see more than particular values, knowledge, and alternatives.

[15] C. L. Barnard, *The Functions of the Executive,* Harvard University Press, Cambridge, Mass., 1938, p. 188.

[16] Herbert A. Simon, *Administrative Behavior: A Study of Decision-making Processes in Administrative Organization,* The Macmillan Company, New York, 1958.

[17] Herbert A. Thelen, *Dynamics of Groups at Work,* University of Chicago Press, Chicago, 1954.

a. Instead of being "procedure-oriented," that is, members are expected to accept a common ideology, resent unorthodox views, and rely on existing roles or customs, the group must be structured to ensure behavior that is "purpose-oriented." Purpose orientation requires that all ideas be tested against the larger purposes of the system and that conflict be resolved by appeal to the best evidence.

b. Members of opposing groups must be brought together to develop a new culture and new agreements, ways of working, and expectations of membership. District committees which cut across levels and areas are cases in point.

Supervisory practices affect organization identification. There is evidence from organizational studies that the more the supervisor facilitates the satisfaction of personal goals by individual members of the organization, the stronger is their identification. The more general the supervision, and the more the supervisor is oriented toward individuals rather than the work of individuals, the stronger the tendency of subordinates to identify with the system.[18] However, ordinarily if a teacher faces a task which is highly complex in relation to his capacities, he will want close supervision.

While the most serious misdirection results when objectives are vague or means to the objectives are unclear, the sharing of goals also tends to be a function of the interaction patterns within the organization. The individual is more likely to identify with a district and its goals when he interacts or has close contact with other members. To some extent, a district can hasten agreement of goals by the careful screening of applicants for positions, hiring those with homogeneous expectations. Once teachers and supervisors have been recruited, continual unity depends upon making clear the specific criteria which will indicate attainment of the goal and arranging for interaction of school personnel.

INTERACTION

Interaction is generally defined as that contact between two or more persons which causes one member or his activity to act as a stimulus to another's activity. It includes the channels of communication between members and the way activities necessary to accomplish purposes are divided among participants.

The Supervisor's Role and Interaction

Increased interaction, friendliness, and similarity of activity tend to

---

[18] James G. March and Herbert A. Simon, *Organizations,* John Wiley & Sons, Inc., New York, 1958, p. 74.

go together. The liking of one person for another depends upon the amount of interaction and the importance of the other's activities. Those who hold favorable opinions of a supervisor are likely to interact frequently with him, and this frequent contact itself leads to favorable opinions. Where a job has little intrinsic interest and the organization creates a feeling of pressure and impersonality, it is believed important that supervisors maintain friendly informal relationships which are not directly related to the instructional task. Building up a feeling of identification with and an understanding of each other's personal problems often augments the supervisor's influence upon a teacher's professional performance. Both those who are highly competent and those who have particularly extensive informal relations have more contacts and exercise greater social control. The factor which predisposes others to associate with an individual also induces them to follow his recommendations. Blau[19] found that the one who is sought by others becomes differentiated in status with the power and prestige bestowed upon him. Frequency of contact not only indicates but determines status.

Scientific explanation of the relationship between liking for a supervisor and the teachers' interaction with him corresponds to our commonsense notions. First, persons generally express a liking for another person to the degree that his activities measure up to their ideas of what his behavior ought to be in the circumstances. In other words, a popular supervisor or an informal group leader is likely to meet group norms or standards of behavior. Not only the supervisor but the objectives and activities of the school system are apt to be rejected when a supervisor does not live up to teacher expectations. Second, most of us think that the actions of the one we like are better than the activities which those we dislike are doing. Third, people have ambivalent feelings about interacting with a supervisor: (1) they admire the status of the supervisor and want to associate with him and (2) they fear his control and move away from him. In most schools teachers hold two different kinds of norms. They believe that a supervisor should be a "good guy" and also that he should make decisions. It is difficult to be a "good guy," yet avoid the negative expressions: "He doesn't supervise at all. He's always praising our work and is satisfied with everything."

Group Interaction

The practical problem of conducting faculty meetings, conferences, and workshops as well as the necessity for dealing with informal groups has caused supervisors to notice patterns of communication and prob-

[19] Peter M. Blau, *The Dynamics of Bureaucracy*, University of Chicago Press, Chicago, 1955, p. 130.

lem solving which are crucial factors in interaction. Channels of communication available to members are directly related to the effectiveness of groups. Studies of small groups, such as the Lewin, Lippitt, and White experiments on the relation between behavior and authoritarian, democratic, and laissez-faire types of leadership,[20] have shown that when the leader directs the activities of the members without either consulting their wishes or informing them of his future plans, groups spend a great deal more time in giving attention to the group task. Also it has been found that persons are more effective in terms of speed and accuracy in solving problems when communication is channeled through a central figure (Y wheel design in which the superior is the hub) than when there is a "wide open" pattern (circle) design.[21] Supervisors do not generally act upon these findings, partly because of the equalitarian bias of teachers and also because the findings are only half-truths. The other half of the story is that members are more dissatisfied under restricted communication patterns. In other words, effectiveness may occur without efficiency. Those who are relegated to a peripheral position can be productive but they are likely to be less satisfied. The more central one's position, the greater the gratification he receives from the activity. Circular arrangements result in more congeniality; networks which do not permit two-way communication leave teachers with the feeling that they are left out and unsure of themselves.

The correlation between satisfaction and performance is not clear. While it appears that in many instances the two are negatively related, the observation might be based on too short a time interval. Over a long period of time one might find that satisfaction contributes to effectiveness. Certainly if a supervisor must depend upon teacher motivation as well as effective organization, he should see that teachers are rewarded for group success. In this connection, there are several findings[22] demonstrating that in the long run both individual and group reward is likely to be less when a group or organization permits individuals to express personal needs instead of directing participants to the group goal or to the solution of the group's problems. It is predicted that there will be much dissatisfaction with the decisions reached, with the procedures

[20] Kurt Lewin, Ronald Lippitt, and R. K. White, "Patterns of Aggressive Behavior in Experimentally Created 'Social Climates'," *Journal of Social Psychology,* vol. 10, pp. 271–299, 1939.

[21] Harold J. Leavitt, "Some Effects of Certain Communication Patterns on Group Performance," *The Journal of Abnormal and Social Psychology,* vol. 46, no. 1, pp. 38–50, January, 1951.

[22] Henry W. Riecken and George C. Homans, "Psychological Aspects of Social Structure," *Handbook of Social Psychology,* Gardner Lindzey (ed.), Addison-Wesley Publishing Company, Reading, Mass., 1954, pp. 786–832.

used, and with the supervisor's handling of the situation when a group's discussion is characterized by self-oriented comments. Self-oriented comments are those by which someone attempts to enhance personal status, dominate the situation, make others dependent, and relieve his own tensions through aggression or catharsis.

Need for Control of the Group

Certain self-expressions must be curtailed if the individual teacher is to receive the rewards which accrue in the form of prestige brought by identification with a school noted for its academic achievements and carefully developed programs. The bigger payoff in personal reward which rests upon group goal attainment is sometimes lost to short-term satisfaction which comes to one who goes off on tangents of personal interest, reducing group effectiveness. Not only the supervisor but the group itself must be alert to those who "talk all the time" and wander afield. When troublesome behavior occurs it should be regarded as an indication of a needed structure within the group. Perhaps the task or purpose has not been clarified. While there is no particular set of procedures which can be used for controlling the quality of work in groups, there are understandings which can aid the staff in looking at itself.

Thelen[23] has described in specific detail a number of useful principles which seem to result in effective group operation. His description of these principles and control devices is a fruitful study which bridges the theory of interaction and its application. Included in these principles are the following ideas which can lead to unified controlling and understanding of group situations.

1. Make each individual statement the property of the group, not the possession of the one who makes the suggestion. The group should determine for itself whether or not the suggestion is a useful one.

2. Emotional expressions by individuals reflect the need of the group itself. If scraps are going on, the chances are that others are getting gratification out of the fight.

3. "In all but extreme cases, problem people are to be considered group problems." If someone bothers everyone, the question should be: "Why does his sort of behavior bother us; why can't we deal with it?"

4. Since individual contributions arise when the group tries to do something, and everyone contributes to the solution, all are entitled to consider how serious a problem is for the group and whether members need to do something about it.

5. "A problem is whatever everyone feels to be a problem."

[23] Herbert A. Thelen, *Dynamics of Groups at Work,* University of Chicago Press, Chicago, 1954, pp. 285–289.

6. "The group moves by consensus and agreement, not by taking sides in disputes."

7. "Steam-roller tactics and persuasion are of no avail because they block the objective evaluation of consequences and possibilities of correction. . . ." Data and exploration of the obstacles individuals see should replace ambiguity, vagueness, and inability to assess the costs of alternatives.

8. "Whenever the group does not know what it is doing, it ought to stop and find out." One way to do this is for the group to describe what it is doing. Members will know how to participate only when they know what the group is doing.

9. All seriously intended contributions should be responded to. "If the contribution seems of no value, it is better to admit an inability to see its implications for the group than to ignore it." Again, a purpose-oriented group can permit rejection of an idea without rejection of the individual.

10. "No individual can speak for the group. . . ." One can report how he feels and thinks and also give his impressions of the group. "But no man really knows how others think and feel. . . ."

11. "The aim of the group should not be to get participation equally distributed among members." The aim should be to deal with the group's problems—although everyone should be allowed to contribute if he wishes and there should be no barriers that prevent needed contributions. Opportunity for more people to achieve prestige is found when there is frequent change of activity.

Cooperative versus Competitive Groups

Both effectiveness and efficiency are maximized when personal and group goals are congruent. Integration of individual motives and group goals is achieved through cooperatively organized groups. A cooperatively organized group is one in which an individual cannot move toward his own goal without also forwarding the progress of others toward their goal.

Cooperatively organized workshops and study groups, for example, invite teachers to attack common problems, plan together, and share the results of their efforts. Most important, evaluation of their group undertakings is a joint affair in which members are told that their "grade" or appraisal depends upon the merit of their performance as a group. This procedure for evaluation is in contrast to the one followed in competitive situations; there members are ranked individually on the basis of how much each contributes qualitatively and quantitatively to the solution.

Deutsch[24] has found that cooperative groups show more productivity per unit of time, greater mutual comprehension of communication, greater attention to fellow members, greater coordination of effort, more pressure to achieve, greater friendliness during discussion, and a more favorable evaluation of the group and its products by the members.

Members of cooperative groups are more likely to maintain strength and regulate the group themselves. Competitive groups engage in self-expression which, as we have seen, often leads to both less productivity and more member dissatisfaction.

A successful supervisor believes that teachers work hardest to meet their own needs and that it is his business to arrange conditions so that they find it to their advantage to work cooperatively. The reward to the individual teacher through group effort will be greater only when the sequential steps necessary to attainment of the group goals are so simple that each one can perform them, and at the same time learn whether the step has been satisfactorily hurdled. This knowledge of results can be a powerful reward. Constructive accomplishment in a group such as a curriculum committee, a class, or a community task organization usually follows these considerations:

1. What do we actually hope to accomplish both immediately and in the future? Are these outcomes stated in terms of particular behaviors rather than as high-level abstractions?

2. How do these efforts fit into the larger context of the school's role? What is the group's defined responsibility? To whom is the group responsible?

3. What will we do differently as a result of this effort?

4. Is the task divided into small steps and is there a plan for evaluating and reporting outcomes from these simple steps?

5. What participants are required?

6. What will each person do?

7. What knowledge, resources, and other assistance are necessary?

8. What information will we need? What consequences must be continuously reported if we are to alter our planning on the basis of knowledge of results? How can this best be undertaken?

Individual versus Group Problem Solving

The overwhelming emphasis upon group work as a means of facilitating individual change and improvement in professional practices of teachers is generally well placed. But the superiority of group solutions

[24] M. Deutsch, "An Experimental Study of the Effects of Cooperation and Competition upon Group Process," *Human Relations,* vol. 2, no. 3, pp. 199–231, 1949.

in the decision-making process over individual solutions is not always demonstrated. The practice of decentralizing responsibility through the establishment of teacher councils and other structures for decision making opens up the matter of individual and group problem solving as well as the factors affecting the quality of decisions.

Accuracy of perception and judgment is not necessarily better because a group pools its intelligence. A minimum basis for making a valid judgment must exist. True, a group solution can be more than a statistical pooling of ideas. The experience of working in the group has an effect which can facilitate individual learning as the individual rejects incorrect ideas that would escape his notice if he were working alone.

One reason for the popularity of group activity as a supervisory process is that it is a convenient way to make public many opinions. But why is it important to share these differences of opinion? Because one will be better able to reach a correct judgment if he is aware of the great variety of judgments possible in any given situation.

The effectiveness of group effort as compared with individual effort depends upon the degree of identification members have with the group, the responsibility they assume for the outcomes, and the kinds of rewards for successfully completing steps in the problem-solving process.

Superiority of group effort has been attributed to the resistance that vague ideas meet in the demands of group communication. The very act of formulating an opinion for communication to the group may lead to a sharpening of an idea. Reduction in errors is also found to be associated with the practice of members' responding to the contribution and not to the status, friendliness, or other personal characteristics of the contributor.

Conversely, the social stimuli of group work may interfere with the task when intellectual processes or concentration is involved. An individual may be more effective alone than with others.

Allport[25] provides evidence that the intellectual responses of thought are hampered as group work continues. While group work heightens motivation to perform the common task, it also presents distractions which make the task more difficult, reducing the quantity and quality of work.

The effects of a work group upon individuals in industry has been well described by Seashore,[26] who found that attraction to a group was re-

[25] F. H. Allport, *Social Psychology*, Houghton Mifflin Company, Boston, 1924, p. 274.

[26] Stanley E. Seashore, *Group Cohesiveness in the Industrial Work Group*, Institute for Social Research, University of Michigan, Ann Arbor, Mich., 1955.

lated to production, anxiety, and attitude toward the company. Members of closely knit or cohesive groups were less anxious and under less pressure to achieve. However, when cohesive groups perceived their supervisors as supportive, they achieved higher production than those groups that were less united. This study suggests that the attraction of a group for its members can be either a force for positive benefit or a negative influence in an organization, depending upon the supervisor's success in establishing a feeling of confidence and security in his official leadership.

Statements like the following indicate that groups are not always effective or efficient decision-making instruments:

"Let's stamp out committees."

"I'm always glad when the meeting is over—I hate the bickering."

"We lost this time, but we'll lay for that guy until we can put him in his place."

"I don't think we can solve this problem by voting. We must get at the real issue of educational standards."

Such comments occur when:

1. *The supervisor is adhering too closely to procedural rules and lacks sensitivity to the interest of individual members, blocking participation and creating apathy.* A formal procedure threatens and leads to a reduction in the number of ideas produced. New ideas and new members need protection. The group should be helped to create jobs and to be aware of talent within its members who are potential sources of help in the matters being discussed.

2. *Conflict between private and public interests,* i.e., there are underlying animosities and "hidden agenda." Conflicting motives of individuals, subgroups, or the group as a whole cannot be fitted into the task. Action is almost impossible while the members work on private purposes, moving illogically on the surface task. Some members are afraid of examining long-held beliefs or practices; others fear they will lose power. In back of some members are invisible social organizations or forceful personalities that control their behavior. One's resistance to progress is often due to the fact that the group is approaching a decision which he knows will be difficult to explain to friends in another group.

3. *The supervisor may neglect to make clear that each person might see things somewhat differently.* It is important to lessen feelings of guilt and increase the tendency to put more concerns in the open. In this connection, it is recommended that the supervisor issue statements such as

this: "Perhaps we haven't said all we feel about the issue. Maybe we should go around the table so that any further ideas can be brought up."

4. *The members are not willing to assume mature responsibility for the way the group acts.* The group has not looked at its own procedures nor devised a method of evaluating so that it can improve its process. Remember, members do not know how to participate until they know what the group is doing. Too much bickering reflects lack of clarity of the group's problems and the behaviors necessary to serve these problems.

5. *The staff is unrealistic in expecting frequent unanimous decisions.* Members should not expect unanimity to follow discussion. It is better to seek tentative agreement or consensus upon the simple steps which might lead to the goal and to encourage dissenters to participate in the evaluating of the effects of these steps.

Before surface acceptance of a decision as opposed to deep level of commitment can be achieved, the group must provide positive satisfaction to the individual rather than constrain his membership or threaten him with the sanctions of tenure and promotion. Also, let's not sell voting short. The superiority of groups may rest upon the process of voting. Gurnee[27] has observed that those persons with high confidence and valid information are more likely to respond and carry more weight in a group vote.

6. *The group is too large for decision making.* In addition to the obvious difficulty of reaching a consensus when the group is large, other changes in structure occur with increased size. Subgroup coalitions representing minority views offer more effective resistance, and members feel their impulse to participate is inhibited.

In large groups only the more forceful ones show their abilities and share ideas. Available investigations[28] of group size and participation indicate that after a group exceeds about seven persons, there is much less participation. Concern for motivation has led to the *principle of least group size,*[29] which recommends the structuring of groups into the smallest number in which it is possible to have represented at a functional level all the social and achievement skills required for the particular activity. The use of subgroups may contribute to effectiveness of

[27] Herbert Gurnee, "A Comparison of Collective and Individual Judgments of Fact," *Journal of Experimental Psychology,* vol. 21, no. 1, p. 110, July, 1937.

[28] Harold H. Kelley and John W. Thibault, "Experimental Studies of Group Problem Solving and Process," *Handbook of Social Psychology,* Gardner Lindzey (ed.), Addison-Wesley Publishing Company, Reading, Mass., 1954, vol. II, p. 762.

[29] Herbert A. Thelen, "Group Dynamics in Instruction: The Principle of Least Group Size," *School Review,* pp. 139–148, March, 1949.

the large group by helping the individual share responsibility and receive the rewards of recognition. Again, however, factional conflict must be expected when the subgroup works out the limits of its power.

The chief question in deciding upon individual or group problem solving is: Does the problem require group action? If the problem is one that calls for change in the behavior of others, it is advantageous to effect group decision rather than to rely upon individual choice. Motivation and thought processes are modified by (1) other members, (2) the social situation, (3) anticipated social reactions, and (4) the responsibility for communicating and implementing the decision. If the problem or decision can be more effectively communicated in a face-to-face situation rather than in writing, a group meeting is likely to be the answer because such a meeting can help clarify responsibilities. If the supervisor does not feel he has the necessary knowledge about a particular problem, he might well consider the organization of a committee composed of those who can best supplement his knowledge.

RECAPITULATION AND PROCEDURES

In this chapter we have tried to indicate those aspects of the school's social structure which must be taken into account if the school's objectives are to be attained and if teachers are to be satisfied. We have seen that supervisory actions which disregard motivation and the personal goals of teachers are responsible for such malfunctions as complacency, inertia, resistance, and withdrawal from teaching. The value of informal groups, participation, interaction, and clarity of objectives has been stressed. Informal groups help to compensate for those supervisory practices or conditions which tend to make teachers feel they are being used or are unimportant. Friendship, leadership, feeling of worth, and a release of tension are among the outcomes from membership in informal work groups. The power of the group in guiding the individual teacher is great both because the teacher values his association with the others for its own sake and because such association enables him to get rewards that he cannot get alone.

Supervisors have attempted to strengthen the official organization by capturing the power which lies in informal associations. Sometimes efforts are made to make formal activities, e.g., workshops, faculty meetings, etc., assume the characteristics of informal groups. At other times, informal leaders are brought into the official family or assignments of teachers are systematically manipulated so that pressures from informal groups are consistent with the system's demands.

Theoretically, if the formal organization can reduce feelings of dependence, provide opportunities for leadership, and release tensions, there will be less likelihood that informal groups will form. If they do, these groups will supplement rather than resist the official norms of the system. The difficulty in such an approach is that it often conflicts with present political and legal structures as well as with the system's need for authority. Then, too, the motivations of teachers are often more complicated than usually contemplated. Some individuals enter groups with attitudes that bias interaction with them. Without common background and outlook, it is difficult to establish free and spontaneous interaction. Teachers who are predisposed to mature self-realization will welcome responsibility and shared leadership; those who have been rewarded for dependent behavior will expect close surveillance and direction. Unless teachers are task-oriented and possessed of the skills and understanding for leadership and membership roles necessary for the functioning of face-to-face groups, there is little likelihood that individual efficiency and instructional effectiveness will occur.

The potential capacities of the teacher will be fully used only when the teacher is a member of a well-knit staff that has high skills of interaction and high performance goals. Where these conditions exist, supervisors should deliberately endeavor to foster cooperative interaction among the total staff, not just among a few friends.

Small groups such as those representing a grade level, department, or school should be linked into an over-all organization by means of which participants hold membership within and between various segments of the school and system: teams of teachers working with special youngsters, teachers of children in the primary grades, study groups for developmental reading, district administrative councils, and faculty advisory committees. Through their own membership and teacher representation in these groups, teachers should have opportunity to exert influence in the school's hierarchy commensurate with their experience and knowledge. To feel that one can exercise no influence, especially over one's own class, department, or school, is detrimental to the school and the system. A reciprocal influence process is likely to weld the system into a more effective organization. All decisions must, of course, conform with broad policies made at higher levels; but decisions affecting only a class or a school should be made without reference to others since the relevant information is present and the responsibility given increases the individual's sense of importance and personal worth.

Ideally, any member of the staff can propose problems for group consideration, but each problem is treated from a system-wide point of view.

In the presence of a group composed of interlocking memberships, it is less likely that the problem will be resolved to the advantage of a particular person or interest and to the disadvantage of others. With the group form of organization, teachers soon learn to seek only those decisions which are in the best interest of the system as well as themselves. In addition, group action is usually accompanied by high motivation on the part of each member to do his best to implement the decision.

Basic to efficiency and effectiveness is a common identification with professional values which make the process of attaining school objectives a source of satisfaction. Such identification rests upon recruitment standards, lengthened periods of service, and evaluation on the basis of results achieved. Unfortunately, these conditions are seldom found in school situations. Provisional credentials, high turnover in staff, and periodic ratings by principals using extraneous criteria are more customary.

Both the public and the school organization will be better served when supervisors and teachers are held specifically accountable for the consequences of their operations. Most teachers want to evaluate the success of their actions because evaluation furthers both learning and satisfaction. At present, since there is nothing definite about the outcomes expected from the performance of teachers, there is no common acceptance of either performance standards or objectives. In other words, effectiveness and efficiency have been hindered by a lack of specific objectives and criteria indicating their attainment.

Inasmuch as the trends for the future will be toward greater effectiveness of schools, we can predict that supervision will take these directions:

1. Supervision by objectives will become the pattern. Every supervisor and teacher will be expected to be concerned with the rational accomplishment of school objectives in which harmony of system, school, and individual goals will be achieved by specifying results rather than techniques.

2. Particular schools, teams of teachers, and individuals will be encouraged to make necessary adjustments in order to attain objectives. Information as to the pathways followed by others to common objectives will be shared.

3. Personnel policies will place greater emphasis upon the adequacy of the teacher's preparation. Those without the necessary academic and professional training will serve as assistants, not as teachers. The professional teacher will share status with others in the school's hierarchy, leading to a diffusion of rationality and identification with the objectives of the system.

4. Supervisors will first recognize the importance of informal groups and then begin to regard them as assets, seeking ways to extend the development and contribution of these groups.

5. There will be a sharpening of the distinction between the authority necessary for (1) coordination and stability and (2) bureaucratic restraints that reduce efficiency by engendering apathy and resistance. Legitimate authority will be made manifest and used along with influence by supervisors.

PART THREE

HUMAN SKILLS
IN SUPERVISION

THE materials in Parts One and Two dealt with social systems and supervisory functions related to these systems with special reference to these functions in schools. Some propositions were offered concerning the nature of the forces which shape positions of authority and determine the direction of planning and action. A careful review of the functions of schools and the tasks to be accomplished indicates that some of the views and ideas about supervision are outmoded, and that knowledge can be gained and statesmanship developed to lead, alter, or reverse trends in teaching and learning. In our deliberations thus far consideration has been given to the individual as a part of group and organizational processes. It is our purpose in Part Three to examine the importance of the individual as an end in himself, since it might be argued that relationships with individuals are among the more important elements in supervisory thought and action. The wisdom for understanding and judging others in order to accomplish the most good and the least harm comes from self-examination and analysis of the many factors affecting what persons do and how and why they do it.

147

Dealing effectively with individuals is not to be achieved by thought alone. Knowledge of the attitudes of oneself and others is not sufficient unless this knowledge is put into practice. It is from on-going behavior with others that a great deal can be learned, not from information *about* behavior. The supervisor tests his ways of acting in the arena of interpersonal relations. How he behaves with others and how he assesses his own strengths, lacks, successes, and failures determine the kinds of skills he develops in working with individuals. It is the degree and quality of his sensitivity and responsiveness to others which influence the way others react to him and in turn to one another. Objectivity encourages objectivity; negativism encourages negativism; understanding encourages understanding. The list is endless.

The supervisor will not acquire behavioral sensitivity merely by getting into the arena with others and "behaving." A primary responsibility in developing human skills is to oneself. The supervisor must make himself the most educated, objective-minded, responsive person that his physiological and psychological make-up will permit. He can give to others only after giving to himself. Giving to himself means that he is a culturally and humanly expanding person. When he has a rich body of knowledge both for and about himself, and can use his experiences with others to incorporate new skills and understandings into his behavior and reject ineffective ones, he is taking steps toward the kinds of self-development which in turn will enable him to influence others in a like manner.

The materials in Part Three relate to the human skills involved in (1) perception of individual motives, personality, and behavior; (2) communication processes and guidelines for effecting desirable behavioral changes among individuals; and (3) factors in learning and appropriate supervisory behavior.

7

HOW SUPERVISORS
AND TEACHERS
SEE EACH OTHER

THE academic preparation and background of teachers throughout the country have some common elements, as reflected in approximate years of schooling, social-class background, and personal interests. These common elements, however, vary in degree and kind. There are no universal thresholds of teacher preparation or levels of competence, and there are wide differences in selection procedures of school districts, the qualities of school programs, salaries, and the kinds of in-service education provided. Any school district is thus affected by a number of forces which may determine the kind and quality of teachers employed and retained. Of course, school districts have a better opportunity to develop teaching staffs of quality when (1) they can draw the best teachers from topnotch institutions whose students are rigorously selected and educated; (2) teaching is looked upon by the community as an important occupation, a view reflected in its support of its schools; (3) the highest possible salary schedules prevail; and (4) the districts are located in centers of culture, with institutions for educational or professional advancement readily available. Superior situations of this kind are not numerous, and school systems are faced with the problem of building and maintaining competent staffs composed of persons with diverse and often uneven education and teaching experience. Understanding the varied characteristics of teachers in any one system is

149

of importance to the supervisor in developing a competent teaching staff. He must take into account the educational backgrounds of the staff, the motives which bring people to teaching, the ways in which the teacher views teaching, the means by which motives may be redirected or behavior changed, and the directions which in-service professional improvement must take.

MOTIVES FOR BECOMING A TEACHER

The motives which cause men and women to become teachers vary; they range from a generalized liking for children, religious beliefs, a desire to impart knowledge or serve mankind, to a need to acquire power and manipulate others. The limitations of applicability of some academic specialties can also serve as motives. For example, a student majoring in music, art, or physical education often turns to teaching, since other avenues for using his education in these fields may be relatively limited and teaching offers one opportunity to make these special skills viable. Some individuals, particularly women, may have entered teaching primarily for economic reasons, such as obtaining "an insurance policy" in the form of a teaching certificate or supporting temporarily a husband while he is establishing himself in a profession. Others enter teaching after graduating from a liberal arts curriculum because their vocational goals are amorphous and there is a demand for teachers, or for want of something better to do until they can develop or afford some other vocational interest.

The initial motives which lead individuals to enter any vocation may change. Motives may become transformed by on-the-job experiences. The person who entered medical school motivated by the possibility of receiving high economic rewards from an exclusive practice may find that medical research or a small-town general practice gives more satisfactions than the "silk stocking" practice he had originally envisioned. The newly trained teacher who enters the classroom with the idea that he wants only to get enough experience to become a superintendent may gain new insights which influence him to continue teaching in the classroom. Other avenues such as college teaching, research, or work as a supervisor or curriculum consultant may emerge. The changing demands of society, the expansion of knowledge, the growing need for new skills in schools are situational forces which may change the original vocational motives of teachers.

Although the motives of teachers, and their personalities, like those of other adults in society, are a complex of traits embedded in the nature and nurture of past experiences, motives are also conditioned by the kind and quality of experiences in a teacher's professional life. Some persons value the feeling of professional worth, satisfactory peer relationships, or the security which teaching can offer, above the greater financial rewards of other professions. Our concern is with the motivating forces of the professional environment which can be influential in changing behavior and determining the degree to which teachers are to be effective, mature, functioning members, not only of the school staff but of society. For example, the mature university graduate who has demonstrated skill in his beginning teaching, who has met certain standards of scholarship, and who has had emotional and intellectual experiences of a cultural nature must find himself in situations where he can continue to expand these patterns of behavior and obtain satisfactions consistent with his personality structure. Unfortunately, beginning teachers sometimes find themselves in a school system or a community which restricts their behavior or requires adherence to a pattern of behavior quite different from that which they experienced previously in associations with other adults. As a result, they may consider themselves to be members of a second-class society and begin to think of finding different ways of earning a living. By way of illustration is the remark of a teacher who resigned from teaching in a school system noted for its rigorous restrictions on the professional development of its teachers and its high turnover rate: "I rejoined the human race after I resigned from teaching and went to work for the XYZ Research Corporation."

Although those concerned with education in schools pay lip service to the idea that the personal and professional life of teachers should in no way be more inadequate or circumscribed than that of any other comparable work group in society, in reality the forces which operate outside and sometimes within the school lead to the conclusion that education has not yet reached the status of a profession. Teachers who come to consider themselves as a "class" of people different from other educated adults may react by suppressing reasonable desires and satisfactions, by developing feelings of inadequacy, or by leaving the teaching field.

Supervisors must recognize how important it is for teachers to have as many opportunities as any other professional group for participating in decisions related to their own welfare, for determining policies affecting their responsibilities, for participating in research which will help them in their teaching, and for assessing their own professional achievement. Teachers whose professional activities and responsibilities are limited or thwarted cannot remain competent, mature adults capable of improving the learning of pupils or contributing to the advancement of knowledge in education. Those responsible for the supervisory operation must provide constant reinforcement for mature teacher behavior and view teachers as persons who are (1) engaged in a mutually vital task; (2) concerned with their own destiny; (3) in possession of various degrees of expertness; and (4) responsible and accountable for achieving results. In like manner teachers must see supervisors as agents of the school using human and technical resources for the achievement of these same ends. Both supervisors and teachers must develop sensitivity to each other's personality and strive to understand others' expressions of feelings and beliefs. To gain insight into the ways each perceives reality is to approach maturity.

SENSITIVITY TO PERSONALITY

Although the dimensions of personality are varied and complicated, the supervisor can learn to be objective in such areas as (1) developing an understanding of the many-sidedness of personality; (2) acting in regard to others in terms of observable behavior and freeing himself from simple, unitary, or categorical explanations for the behavior of others; and (3) understanding that, no matter what the behavior of others may be, as long as he accepts all such behaviors as expressions of individual personalities, he cannot be really hurt, threatened, or contaminated. The objective acceptance of others is the key concept implied here.

Being able to recognize the constituents of individual personalities, both of oneself and others, is one of the most critical, and at the same time most difficult, skills a supervisor can develop. Many aspects of personality are hidden, or not cultivated, or not consciously recognized. Sometimes personalities are perceived from what appears on the surface. Yet much of what determines behavior may be hidden from oneself and others, like an iceberg with just a small part visible. The supervisor can develop sensitivity toward others and insight into his own behavior by an awareness of the different manifestations of personality and the significance of behavior in varying situations.

Each of us has an individual personality which is unique and can be viewed from different directions. According to Guilford, ". . . *an individual's personality, then, is his unique pattern of traits.*" [1] These aspects, or traits, of personality are defined as

. . . any distinguishable, relatively enduring way in which one individual differs from others. . . . "Trait" is thus a very broad general term. A trait

[1] J. P. Guilford, *Personality,* McGraw-Hill Book Company, Inc., New York, 1959, p. 6.

of personality may be as inclusive as a general attitude of self-confidence or as narrow as a specific habit, such as a conditioned muscular contraction in response to a sound. A trait may be a characteristic indicated by behavior, as in the two examples just given, or of physical make-up. The former is a behavior trait, the latter a somatic trait.[2]

The modalities of traits which make up the aspects of human personality are presented in Figure 7-1. Adapted from Guilford's work, these traits can be defined briefly as follows:[3]

[2] *Ibid.*, p. 6.
[3] *Ibid.*, pp. 7 and 8.

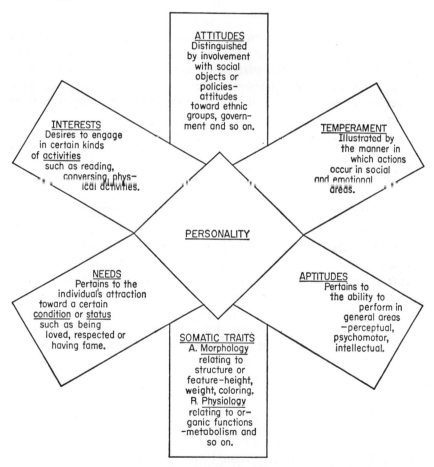

Figure 7-1. Modalities of traits representing different aspects of personality. (*From J. P. Guilford, Personality, McGraw-Hill Book Company, Inc., New York, 1959, p. 7.*)

1. *Somatic traits.* These are of two kinds—morphological and physiological. Traits of morphology are those relating to bodily structure or features, such as height, weight, and skin coloring. Traits of physiology relate to organic functions, such as heart rate, basal metabolic rate, and body temperature.

2. *Needs, interests, attitudes.* These are motivational traits which pertain to what a person does—to things one strives to do or to obtain —rather than to how one feels. Needs are continuing desires for certain conditions, such as being comfortable, receiving recognition, or being respected. Interests are long-standing desires to indulge in certain kinds of activities, such as handwork, sports, thinking, or conversing. Attitudes are distinguished by the fact that some social objects or policies are involved, as seen in attitudes toward birth control, income tax, or certain ethnic groups.

3. *Aptitudes.* These traits pertain to the ability to perform and to how well a person performs. Although there are as many aptitudes as there are actions to be performed, they can be described in a limited system covering three general areas: perceptual, psychomotor, and intellectual.

4. *Temperament.* Traits of temperament relate to the manner in which actions occur. They can be defined broadly as one's disposition —being confident, cheerful, impulsive, or other similar emotional or social behavior.

Attempting to understand the forces controlling the needs, interests, and attitudes of others, in particular, without judging or categorizing, will enable the supervisor to place the right or relative value on these behaviors as they are manifested in varying situations. To know, also, that a particular individual's temperament is so constituted that he is hostile and emotionally disturbed by certain ideas or, on the other hand, receptive to such ideas is a real step in understanding. There is no reason for the supervisor to probe the "why" of such behavior or to type persons as those who resist or accept ideas. Rather, it is important to be sensitive to the *kind* of behavior which is being manifested—to the situations which elicited it—and to meet this behavior with requisite and reasonable responses of a questioning or additive nature. It is in the *acceptance* of an individual's behavior that the supervisor has a basis for better understanding and for maintaining the lines of communication, so that he can continue to work *with* individuals. No matter how much it may relieve the supervisor's own feelings, it does no good to label the behavior of others. When certain behaviors are frankly displayed in group or person-to-person communication, it is of little value for the supervisor to tell another person that he is showing such-and-such behavior (or to categorize him unconsciously). *The behavior itself tells the supervisor what he needs to know.* Any labeling of a behavior helps neither to control the behavior nor to change it.

To welcome or at least accept from other individuals every kind and form of behavior called forth by the tensions which occur in problem situations is to have a basis for better understanding and communication. If varied behaviors are not accepted, or, in other words, if they are screened out or rejected by either direct or subtle means, the other person's defenses may be mobilized, resentments precipitated, and the channels of communication closed. A hard lesson to learn in working with others is to accept their statements of position, their concepts, and their expressions of temperament. If, for example, an individual holds the view that pupils of a certain ethnic group cannot learn certain concepts, he must be allowed to state his position until he himself discovers why he had to cling to his belief. Rejecting or categorizing responses with terms such as prejudice or stereotype will not help. Aggressive action to change this particular behavior will be fruitless. Argumentation and confrontation are to be avoided even if these approaches appear to succeed in breaking down the individual's barrier of ideas. The only achievement may be an eruption of emotions and a blockage of communication. Rather, the overt behavior should be recognized as an opportunity to bring the views of the other individual to a conscious level where they can be tested against facts and knowledge in due course. Discussion should take place in as unemotional a climate as possible, until the individual may eventually arrive at a changed configuration of behavior as a result of his own insights.

Reflection and acceptance are, therefore, important behaviors on the part of the supervisor. He tries to develop insight about *his* feelings toward the other person and to understand his *real* conception of the other person. Understanding another person so that one can relate what one says and does to the other's behavior in specific situations is a skill of singular importance. The supervisor who has this skill invites a climate in which the other person is taught something about himself, about the supervisor, and about how to get along with others.

TECHNIQUES OF MANIPULATION
AND PERSONAL THERAPY

In working with others the supervisor should not view himself as a manipulator of persons. If he believes that changes in group behavior can be effected by procedural manipulations alone, he may find that such mechanical approaches lead to dissatisfactions and group tensions, and that he produces ineffective results. Examples of manipulative process-procedures are numerous and are to be found in lists proposed as techniques for handling individuals and groups; for example:

"How to arrange the environment for a committee meeting"
"Procedures to be used in warming up a group"
"How to get everyone in a group to talk about something"
"How to praise an individual for a contribution"
"How to handle the hinderer or excessive talker in a group"
"How to open a meeting and what questions to ask"
"How to close a meeting"
"How to be a good leader without letting others know you are directing them"

Dependence upon these or other similar mechanical, prescriptive, or formalized procedures may lead to stereotypes of leadership behavior. Since they are not directly related to tasks and the involvement of individuals with purposes, they tend to subvert the essential reasons which bring groups together. They represent an outward simulacre of the communication process and depend upon fixed mechanics. They are not germane to a rational, direct attack on problems or to the needs of individuals.

In essence, dependence upon process-procedures as *the* way of working with others may not have the desired effect in terms of achievement, because such procedures are generally focused on operations which are peripheral to or unnecessary for realizing the purposes of a work group. The emphasis, instead, should be on the implementation of the indigenous concerns of a group; for example:

1. For what purpose have we as individuals come together?
2. What problems need to be defined?
3. What hypotheses should be developed?
4. What plans need to be formulated to attack the problem?
5. How will the results be assessed?

Teachers, like other individuals, may be plagued with psychological or personal problems, and the question sometimes arises whether supervisors should behave as therapists. A therapist is one who engages in the act of counseling others on personal problems. The supervisor who sees himself as a therapist or "junior clinician" is assuming a responsibility which is questionable. It seems fundamental in working with others that one should not engage in counseling on personal problems unless one is professionally qualified to follow through with the counselee. The personal and psychological problems of individuals are outside the purview of the supervisor's professional responsibility. Supervision, like teaching, is not therapy. The supervisor should clearly differentiate between giving professional counseling and giving personal therapy. Professional counseling about matters directly pertaining to teaching is one of his prime responsibilities; personal counseling or clinical therapy invades the private and personal life of an individual and has no place in the supervisory function. Amateur therapists can produce miscounseled and misled individuals. For example, the teacher who is disturbed because of difficulties in planning a systematic classroom program can be given professional counseling by the supervisor. On the other hand, the teacher whose spouse drinks excessively and whose professional work is affected becomes the concern of the supervisor only to the extent that the teacher is asked to seek help from agencies equipped to handle the problem. The supervisor in this situation focuses his assistance on relieving the teaching concerns of the teacher but avoids involvement with his personal problems. Visiting the home of a teacher to be helpful or to listen to his problems may be opening a Pandora's box of trouble. Even in such a seemingly innocent gesture the supervisor *is* initiating a counseling relationship for which he is not qualified. When the supervisor indulges in personal therapy he contaminates his professional role and may lessen his effectiveness as a leader. He is assuming a function of being all things to all persons and setting expectations which he should not attempt and cannot fulfill.

THE INDIVIDUAL IN THE GROUP

It has been stated that in this section of the book we proposed to give special attention to the individual as an end in himself. Without overplaying the issue of the group versus individual autonomy, it seems just as unreasonable to reject the significance of the individual as it would be to reject the importance of the group. Individual diversity and mutual cooperation as represented in the group are not in conflict essentially. It may be true, and extremely clever to say, as persons have noted, that a committee could never have written *Hamlet* or that the camel would appear to have been designed by a committee. Having been raised in groups, most persons have worked effectively in groups at one time or another. Group processes, depending upon purpose, are important in any society or organization. To hold the view that the individual should work in his own psychological tent, and that individual thought is to be valued most, seems as unwise as to hold the view that only groups can engage in effective action. In reasonable terms both the productivity of individuals and that of groups have a place in problem-setting and problem-solving tasks. The relative emphasis to be placed on the individual or the group relates to (1) the purposes and dimensions of any particular task; (2) the expertness of the individuals involved; and (3) the differentiation of responsibility. Overlooking the possibility of a continuum of individual and group processes leads to emphasis on one or the other and sets up a false dichotomy.

Reports of research on major issues in education and science conducted by foundations and commissions exemplify individual effort embedded in team operations. In such studies planning may have been a group act, research an individual task, the production of content the result of both individual and group effort, and the collating of data a product of either individuals or groups. The final agreements represent both individual expertness and the wisdom of the group. For example, the production of a large lens for an observatory telescope involves both the specialized talents of individuals and continuous group cooperation in the planning stages and during production. The tasks involved in the firing of a space rocket require that individuals in such an operation plan and flow in and out of groups, assume individual responsibility, cooperate on tasks where complete unity or understanding is vital to success, and evaluate results both as individuals and in groups. It is the talent of the individual which makes an emergent group viable, not the reverse.

We know that groups can be used to develop cooperation among individuals where there is effective communication, easy access to all necessary information, and opportunity to participate fully in shared tasks. The individual is unique and the use of his talent may be of critical importance, but in certain operations mutual identification is required for successful task accomplishment. For example, a military patrol is assigned to take Hill Number 8 and report back to headquarters. This group of men must have complete understanding and agreement on the operation. They must have all available reports on the route, the hazards to be avoided, and they must reach precise agreement on the responsibility of each individual. In carrying out the operation each individual has an assigned task. One will use the radio to report back to headquarters, another will read the map and lead the patrol, still another will act as observer, and so on. The members of this patrol have individual responsibilities according to their abilities, yet they are engaged in a group task the success of which, in the final analysis, depends upon the quality of individual performance. The group is a matrix of individuals cooperating to achieve a common end. Groups thus become vehicles for the expression of individual needs and talents and not controlling organizations to which the individual is subservient.

Groups come into being because of the demands of individuals to multiply human talent, to diversify work tasks, and make possible the testing of an individual's hypotheses against the ideas of a larger consultative body. Such operating bodies are more apt to be successful when they have a common purpose and are made up of persons whose technical competence relates to the group task. But the quality of groups rests on the quality of individuals. It is the individual who should be central in all cooperative staff endeavors. It is said that Hitler once noted: "The group is everything and the individual is nothing." The German man-in-the-street wisely asked: "How can the group be everything if I am nothing?"

MODES OF INDIVIDUAL BEHAVIOR

In working with individuals, supervisors can make conscious efforts to become aware of individual reactions which are related to better communication, facilitate adaptation to various learning situations, and improve the process of working together. The supervisor can assess the dimensions of hindrances to learning by careful observation of how individuals react to various situations, by obtaining feedback on proposals for action, and by informal inventories of how others view particular problems or tasks. The establishment of the kind of atmosphere which makes it acceptable and possible for mature teachers to assess objectively their accountability to the job will help immeasurably to increase understanding not only between the supervisor and other persons but among the professional staff members as well.

By getting constant feedback from individuals on how they view problems, conflicts, or tasks is not to imply that the supervisor has a select group of informants who provide privileged views of the behavior of others. The supervisor establishes the climate of freedom for individuals to express needs and to suggest openly better ways of working together. He develops insight into the behavior of others and improves his own behavior by consciously seeking to have others communicate their reactions to situations without fear of reprisal and by accepting all proposals or personal reactions as hypotheses or generalizations to be tested.

The supervisor will recognize that the varied forms of overt behavior which individuals display are, in general, modes of adaptive behavior for handling situations. Thus traits of personality represent characteristic reactions to problems and situations. Modes of behavior which seem negative in social situations should not be judged necessarily as forms of malingering; rather, they may be ways to get persons out of a dilemma. Suppression of a mode of behavior, i.e, overt expressions of hostility toward the leader, by domination, coercion, or threat, may well cause the hostility to become suppressed and do harm to the individual.

Most specific modes of behavior, like over-all social behavior, are characterized by compromises. Individuals rarely achieve complete satisfactions, and their modes of behavior represent their compromises. Fortunately, these compromises are usually at a conscious level and if the constituents which make up the compromise are known, behavior will be better understood. Negative modes of behavior occur when the achievement, recognition, security, sensory gratification, or response opportunities of persons are thwarted. The need for satisfactions develops early in life, and the individual becomes consciously aware that getting many of these satisfactions is fraught with painful experiences or guilt. Thus some modes of behavior become disguised outlets for painful conflict. Sometimes the ways of meeting situations may result in habitual patterns of behavior, and although the original stimuli which brought forth the behavior disappear the habit of responses remains.

Knowing the nature and the components of conflict which create and sustain certain modes of behavior is important in trying to understand others. Persons react to situations in various ways in terms of their personality make-up. Some avoid problems because they do not know how to meet contingencies or have rarely had success in such endeavors; others must be supported and given help; and still others attack problems vigorously on their own. The supervisor who anticipates the various modes of behavior which may occur is in a better position to arrange an environment conducive to effective responses. He will take into account the requirements of individuals and the ways in which they work best, and face the fact that many modes of behavior are inevitable even though they may seem inappropriate. The recognition that there are wide differences in behavior will help the supervisor differentiate tasks among those who are aggressive, those who are self-assertive, and those who express feelings of weakness or inadequacy. His work with individuals will be less concerned, therefore, with the symptoms of behavior and more, with helping others to express their views of problems. He directs conflicts with reality into productive channels by understanding personality characteristics realistically as possible strengths and not as shortcomings.

The supervisor demonstrates that he is aware that all persons have conflicts and varied modes of response to particular situations and that there is value in releasing these conflicts to a conscious level—by talking them out in an atmosphere of acceptance. However, there are times when individual behavior can block effective understanding and appropriate group action if not recognized and redirected. A directive approach becomes imperative in cases where important outcomes may be jeopardized by individual behavior. No mode of behavior is considered to be permanent; a different situation may result in hoped-for changes in behavior and in a new respect for individual capabilities as well.

When teachers are worried about their teaching competence they usually show their concern in one form or another. The informal statements of teachers themselves can often provide the supervisor with insights for helping them achieve more success. Behavioral difficulties may affect the competence and effectiveness of individuals unless they are helped to overcome their problems. These difficulties may be categorized for purposes of illustrating the modes of behavior which are likely to occur. In the list which follows each category is accompanied by personal factors or individual characteristics reported informally by teachers as being in their own minds obstacles to their learning.

1. *Dependence upon definite instructions.* A person who feels highly uncertain and hesitant, who blocks or worries excessively when he does not know exactly what he should do and how he should do it or what is expected of him or what to expect of others, may worry or get mixed up and be unable to perform as efficiently as he would ordinarily. Reactions which reveal this difficulty are:

If the supervisor would only be more definite and stress the main points in his discussions so that I would have some idea of his explicit points—instead, everything he suggests is vague and open-ended.

Why doesn't he tell us what he would like us to do in the workshop instead of suggesting we develop *any* problem.

He asked me to do a series of demonstrations for the visitors from India, but did not tell me the purposes of the demonstrations or what the visitors would have liked to observe. I'd get up in front of the class and wonder what the expectations were; then I would get confused and fumble the ball. I did not find out until later from some of the foreign visitors that he had told them that I was going to emphasize the use of materials.

2. *Dependence upon a solid foundation or systematic steps.* Such a person needs to have complete certainty about one step in the process of learning before proceeding to the next.

I always have a psychological block to overcome. I have to practice and rehearse one thing at a time before I feel free to go on to the next.

If the principal would only suggest one thing at a time—let me get real proficient on that, and then go on to the next thing—I would do a better job.

I never feel I develop competency in anything. One week the supervisor stresses writing anecdotal records like mad, the next week, pupil observation, and the next week something else. There is no continuity or central purpose to his suggestions.

I don't have time to read the research on one problem before the supervisor is off on another tack.

3. *Difficulty in building confidence.* Such a person can establish a stable confidence, but he requires considerable reinforcement or concrete experience before he can so achieve.

Confidence is of the utmost importance to me. I can develop confidence and maintain it, but first I have to prove definitely that I can do a job; until I do I feel confused and tense.

I like to be sure of myself before I go ahead.

I was asked to make several reports for the teachers' seminar and I was afraid of making mistakes, but the supervisor had me rehearse what I was going to do. When I did make some good reports after that it was o.k., and I did not have any trouble with succeeding reports.

4. *Anxiety about progress.* A person expressing this behavior needs to see ahead clearly before proceeding. He wants to know the target at which he is aiming.

I felt ill at ease when I first started the workshop. But once I saw that some progress was being made and could anticipate what to do next with the group, I was all right.

If only the supervisor would let me know how I stood in the arithmetic program he helped me to initiate. I never was sure whether or not I was making progress. If he had merely asked me how I was doing I would have felt better about the whole program.

5. *Confidence easily disrupted.* Such persons have the ability to conduct worthwhile teaching activities, but require intelligent support and satisfactory reinforcements for their efforts. Lack of such support may result in worry, withdrawal, and loss of motivation.

I spent nearly two years developing a special reading program with my high school classes and the test results showed progress beyond expectations. The supervisor's only comment was: "Apparently your program has resulted in good achievement, but you push your pupils too hard; you should give more emphasis to making them like school—that is one of our major purposes."

Every teacher at my demonstration complimented me on the overhead chart showing relations among the heavenly bodies. My supervisor noted that all displays should be at eye level and in not more than two colors. He made no comments about the content which I felt was of more importance than the physical arrangement.

6. *Oversensitivity to change.* Some individuals react strongly to any change, whether it be a change in person-to-person relationships, such as a change in supervisors, or changes in methods of teaching. They react by losing efficiency in their teaching.

If they only hadn't changed supervisors on me. I was doing fine and could really communicate with Mr. X. Then I got a different supervisor and now I am all mixed up.

I don't care what the superintendent says about everyone's having similar objectives in this system. Every supervisor has his own way of doing things. You cannot do it both ways at once—so you get confused.

If the general and special supervisors would only unify, that is, get explicit ideas of what we are all trying to do, so that I wouldn't have to react differently every time I work with a different supervisor, I could do a better job.

7. *Sensitivity to criticism or to suggestions interpreted as criticism.* Certain individuals become tense or annoyed at suggestions which they interpret as criticisms, or conversely, the absence of suggestions.

When the supervisor raises questions about my work, I get tense and overanxious.

Supervisor X is always quick to comment before he hears my side, and it makes me ill at ease.

Supervisor X has the "goody-goody" approach to everything. When I give a reaction to something, his immediate response is: "Good thinking!" or "That's good!" He has no values. He can't tell the real good from the goody-goody. How does he know it is good? I wasn't sure of my proposal and wanted to ask some questions, but he shuts me off. His value judgments leave me hanging.

8. *Desire for independence.* Some individuals find it difficult to tolerate being in the position of student or learner and their inner rebellion is shown by unwillingness and resistance to learning.

Every time I work with Supervisor X I feel like a passenger in my own automobile. I may have the wheel in my hands, but he is doing the driving. I don't feel independent. He gives me no opportunity to show what *I* can do nor does he let me test my ideas.

I guess there are some of us who just have to do things by ourselves and can't take directions from others. A fellow has to test his own hypotheses once in awhile.

I am sort of a rugged individualist. I want to have a few things my own way—want to do things myself. I don't want anybody telling me what to do. My supervisor has never recognized this trait in me.

9. *Tendency toward self-analysis and self-consciousness.* Some persons appear to be overly self-conscious and self-analytical. The attention to self may impair one's efficiency in professional activities. The self-conscious person is hesitant to secure information or ask for help. He is tense and worries about failure.

I am self-conscious at times. I don't like to ask too many questions. If it is something I don't know anything about I would rather wait to figure it out myself.

I would be willing to discuss things more with my supervisor, but he never tries to draw me out. He doesn't seem to recognize that I am a withdrawing person. He ignores me in any group and always talks to his cronies. I would be willing to participate more in his projects if he would only recognize me once in awhile.

I tried too hard—got too tense—worried about the stigma of failing. As a result I didn't do well at all in the job of leading the discussion group. If the supervisor had helped me a little, it might have come out differently.

10. *Oversensitivity to leader direction.* Some persons tend to be more attentive to the presence, opinions, expectations, and reactions of the supervisor than to learning the task at hand. This may produce a general emotional tension involving overanxiousness to please or fear of displeasing, and hypersensitivity to criticism and opinion.

I am more afraid of the principal's reaction than of how I might perform.

The supervisor talked too much. One meeting day I took the bit in my teeth and asked him if I could talk, and I improved a lot in self-confidence as a result.

I can never concentrate on a task when the supervisor is listening to what I have to say. I feel I am not expressing my true feelings, but only talking to please him. I find myself trying to confirm his beliefs rather than trying to express my own.

11. *Overdependence upon the leader.* This factor is related to the previous item, with the addition of a strong desire for individualized attention from the leader and a consequent sense of frustration and tension when this desire is unsatisfied.

Anyone could be a better teacher if the supervisor and principal had an interest in your teaching. Just makes me wonder if it is all worthwhile. The supervisor ought to fit himself to what we teachers want to do, not the opposite.

It seems to me that the supervisor is not interested in whether or not we are good teachers. Maybe I am too new at teaching, but I feel every beginning teacher should have someone he can look up to. I don't seem to have anyone.

I did much better the first year I was teaching because I felt my supervisor tried to help me and I learned. This year my new supervisor seems indifferent to me. If I had someone always supporting me and showing confidence in me, and I could place confidence in him, I would do 100 per cent better.

I have to get my support from my husband. My supervisor has no interest in me whatsoever.

Broadly interpreted these statements of teachers appear to reflect (1) reactions to lack of definiteness and to the presence of unknown elements in situations and persons; and (2) unsatisfied personal, social, and professional needs. The demand for definiteness may apply to (1) the situation as a whole or to orientation in general; (2) specific ways of performing particular tasks, i.e., giving demonstrations or leading a group; (3) need for a feeling of certainty in an immediately preceding step, such as the extent of preparation before a demonstration; (4) certainty pertaining to a following step in terms of what to anticipate; or (5) specific knowledge of progress, such as "Where do I stand?"

Obviously, individuals will vary in the degree to which they require definiteness, some tolerating more unknown elements than others. The supervisor must determine the preferences of individuals concerning how they feel they can best work in specific problem areas. Some of the questions the supervisor asks himself frequently are:

1. Do they prefer situations where requirements are definite, including assignments or outlines which are provided by the supervisor or by their peers?

2. Do they operate best in group-centered or individual project approaches to problem solving?

3. Do they learn best by immediate involvement in tasks, or do they prefer considerable orientation before engaging in an activity?

Such information helps the supervisor know where and how to start. The free discussion of each individual's role or goals can lead to better performance. Raising to a conscious level the assumptions with which each person approaches a task avoids starting in the dark, takes cognizance of human talent, and reinforces each person in what he knows he does well.

The comments of teachers relating to unsatisfied personal, social, and professional needs reflect various kinds of tensions and may cause a consequent reduction of the individual's ability to function adequately in his professional role, although in some cases the individual may actually perform better than his self-assessment would indicate. In general, the reactions of these teachers serve to illustrate the areas in which tension or conflict arises and some of the conditions which bring forth certain modes of behavior. These kinds of reactions are inevitable in some degree, and supervisors should not be dismayed when they occur. Many responses are beyond one's power to change, control, or direct, since they arise from remote causes. However, the supervisor can reduce the impetus for such behavior by recognizing the diversity of individual behavior, by being flexible in changing situations and his own behavior as required, and by placing himself and others in an environment where mutual success can be attained.

There are a number of ways by which the supervisor can develop sensitivity to the conditions and behaviors we have described. For example, he might evolve a figurative framework for seeing himself and others, as shown in schematic form in Figure 7-2. Within this framework, the supervisor starts with behavior known to himself—in an area of understanding in which personal behaviors are clearly communicated to others and actions are explicitly understood. In this area there is mutual agreement and acceptance. The pathway from this area is open to that in which behavior is known to others. But from this point on the pathways must be found and opened, leading not only to areas in which behaviors are unknown to oneself, but also to areas unknown to others. Opening these pathways by purposeful thought and dedicated effort will help the self and others to work more comfortably together. New areas are opened along pathways of personal sensitivity, improved communication skills, and conscious recognition of the individual in the formal and informal group. How we see ourselves and others, and how others see us, are factors which determine behavior and satisfactory relationships. The individual in testing his perceptions against this model will ask himself to what extent he has developed self-visibility and more reliable insight into the behavior of others. Careful assessment may reveal that the behaviors known to oneself and to others are extremely limited. Conscious application to a self-study of ways to open new pathways will yield personal dividends.

Effective supervisors face up to their limitations. They do not pretend

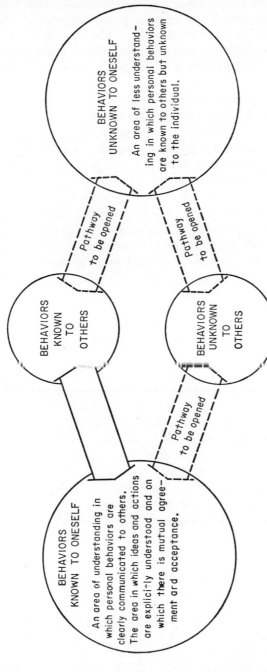

Figure 7-2. A framework for seeing oneself and others.

to know all the answers or to propose propositions or give advice in areas beyond their knowledge or ability. They make every effort to define their area of influence and to acquire the requisite skills for implementing purposes. By readiness to admit difficulties, to concede failure at certain times, and to try to solve problems through discussion, supervisors can help the teacher to feel less guilty about his difficulties. They help others to face facts, to take the consequences, and to persevere at tasks. The supervisor works closely with the teacher to develop hypotheses and to examine the results of mutual predictions; he does not encourage the teacher to abrogate his responsibility to carry through on his commitments by taking over or assuming command. The supervisor targets his assistance at the teacher's task; he does not do the job for the teacher. The supervisor gives technical support within a humanistic framework; but he keeps clearly in mind that the performance and the validation thereof are the teacher's own responsibility.

The teacher's job satisfaction within his own dimensions of competence in teaching should not depend solely upon the support, advice, or directives of the supervisor. The supervisor stresses firm accountability to agreed-upon commitments and the importance of task fulfillment, and reinforces the teacher when tasks are accomplished. He recognizes that some teachers are more concerned about their performance than others and that some teachers need special assistance in particular areas. Therefore, he differentiates his assistance and concentrates on getting the best possible performance from teachers (and himself). He ignores personality factors that bear no relation to professional problems and to the teaching process. He recognizes that improvement and teaching success will lead to teacher satisfaction and reinforce continuance of like behavior. In the final analysis, the supervisor recognizes that the quality of his own behavior in all person-to-person situations can be a model for emulation by others. The "goodness" of this model rests in some measure upon the supervisor's perceptions of the kinds of factors which have been discussed.

8

COMMUNICATION AND GUIDELINES FOR EFFECTING CHANGE

ONE important task of those holding supervisory positions is to get things done effectively with and through others. An essential process toward accomplishment of this task is the practiced use of communication media, whether auditory, written, or visual, by means of which individuals or groups are placed in contact with various proposals or data. Considerable material about the communication process between persons and among groups or organizations is available in the literature, some writers being concerned with developing theories of communication, others with reporting the results of research and experience.[1] It is generally agreed that adequate communication processes are an effective means for influencing persons toward organizational and personal goals, and that they serve to engender a climate wherein persons are encouraged to make full use of their thinking processes. Communication processes occur in social situations and are conditioned by the different expectations of persons.

[1] Roald F. Campbell and Russell T. Gregg (eds.), *Administrative Behavior in Education,* Harper & Brothers, New York, 1957, pp. 294–302. See also Nathaniel Cantor, *The Learning Process for Managers,* Harper & Brothers, New York, 1958, pp. 20–25.

In brief, communication processes may be viewed as a moving of ideas translated into symbols from a communicator who formulates a message to an interpreter who, in turn, interprets the message. In operative communication the *intent* of the communicator and the *effect* received by the interpreter should be the same. In other words, communication is most effective when the sign-symbols closely represent the same things in the experience of the communicator that they represent in the experience of the interpreter. However, the communicator must recognize that there is a constant selective process going on in the mind of the interpreter whose assumptions, points of view, and feelings are apt to color his responses to any message.

HOW TO USE THE COMMUNICATION PROCESS

In order to function well, any systematic program of communication should be designed in terms of the purposes of an organization, the differential functions of the staff, and the degree and kind of information to be disseminated. Inclusive communication programs characterized by systematic procedures (1) develop explicit understanding of duties, responsibilities, and privileges among all persons; (2) provide a place or source to verify facts so that misinformation will not arise (i.e., rumors); (3) supply channels whereby persons can contribute information, proposals, and reactions for consideration in decisions whose consequences affect them; and (4) make provision for free expressions of feelings about problems, issues, and proposals. Communication programs which take these factors into account are more likely to obtain wholehearted commitment to purposes from staff members than more restricted programs. In the latter, the system of communication is apt to have these characteristics:

1. Information flows only in and among selected echelons. For example, information is restricted to persons in an inner advisory council or to members of the top echelons, who in turn pass on selected items of information and withhold other information as they desire.

2. Communication is downward and the channels are limited in provisions for upward feedback. For example, persons in lower echelons may receive information relative to organizational goals as these are seen by the top hierarchy, but in turn have little opportunity to react or furnish feedback. This restriction leads to limited interest or commitment to proposals.

3. Communication is strongly status-centered and inviolate meanings are attached to the pronouncements of a central office or to the state-

ments of particular individuals. For example, the validity of information depends upon who gives it, and the tendency of communicators in this instance is to discuss or report only those matters which support status and to avoid communications which may threaten status maintenance.

Restricted communications systems which are characterized by these three factors almost inevitably lead to mistrust, misunderstanding, and conflict between teachers and administrators as well as among individuals in the organization.

The written, oral, or visual expressions of ideas employed in the communication system may be either formal or informal, as determined by the occasion. Where there are uniform expectations on the part of staff members and the problems are structured or concerned with previously determined content, communication can generally be in either written or oral form, e.g., a supervisor's report summarizing research findings or an oral summary of committee findings. A problem of change, an analysis of conflicting issues, or the determination of objectives may require more than one type of communication, including any or all of the following: (1) person-to-person discussion to explore or structure the ideas and feelings of a person or group about a topic; (2) written proposals or summaries presented as a basis for discussion; and (3) the use of audio-visual media, e.g., displaying a chart to provide information or to study a problem, or showing a motion picture to elicit responses and obtain emotional commitment to an idea.

In employing communication processes, the supervisor encourages freedom of expression by individuals and groups, and strives constantly to obtain feedback. In those areas where he is responsible for the final plan of action he makes his position clear. He shows by his behavior that he respects the opinions of others. His statements about accountability, however, are explicit: "It is your privilege to say what you think, whether or not it agrees with the points of view of others. I respect your judgment, as well as the judgments expressed by others, but I am responsible in this instance for weighing all ideas or proposals which we may develop in light of purposes or goals and for making the final decision."

Any one of the communication media has both strengths and weaknesses. The supervisor, sensitive to human relations, tests the effects of each by carefully observing the behavior of other persons or groups which results from his messages. Some suggested ways to improve the communication process follow:

1. *Use several media for the same target if necessary.* Among the

possibilities are written information, audio-visual techniques such as schematic materials and diagrams, person-to-person discussions, and group meetings.

2. *Obtain feedback whenever possible.* Obtain written or verbal responses to determine understanding, and constantly encourage suggestions and criticisms.

3. *Know the precise purposes for preparing the communication.* Limit memos to essential items in order to avoid confusing or diverting the interpreter by an unprogrammed miscellany. Give attention to major needs or information required to carry forward a particular operation in preparing other forms of communication.

4. *Write or speak only to the essentials.* Be parsimonious in using communication media. Do not meet every problem with an open mouth or with a ball-point pen at the ready position. Overimpacting a staff with a barrage of verbal and written information, ideas, or proposals, especially without follow-up, results in extinction of discriminatory responses to such stimuli. Avoid repeating information available in prior communications or available by reference to other sources.

5. *Develop a systematic set of communication techniques.* Be sure that all persons know that certain classes of bulletins deal with particular areas of thought, that memos deal with other specific areas, and that working papers are used for primarily the presentation of content materials. Labeling or giving a series listing for bulletins, reports, and other materials in terms of their purposes and targets provides focal points of attention. The interpreter is helped to attend to the message if its label defines its intent.

PERSON-TO-PERSON COMMUNICATION

One important communication process for the supervisor to use is that of person-to-person communication. He may employ this process to effect changes in staff behavior, to discuss various problems, to discover vis-à-vis the ideas and feelings of others, or to transmit his own ideas. The description of person-to-person communication which follows is primarily concerned with the role of the communicator and interpreter in oral discourse.[2] However, many of the factors which operate in this process operate in other forms of communication as well. In any communication process—when persons are communicating—a kind of

[2] Information based on Robert Tannenbaum and Irving R. Weschler, "Developing Effective Communication," *Report of the Western Regional Conference for Nurses in Administrative and Supervisory Positions,* University Extension, University of California, Los Angeles, Calif., June, 1956, pp. 25–32. (Mimeographed.)

transmission belt is operating. Ideas themselves are not communicated by means of this transmission system, but ideas which have been translated into symbolic forms, such as words or signs. Symbolic representation is used with the hope that it will generate in the minds of others the ideas that the communicator holds in his own mind.

To highlight essential elements in person-to-person communication, a model showing the flow of ideas, or symbols which stand for ideas, in the message channel and the factors affecting communication is presented in Figure 8-1. Two persons are represented: the *communicator* and the *interpreter*. These two persons are faced with the problem of communicating with each other and providing content in the message channel, content which represents, stands for, the same things to both persons. The communicator starts with an idea which he wishes to communicate. If the idea generated by him is not clearly formulated, communication effectiveness is reduced from the beginning of the process. The communicator must then translate his idea into message form. He will have to use symbols in his message, generally either spoken or written, for representing the idea. After the communicator has translated his idea into a message, he transmits the message to the interpreter. Various factors may hinder or help movement of the message through the message channel and affect its interpretation. These factors may be classified as mechanical, semantic, or psychological. Mechanical factors include the kind of situation in which communication takes place, how the voice is used in oral communication, and such hindrances as mannerisms and external noises. Semantic factors have to do with linguistic skills, vocabulary, nomenclature, and the interpretation of symbols. Psychological factors include needs, beliefs, attitudes, and expectations, as well as feelings of security or lack of security, and the status system.

The message becomes a stimulus to which the interpreter responds with a discriminatory response. He translates the message into an idea by a selective process. In effective communication the idea from the communicator's mind (intent) ends up in the interpreter's mind (effect) equivalent in meaning to the original idea of the communicator. However, in the actual communication process this sequence does not occur regularly or systematically because of distortions resulting from negative factors operating in the communications network. Obviously, when distortion is reduced, communication is improved.

Problems Faced by the Communicator

When recognized, factors which lead to distortion can be reduced.

1. The communicator may face difficulties relating to his feelings about *himself.* For example, he may feel that he is seldom able to make

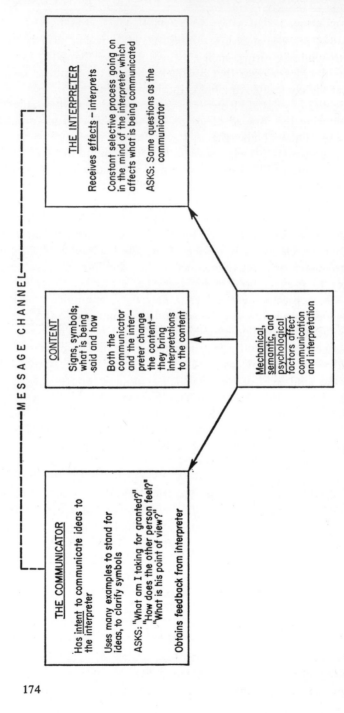

Figure 8-1. Person-to-person communication.

THE INTERPRETER

Receives effects – interprets

Constant selective process going on in the mind of the interpreter which affects what is being communicated

ASKS: Same questions as the communicator

MESSAGE CHANNEL

CONTENT

Signs, symbols; what is being said and how

Both the communicator and the interpreter change the content— they bring interpretations to the content

Mechanical, semantic, and psychological factors affect communication and interpretation

THE COMMUNICATOR

Has intent to communicate ideas to the interpreter

Uses many examples to stand for ideas, to clarify symbols

ASKS: "What am I taking for granted?" "How does the other person feel?" "What is his point of view?"

Obtains feedback from interpreter

himself understood, that he typically has difficulty in communicating his ideas to others. Because of this concept of himself, he may find it necessary to formulate his messages several times over and in several different ways. He may send a message phrased in one way, but not being satisfied that it is clear he rephrases it, and so on through a number of changes. Thus, the interpreter is confronted with a number of formulations of an idea, each of which may be different from the others. He has difficulty in knowing what is being said. The communicator, in attempting to be understood, displays his lack of skill in formulating the statement of his ideas and is more often than not misunderstood.

2. The assumptions held by the communicator and the feelings he has about the interpreter may have the effect of distorting an idea as it gets translated into a message. For example, the communicator may dislike the interpreter, yet does not wish to or is not able to express directly this hostility because it is a relatively submerged feeling. Nevertheless, this hostility may be reflected in the message which is transmitted. He may say, "Do you know what procedures our former supervisor used to study this problem?" To the casual observer, this may sound like a reasonable question, but what comes through to the interpreter of the message is a feeling of comparison, a criticism of his way of working. The person who asked the question may not have been aware of its impact, but because of his buried hostility he managed to give the impression of hostility in his statement.

3. As communicators, we may or may not be aware of the kind of person with whom we are communicating. To communicate effectively, we must learn to take into account the other person's point of view and his personality make-up so that we can frame messages which will more accurately target him. We have to take into account such factors as the kind and degree of knowledge the interpreter possesses regarding a particular topic. We have to know with what nomenclature he is likely to be most familiar. If the communicator uses technical terms unfamiliar to others, his message will appear in symbols unfamiliar to them. For example, if one is talking about learning theory to a group of experts in the field, his messages would contain symbols of one order; if talking to a group of lay persons on the same topic, his messages would have a different content. The communicator has to know as much as possible about the interpreter's frame of reference, because it is in this personal framework that messages will be decoded or interpreted.

4. The communicator needs to know how the other person perceives him. If the interpreter respects the person to whom he is giving attention or has generally good feeling toward him, he is more likely to be favor-

ably disposed toward the messages he receives. If his feelings are negative toward the communicator, it may be difficult for the communicator to get any messages through, even though they are, in an objective sense, basically good ideas. Most persons have experienced this kind of frustration.

5. Another factor affecting the communication process relates to the assumptions or expectations about the organizational system in which persons are operating. All of us need to be sharply aware of the ways in which individuals behave in the organization. What kinds of things are valued and what are not valued in the organization? What kinds of actions are expected and valued and what not accepted on the part of individuals? If an organization is one whose operation is based upon widespread communication and the development of skill in discourse, individuals will reflect this atmosphere in their actions. If the organization is restrictive and only limited kinds of communication are encouraged, this atmosphere will be reflected. The implications for the supervisor seem clear. If the only way for teachers to get along is to keep their mouths shut, the expectations and atmosphere of the organization may need examination.

6. The actual communication skills are also critical to effective communication. An individual's facility with words and the precision with which meanings are attached to words are determinants in skillful communication. Since words stand for ideas, their choice and patterning are critical. The constant sharp definition of terms is necessary. Using words in bulletins or memos requires as much thought as in oral discourse, if not more. Individuals read only that which "they bring to read with." Further, written communication is based on the assumption that one can write; this is not always valid. Whether in spoken or written form, the extent to which a communicator makes skillful use of examples will help communication. Examples which illustrate or stand for an idea enable others to understand the idea. Feedback techniques also help the communicator to discover how much has been understood and to adjust his messages accordingly.

Problems Faced by the Interpreter

The factors affecting the communicator also exist for the interpreter in a number of ways. The interpreter is faced with understanding such factors as the following:

1. The conscious feelings he has about himself. For example, a supervisor may have excellent technical skills, but he feels that teachers really do not care for him as a person. They respond to his technical behavior, but show little interest in him as a human being. This is the way the

supervisor views himself. Because of this self-view, whenever others communicate with him he assumes that they personally do not like him. And so he misinterprets the messages he receives, thus contaminating them with what he *thinks* others feel about him, even though others may not have these feelings at all. The feelings we have about ourselves affect the way in which we interpret the messages of others.

2. There are unconscious processes operating within the interpreter. He may have self-doubts about his own competence, including short-comings that he can never examine too closely or accept. He may deal with his shortcomings by diffuse activity, by driving others, or by avoiding mechanisms. When someone offers a suggestion or raises a question to help improve a particular situation, he may interpret it as a criticism of his technical competency or an attack on some imagined area of sensitivity. He may react by rejecting the suggestion outright or by saying: "This does not concern you; it is my problem." Responses such as this are a defense against his own feelings of inadequacy and are unrelated to the content of the communication messages he is receiving.

3. The interpreter also makes assumptions about the communicator as he listens to a message. The other person's personality traits, knowledge, or attitudes are assessed as he receives the message, or even before the message is formulated. The quality of assumptions and their relation to the message can affect strongly his interpretation, leading either to wrong conclusions or, hopefully, to more effective understanding.

4. The assumptions which are made about the organizational and social situation will affect interpretation. If the supervisor feels that the teacher's suggestions or decisions are critically important to successful operations, he will respond differently to communication messages from the way he will if he considers himself the supreme decision maker and treats the teacher's ideas in accordance with this self-centered view.

5. Many communication skills are of equal importance to both the interpreter and the communicator. Most important is the skill of really listening—the ability to hear what is being said from the other person's point of view, and to draw only those conclusions which are validated by mutual understanding and agreement.

Although there are many barriers to effective communication, there are also communication gateways available to all.

In order to provide gateways, it seems to me that both the communicator and the interpreter have to learn how to understand each other. They have to find ways and means of "getting inside" the other person, of understanding him as a unique individual with his personality, his frame of reference, his knowledge and his experience. This is something that is not easy to do, but getting real understanding of the other person provides an exceedingly helpful gateway to effective communication. Also, understanding of self is another exceedingly meaningful device for opening gateways to effective communication—really to understand what one's own unconscious processes are, to bring them up to the conscious level, to become aware of one's own distorting mechanisms.

To the extent that we can create an atmosphere around ourselves that makes it possible for other people to express their feelings and attitudes about themselves and others, to this extent I think we can vastly improve the effectiveness of our communications. This type of gateway is hard to come by—it is something that we cannot open up overnight—but it is one which yields rich rewards.[3]

GUIDELINES FOR EFFECTING CHANGE

Supervisors are constantly faced with the problem of effecting changes in the beliefs, attitudes, and feelings of others, as well as the problem of initiating and implementing changes in organizational structure, curriculum programs, and other important areas. The supervisor's effectiveness in achieving changes in persons and in organizational functions is related to his understanding of personality, awareness of individual behavior, and skillful use of inclusive communication media. The kinds of questions and premises which are proposed in this section represent a framework in which the supervisor seeking change can generate hypotheses and predict outcomes.

1. *Be aware that changes are needed.*

What educational, psychological, and sociological findings show that changes are required?

How have I made it easy for persons to register disapproval of existing conditions?

Have I sensed the needs of others?

How do I stimulate persons to seek change?

Have I provided a map of the possible routes toward change which we might take?

Have I tentatively projected possible consequences and implications of the proposed change?

2. *Recognize that the individual may have a different view of the situation.*

What experiences has he had?

In what social role does he see the school?

What attitudes and interests does he hold?

[3] Tannenbaum and Weschler, "Developing Effective Communication," *Report of the Western Regional Conference for Nurses in Administrative and Supervisory Positions,* p. 32.

Is the proposed change based on what he thinks the problem is?

Do I constantly seek to get feedback on how others view the accuracy of my perceptions of a situation?

3. *Respect other points of view and grant security for expression.*

Is the setting one which permits clarification of values and goals by letting individuals seek reasons for disagreement?

Am I sensitive to the real feelings of others in both their observable and hidden reactions?

Am I genuinely interested in what the other persons are proposing and doing about the problem?

Am I making every effort to encourage others to arrive at their own hypotheses and conclusions and not to give them answers every step of the way?

Can I demonstrate that personal security will be increased because of the proposed changes?

Do I respect the right of persons to be different and maintain a consistent behavior in myself?

4. *See that helpful mechanics are established.*

Have I provided a leadership which encourages all teachers to participate?

Have I prepared participants for discussions of problems?

Have I made it easy for persons to get together for communication of ideas?

Have I done my utmost to remove conflicting pressures of other responsibilities?

Is the physical setting pleasant and reasonably appropriate for the business at hand?

To what extent am I prepared to backstop the group with resources and assistance?

5. *Get participation.*

Can I interest others by sensing their dissatisfactions and desires?

Have I helped individuals feel free to participate even though their ideas and actions are not what I had expected?

In the discussion of a particular problem have I made certain that all those who should be present are present, including those who will be most affected by the change?

Have I avoided exercising leadership by cronies?

Have I set a relaxed atmosphere but at the same time concentrated on specifics?

Have I avoided being concerned with trivia or nonessentials?

6. *Unify the attack on the problem.*

Am I helping to delineate the problem?

Is the problem really of concern to the group?

Can we weld the divergent points of view and build a common problem from them?

Am I willing to face the facts and not push on for unwanted action?

Is my contribution to problems helping others and not just myself?

Are group members encouraged to suggest possible outcomes so that we are all developing the same vision?

Am I certain that everyone sees the immediate limits to an undertaking as well as the long-range goals?

Did the group set these goals itself?

In pointing out logical errors or limitations, do I still preserve the atmosphere which fosters initiative and does not push the group against a wall from which there is no escape?

7. *Sense the forces operating and evaluate what is happening.*

What external or internal forces are restraining the group or urging it on?

Why do these forces exist?

How can they be lessened or modified to permit change?

What part are personal needs playing?

What attitudes are being challenged?

What facts are needed?

Are the efforts in which we are involved promoting teacher growth?

Is the activity, whether an immediate undertaking or a long-range goal, likely to promote pupil growth?

8. *Recognize that change might be slow.*

Do I keep constantly before me that new values and skills may develop only after much participation and that a small beginning might lead to larger developments?

Have I resolved the classic conflict: a program cannot change faster than those involved and a change must occur as rapidly as necessary?

9. *Give persons the opportunity to operate in the way in which they do best.*

Are we going in the direction in which we really want to go?

Am I certain that the teacher is accepting a change because he wants it?

Do we know the responsibilities we are to accept in connection with our decision?

How will our decisions be communicated to others proximate to the task?

What provisions are being made to get feedback from others?

How is our plan to be coordinated with the rest of the program?

Have we made specific provision for further personal interpretation, expression, and development of the proposed change?

Have we given recognition to the contributions made by individuals?

10. *Recognize that change is more continuous than permanent.*

Have we provided for follow-up?

How will we evaluate the effectiveness of the change?

Have we taken specific responsibilities in these tasks?

What is the relation of others to the proposed change?

What new forces and other persons may already be altering the situation?

11. *Determine those factors of behavior which do not change radically from one situation to another.*

Am I able to determine the goals (specific premises, beliefs, facts) of others?

Do I know the generalizations being employed?

Can I assess the thinking processes of each member of a group?

Can I describe thinking processes so that I can predict the behavior of persons when confronted with a new problem?

A further illustration of the ways in which supervisory action can be derived from theoretical propositions is shown in the following list of matched items:

TABLE 4. How Supervisory Action Can Be Derived
from Theoretical Propositions

Sources and propositions	*Implications for action*
1. *Phenomenological psychology:* "One acts as he perceives himself."	The supervisor makes every effort to provide opportunity for others to express their beliefs and feelings; he tries to understand how the teacher perceives reality.
2. *Organizational theory:* A leader must be seen as an influential member in the system if he is to be influential with others.	The supervisor must carry weight with higher authorities if he is to exercise influence with teachers. The supervisor holds a place in the hierarchy, and his effectiveness is related to the stability of his status role with those above him—and his consequent security is so reflected in the confidence shown by teachers. He is not a member of the peer group, but holds special status with rights, privileges, and responsibilities ordered to him as an agent of the system.

TABLE 4. HOW SUPERVISORY ACTION CAN BE DERIVED
FROM THEORETICAL PROPOSITIONS (*continued*)

Sources and propositions	*Implications for action*
Hierarchical organization frequently results in developing a "trained incapacity."	The supervisor who adheres to regulations and the propriety of procedures as ends in themselves will be associated with timidity, conservatism, and conformity in his own behavior and will influence teachers in the same direction.
3. *Role theory:* Role is usually defined in terms of patterns of behavior or expectations others have of behavior. Expectations define how an individual should act in given situations: roles are complementary.	One is successful in supervision to the extent that he fulfills the role expectations of the teachers.
4. *Theory of leadership:* Autocratic leadership results in (1) hostility, (2) identification with the leader rather than with the group, (3) anxiety about the future, (4) rigidity of behavior, and (5) formalized productivity.	In selecting a supervisor, the likely consequences of choosing a person who sells, pushes, pressures, and persuades teachers to improvement and loyalty to the system should be considered. It is well to select a supervisor who predicts the logical consequences of his proposals and demonstrates that he is a fact-facing person when his predictions do not come true.
5. *Theory of group dynamics:* Conflict is desirable because it brings involvement and develops creative alternatives. The individual's loyalty and identification with the group's goals occur when he is dependent upon the group. He will be more likely to persist in carrying out decisions when these decisions are formulated by him and his group.	As the expert leader, the supervisor seeks to establish a free, permissive, informal atmosphere, yet the cherished beliefs of individuals are not considered unassailable. The same persons who work on problems also have opportunity to participate in formulating the goals, planning how they will work, and carrying a task through to completion.

The supervisor who tests his actions against a set of propositions may be more likely to achieve consistent and logical ways of working for change. However, the supervisor also recognizes that principles and propositions are not absolute, and that better ones will evolve as (1) research continues in the disciplinary sources which give rise to new ideas about human behavior; and (2) new principles suggested by the behavioral sciences are proposed.

9

FACTORS IN LEARNING AND SUPERVISORY BEHAVIOR

IN this chapter we propose to examine some of the current thinking about learning. It has been said that those working in learning theory have been responsible for "mapping the boundaries of our ignorance as well as providing workable theories and information." At one time "laws of learning" were confidently put forth as the basis for approaching all learning situations. Confidence in universal theories, however, has lessened and given way to more interest in testing various principles in light of unique situations. Frequently, workers in the field of learning have noted that many of the major contributions of the different schools of learning are largely reconcilable in the sense that an increasing body of knowledge about learning is available for practical application in school situations. In general, there is increased information on factors in learning, such as (1) what learning is—a changed behavior and concomitants which function effectively in new and recurrent situations; (2) the force which systems of reinforcement have for developing motivation; and (3) the contrast between "learning about," through memorization, on the one hand, and "learning to use" information to solve problems, on the other. Selected references pertaining to contemporary learning theories, including summaries and analyses of the changing views of the various systems, are listed in the bibliography should the reader wish to inquire further.

Illustrative of useful principles to be derived from studies about learning are those described by Miller and Dollard,[1] in which the factors in learning were divided into four steps—drive, cue, response, and reward. Miller,[2] in a report on the effectiveness of motion pictures as instructional devices, asked a series of questions related to these four steps. In adapted form these are as follows:

Drive (motivation). Do they motivate? The learner must *want* something.

Cue (stimulus). Are the cues relevant? The learner must *notice* something.

Response (participation). Do they call for participation? The learner must *do* something.

Reward (reinforcement). Do they provide some form of reward for performance? The learner must *get* something.

(Since a person must want what he gets in order for it to act as a reward, drives (motivation) and rewards (reinforcement) are closely related.)

Miller's proposal is a reasonable and testable model for assessing learning, since the factors in this theory are essential in one way or another to processes of learning. Certain implications of these learning factors will appear in the discussion of reinforcement principles of learning.

Hilgard has listed fourteen generalizations about learning which are of practical significance:[3]

1. In deciding who should learn what, the capacities of the learner are very important. Brighter people can learn things less bright ones cannot learn; in general, older children can learn more readily than younger ones; the decline of ability with age, in the adult years, depends upon what it is that is being learned.

2. A motivated learner acquires what he learns more readily than one who is not motivated. The relevant motives include both general and specific ones, for example, desire to learn, need for achievement (general), desire for a certain reward or to avoid a threatened punishment (specific).

3. Motivation that is too intense (especially pain, fear, anxiety) may be accompanied by distracting emotional states, so that excessive motivation

[1] Neal E. Miller and John Dollard, *Social Learning and Imitation,* published for the Institute of Human Relations by Yale University Press, New Haven, Conn., 1941.

[2] Neal E. Miller and collaborators, "Graphic Communication and the Crises in Education," *Audio-visual Communication Review,* Department of Audio-visual Instruction, National Education Association, Washington, vol. 5, pp. 63 and 95, 1957.

[3] Ernest R. Hilgard, *Theories of Learning,* Appleton-Century-Crofts, Inc., New York, 1956, pp. 486–487.

may be less effective than moderate motivation for learning some kinds of tasks, especially those involving difficult discriminations.

4. Learning under the control of reward is usually preferable to learning under the control of punishment. Correspondingly, learning motivated by success is preferable to learning motivated by failure. Even though the theoretical issue is still unresolved, the practical outcome must take into account the social by-products, which tend to be more favorable under reward than under punishment.

5. Learning under intrinsic motivation is preferable to learning under extrinsic motivation.

6. Tolerance for failure is best taught through providing a backlog of success that compensates for experienced failure.

7. Individuals need practice in setting realistic goals for themselves, goals neither so low as to elicit little effort nor so high as to foreordain to failure. Realistic goal-setting leads to more satisfactory improvement than unrealistic goal-setting.

8. The personal history of the individual, for example, his reaction to authority, may hamper or enhance his ability to learn from a given teacher.

9. Active participation by a learner is preferable to passive reception when learning, for example, from a lecture or a motion picture.

10. Meaningful materials and meaningful tasks are learned more readily than nonsense materials and more readily than tasks not understood by the learner.

11. There is no substitute for repetitive practice in the overlearning of skills (for instance, the performance of a concert pianist), or in the memorization of unrelated facts that have to be automatized.

12. Information about the nature of a good performance, knowledge of one's own mistakes, and knowledge of successful results, aid learning.

13. Transfer to new tasks will be better if, in learning, the learner can discover relationships for himself, and if he has experience during learning of applying the principles within a variety of tasks.

14. Spaced or distributed recalls are advantageous in fixing material that is to be long retained.

Hilgard's principles, like those proposed by others,[4] can help to (1) provide a *framework* against which experiences and the results of investigations can be tested; (2) serve as a *point of reference* so that experiences, observations, and data on learning situations can be assessed; and (3) provide a *systematic basis* from which generalizations can be made and hypotheses developed and tested in new and recurrent settings. Principles of learning are not ready-made, nor do they prescribe precisely what is to be done to resolve practical problems. The following cautions might be noted:

[4] See William H. Burton, "Basic Principles in a Good Teaching-Learning Situation," *Phi Delta Kappan,* vol. 39, pp. 242–248, March, 1958.

The supervisor must be explicit about the kinds of learning which are sought in order to determine learning principles or procedures that are to be most appropriate and effective.

2. Rationalizing a particular educational practice on the basis of unsubstantiated theories of learning is to be avoided. Untested acceptance of "what psychology says" can lead a supervisor up a cul-de-sac from which return is difficult.

3. The "learning" psychologist is not going to do the supervisor's job for him; he may make proposals and provide hypotheses, but the supervisor will have to use rational thought in their application.

4. Regardless of how adequately learning principles have been validated in laboratory situations, it will be necessary to validate them at the point of application. Supervisors and teachers must continuously examine all learning practices under actual conditions of use in the school —autoinstructional devices, listening centers, self-instructional materials, for example.

5. Theoretical principles need to be *adapted* to practical learning situations, not *adopted*. The appropriateness of learning principles is assessed in terms of both purpose and desired outcomes.

6. The supervisor cannot examine learning problems alone. The involvement of teachers is always sought. The teacher, above all, is a learner himself and is in a position to question practices and to test theories in his own classroom laboratory. His experiences and observations can provide testable hypotheses which are subject to verification.

REINFORCEMENT PRINCIPLES OF LEARNING

One approach to learning problems, that of reinforcement theory, will be described with particular reference to some of its applications for supervision. One of the major sources of information has been the work of Skinner.[5] Reinforcement theory is a behavioral point of view in which learning can be defined as changed behavior resulting from or accompanying practice or experience; learning is analyzed in terms of observable events and not in terms of internal factors. According to this definition change in behavior is the important element, although it might be added that the behavioral changes should be in a given direction. Consequently, to be certain that learning has occurred, there must be some measurement or evaluation of the behavior before and after the

[5] B. F. Skinner, *Science and Human Behavior,* The Macmillan Company, New York, 1953.

experience. Teaching can thus be defined as the presentation of stimuli which result in a change of behavior in a predetermined manner.[6]

The supervisor applies these principles in staff learning so that (1) stimuli are presented to change the environment to ensure a change in behavior; (2) behavior changes occur on the part of the learner; and (3) the behavior is predetermined, intended, and explicit. The supervisor who only incidentally and unintentionally influences staff members is not teaching. For example, if a staff member acquires from the supervisor a particular technique or nomenclature that was not planned for, he has been influenced but not taught. Learning acquired accidentally is not the consequence of teaching. For systematic staff teaching, the supervisor, therefore, must have clearly in mind what changes in the behavior of others are to be sought and arrange the environment to effect this behavior The desired changes in behavior have to be specified, that is, not only brought to a conscious level in the supervisor's own mind but communicated to the learners. This requires that objectives be stated in behavioral terms and not as vague generalities, and that the ways of assessing behavioral changes be clearly defined.

One of the greatest problems facing the supervisor is to determine the degree to which he has been successful in his supervisory teaching. As long as objectives are stated in vague terms: "The objective of our in-service program is to have teachers love and understand children" or "Our objective is to develop perspective among the staff in teaching social studies"—the teacher may never be able to find out what he is aiming toward or whether or not he did well. Unmeasurable objectives lead to a dilemma. Since the teacher cannot discover how well he did, he cannot improve. The supervisor who recognizes the importance of measurable goals in the learning model will be more successful in accomplishing objectives.

According to the reinforcement point of view the two kinds of learning are: *respondent conditioning* and *operant conditioning*.

Respondent Conditioning or Learning

Respondent conditioning applies to the conditioning of the respondent behavior described in terms of elicited behavior—behavior that is controlled by a stimulus, such as a knee reflex, a visceral autonomic response. This sort of learning is exemplified by the classical conditioning

[6] Acknowledgment is made to Evan R. Keislar, School of Education, University of California, Los Angeles, for the summary of reinforcement theory presented in this section.

of Pavlov and Watson. The learning of fears, likes, and dislikes is an example of respondent conditioning. It is illustrated by the type of mass advertising in which one stimulus is paired with another with the intent of molding the opinions or emotions of the particular audience. This kind of learning is indeed a powerful one. In it the organism appears to be passive. Something happens *to* the learner. The learner is not trying to solve problems: things just happen to him; he is being shaped or molded. Respondent conditioning is the way in which one might best think of emotional learning—the learning of attitudes or reactions to a subject, a problem, or an issue. It operates on an association basis. If the supervisor is visibly interested in the problems of teaching science (finds science stimulating and exciting), the chances are greater that teachers upon whom he has impact will also acquire these same types of emotional responses toward science. On the other hand, if the supervisor ignores or is uninterested in a particular field, teachers may acquire like attitudes. Awareness of the power of this kind of learning should help avoid gaps or misdirected emphases in staff learning.

Operant Conditioning or Learning

Operant learning is probably more dominant for the purposes of education than respondent learning. In this particular area of learning we are dealing with the striated muscles—the muscles that are under the control of the central nervous system (respondent behavior is under the control of the autonomic nervous system). Operant learning, therefore, includes the whole area of motor skills—language, for one. In operant behavior the key to whether a person learns a certain motor response is what happens *after* he makes that motor response—the *consequences* of it. This means that to teach operant motor skills, we must pay particular attention to what happens after the motor response has been given. This consequence is referred to as a *reinforcement*. It is called a reinforcement because it strengthens, or reinforces, the response that preceded it. It makes that response more likely to occur in the future; it makes it more probable. Therefore, in educational practice we have to keep our mind clearly on the reinforcements. What are they? Do they occur or don't they occur? Are they truly reinforcements? It should be noted that the definition of reinforcement is in terms of *effect upon the response*. If the reinforcement strengthens the response, if it makes the response more probable, it *is* the reinforcement. Reinforcement in one situation may well be depended upon in others.

Reinforcements are most effective if they are immediate or if there is a minimum delay between the response and the occurrence of the reinforcement. Studies with human subjects have shown rather clearly that the closer the reinforcement occurs to the actual response, the faster that response is learned. One of the difficulties that supervisors and teachers meet in working together on problems is the gap or delay between re sponse and reinforcement. It may take the teacher a week to discover whether the materials he prepared or the demonstration he gave was correct or acceptable. The staff team may prepare a revision of a report card only to wait indefinitely for a curriculum council's evaluation. The sooner a teacher knows whether or not he has done some task satisfactorily, the more opportunities he has to improve his performance in staff and classroom operations.

Extinction

Closely allied to the concept of reinforcement is the concept of extinction. If an undesirable response occurs, a poor work habit, let us say, it is obvious that this kind of response should not be reinforced. We want to be certain that there is no positive reinforcement for such behavior. If there is no reinforcement on repetitions of this response, it gradually weakens, illustrating the process of extinction. One way to extinguish an undesirable practice is to make certain that no reinforcement for ineffective habits or unwanted responses occurs. For instance, responses that deter a group from its central effort or that hinder individuals in meeting their commitments should not be rewarded in any way. The supervisor must arrange the environmental conditions so that the reinforcements for resistance which come from fellow teachers and other sources are not permitted to operate. In ordinary trial-and-error behavior, the person who gets immediate feedback on whether he is doing the right thing or the wrong thing automatically has his correct responses strengthened and his incorrect ones weakened. In this way proper patterns of behavior are built up and incorrect ones are dropped out. Reinforcement and extinction therefore go hand in hand in any kind of motor skill or trial-and-error learning.

Successive Approximation

Persons must actually do something—give a response—in order that the response can be reinforced. There are various ways to meet the problem of obtaining desired responses; one is to use the successive approximations technique. The supervisor does not initiate the study of a difficult task by a description of its total complexity or by a detailed or involved analysis of how the problem will finally be resolved, if by so doing staff members become lost and cannot make the appropriate responses. Teachers cannot be expected to visualize all the dimensions of a complicated task when a proposal is initiated. Therefore reinforcements, even though available, never occur since the staff is in no position to earn them. This is not to suggest that teachers are any more incapable of understanding purposes than any other group of professional persons. It is the complexity of "hardware" which can be discouraging to any person if learning situations are not well ordered. The supervisor learns to approach the study of projects, research investigations, or curriculum revisions step by step in a manner which will bring forth successful approximations of the more complex behavior to be demanded later. The probability of correct responses in complex learning situations depends upon the direction given in leading from one task to another. Care to ensure that movement from simple to complex tasks is properly paced prevents wasted time or lowered morale on the part of a busy teacher or staff. This means sensitivity in noting when staff members are ready to move ahead. In short, the supervisor secures optimum results by ensuring that the response will be correct; yet he must change the task as rapidly as possible, always holding high the probability of the correct response.

Use of Prompts

Assurance that a learner will develop desired responses can be provided through the use of "prompts." A prompt is simply a stimulus that helps one produce the desired response. Outlining or calling attention to certain features of a problem and giving specific suggestions as to what should be done, making certain to provide reinforcements for behavior, are such prompts. When a person accomplishes a task successfully, the prompt can be removed in subsequent situations. Prompts can be a valuable means of speeding up learning. Their use is an important way of teaching, but they must be removed as soon as possible so that the person can become self-operative and can accomplish the task without any direct help. As the teacher continues on his own, be it self-study or the preparation of a teaching program, the supervisor makes certain that he continues to get reinforcements for appropriate behavior.

Interverbal Associations

Desired responses can be obtained through interverbal associations, i.e., by getting learners to use their own prompts, to supply their own stimulation. They can do some thinking or problem solving, supply their own verbalizations, and produce their own prompts. They can be given a theory, a way of thinking about problems, a terminology, a set of principles, definitions, or procedures for which they will supply their own words or thoughts, and thus produce for themselves the prompts needed for responses. Again, it is important to supply the reinforcement for such responses so that the learner will know whether or not his responses are correct.

Obtaining Transfer through Simulation

Another factor important to teaching is the problem of transfer. How does the supervisor transfer from a training situation to the real life situation he has ultimately in mind? The simplest way is to make certain that the training tasks which are set up are similar (physically) to the final plan for which they are being prepared. How often have teachers worked on curriculum problems in isolation from the point of application? They talk "about" but do not relate their model to the situation in which it is expected to be applied. Again, the task may be too complex to ensure that the nonobvious but more important details will be seen and understood. It might be noted in passing that one of the strengths in action research studies is that they involve staff members in transfer operations at the point of application.

Although the learning tasks in which teachers engage, such as writing curriculum materials or studying linguistic theories for second language teaching, should simulate as closely as possible the actual problem, they should simplify the environment, permitting one to see relevant factors and avoid getting lost in details. Simulated activities involve application, tryout, and continuous relating of the proposals under way to specific situations; but they have the valuable simplicity that permits the learner to stand aside and examine the critical factors.

The armed services have found simulation techniques effective in training men. For example, one gunnery school reported using a large dome with a motion picture projected in front. The trainees stood behind a 20-millimeter gun and fired bullets of light at the screen. A mechanical device calculated whether the trainees were getting the proper lead and the proper tracking on the planes which were shown attacking in the motion picture. To make the situation as lifelike as possible a sound track provided the sound of the guns. This was a training problem which encouraged transfer. Each student was reinforced by hearing a click each time he was on target. Because he got reinforced for making the right response, training was better than the battle itself for learning. In an actual battle with twenty men all firing at and downing the same plane, all of the gunners would get a reinforcement, even though nineteen of the twenty might have missed the target.

One could thus argue that simulated ways of learning provide better learning opportunities than life itself, because in a carefully designed simulation situation with controls we can be certain that those involved meet critical incidents and receive the right reinforcements for their responses. At least, we can provide realistic but controlled learning so that there can be generalization and transfer of ideas to actual situations. Case studies, anecdotal records, tape recordings, and motion pictures can be used as study materials and principles derived from them applied to practice. Role playing, action research studies, demonstrations, and rational discussions also can be used to practice the responses desired.

Transfer is helped by the way in which supervisors and teachers use language or words. Because of language it is possible to generalize from situation A to situation B, even though they are different physically. Both have been given the same label—the same words to stand for a class of objects or events. We can, therefore, generalize from one situation to another. Learning a terminology for characterizing incidents and labeling them appropriately, using the theoretical language or principles for categorizing, explaining, and predicting these incidents, is required. Transfer is possible when the principles or the terminology can be used by the learner because they relate to events, and the learner is able to recognize instances of the class of objects. There must be conscious practice in this kind of behavior. Learners must be reinforced, in other words, for using these principles in practice. A staff discussion, for example, regarding principles of child study, or a lecture on a particular teaching skill, can result in transfer to an actual class or clinic situation if the right language has been acquired and is used appropriately so that generalizations occur.

Interference

Another consideration in the learning environment is the factor of interference. Interference slows up learning; it is the basis for forgetting. Interference inhibits the correct responses and leads to error. The better a person learns one thing, the more likely it is that his knowledge will interfere with the learning of other things. The geology professor who said that every time he learned the name of a student he forgot the name of a mineral illustrates the point. Interference operates all the time in almost every learning endeavor. One of the ways to reduce interference is to separate potentially confusing materials in time and space. If there are two similar concepts that may lead to different results or cannot be related, it is better to discuss them at different times. If the supervisor, for instance, says: "Let us not mix up this idea with this other idea," there is the danger that the teacher will do just that, particularly if both ideas are presented at the same time. Using one idea or concept at a time to make each stand out is an advertising technique. The presentation of too much material at one time, or the injection of unrelated items, may induce interference. In this instance we recall the story about the teacher of statistics who was discussing a particular formula, but then proceeded to fill the entire blackboard with equation after equation. One confused student asked: "But, Professor X, how do all these equations relate to one another?" And the instructor replied: "Really, I don't know, but aren't they beautiful?"

One way to make ideas clear is to make materials distinctive. An experiment conducted in Russia on teaching children the parts of a flower illustrates this technique. One group studied the parts by looking at a real flower. This sounds reasonable since it is lifelike. The other group learned by means of a diagram. The group using the diagram were reported to have learned to identify more parts of the flower than the group which studied the actual flower. The distinctiveness of the schematic presentation was partly responsible. The parts in the diagram were larger and their differences were clear. It is evident that the use of several modalities—sound, touch, sight, color—if carefully chosen can help learning, because they differ in more than one dimension. Words, associations, and ideas which are logically supported by the background and experiences of the learner also help to reduce interference. Meaningful materials, concepts, or theories which are related to other responses already acquired are better retained and used.

Intensity Factor

The use of respondent effects can be important, that is, an effort to see that staff members get emotionally involved—emotionally committed to a task. The emotional experience that stands out is not easily forgotten. Determination of the kind and nature of appropriate emotional experiences is the supervisor's concern. Viewing and discussing a worthwhile film or observing a competently programmed demonstration of some particular concept is an experience which can have emotional concomitants of persistent value.

Overlearning

Interference can be prevented by means of overlearning, the kind of learning produced not by simple rote repetition but by learning beyond the point of mastery, i.e., reviewing, using and extending the knowledge gained, and providing requisite reinforcements. The supervisor, in reviewing materials with a staff in order to prevent forgetting or interference, makes certain that the proper educational conditions of reinforcement are present. Recognition of the need for distributed practice is important in retention also. If the staff spends a number of study sessions on a single subject and then does not encounter that subject for another school year, little of what was learned is likely to be retained. On the other hand, repeating or reviewing and applying learning on a particular topic periodically over a period of time leads to retention. In short, presenting all the material at one time is not a good way to obtain long-term retention.

Motivation

Mature adults have learned how to learn, and they can learn, therefore, without some of the conditions described herein. They have a history of prior reinforcements, having learned to teach themselves to discriminate among various ideas and events. They have already learned how to learn by being self-operative; they can absorb information by study, listening to lectures, reading, and working in groups. The learning set, however, had to be learned, and teachers can be helped to acquire new learning by making clear expected behavior patterns and rewarding responses which meet these expectations. If a teacher has read a research study of particular interest to him and has applied the findings to his teaching successfully, he has been reinforced. His experience has paid off; therefore he has learned to learn under similar circumstances. When the supervisor makes certain that professional workers get reinforced for what they learn, self-operativeness is extended. It is paying off for the participants by demonstrating that skills learned can be applied to classroom situations or other tasks of importance to the teacher.

The teacher's existing behaviors are largely the functions of prior motivation and reinforcement history reflecting his personal and professional experiences. Has the teacher been motivated to achieve, or has he become apathetic toward learning tasks? There can be numerous reasons for the presence or absence of motivation. One reason for failure is that the so-called reinforcements were not so in reality; past behaviors were not reinforcing. Some teachers, for instance, are not at all affected by public recognition of their special contributions. They just do not care about these kinds of reinforcements. Supervisors need to find out what teachers *do* care about—exactly what does act as a reinforcement. It might be that the teacher does not value a reinforcement like social approval, because this consequence has not occurred in the past when the teacher exhibited what he considered appropriate behavior. He might have done a really superior job of teaching or preparing curriculum materials, but nothing happened. He never learned whether he was right or that anyone cared. There is the story about a secondary school teacher of mathematics who gave a series of skillful demonstrations showing how slower learning pupils could be taught to grasp the meaning of certain mathematical concepts, after which the new supervisor's only comment was: "The blinds in your room were not straight during your demonstrations." The supervisor who provides controls and direction in learning situations can discover those elements which do act as reinforcements.

Another possible cause of apathy is that the materials with which the teacher was confronted may have been too difficult, or the proper environmental stimuli were not provided to bring out the behavior that he was capable of giving, or what he was doing was not important to him. Perhaps the consequences of a particular pattern of behavior came entirely too late. Or, as noted earlier, there was too large a gap between execution and recognition.

Negative Respondent Conditioning

Another hindrance to learning is negative respondent conditioning. Fellow teachers may have a negative attitude toward the topic or subject which interests a teacher, or even a negative attitude toward the whole teaching job. These are emotional responses which the individual may be in the process of developing or accreting for himself from other teachers or supervisors with whom he comes in contact. The desirability of building individual teacher resistance to negative pressure is one reason why the supervisor tries to help teachers learn to be their own teachers, to be self-dependent, self-operative, and to develop clear-cut criteria for their own behavior. This calls for helping the teacher provide his own stimuli as he studies materials, prepares reports, conducts research studies, and selects references pertinent to his purposes. The teacher should be helped to provide his own reinforcements, to pose problems for himself of appropriate difficulty, and to develop reasonable expectations of himself in light of the mission of the school in which he works. It is unfortunate for education when the teacher who starts with high-level aspirations either has not been taught how to reach his goals, or lacks reinforcement for his success because he lacks the skill of learning when he is successful.

PROMOTING LEARNING IS EFFECTIVE SUPERVISION

We have presented some of the principles derived from reinforcement theory for guiding the supervisor in applying learning principles in operational situations. These principles indicate the importance of the following factors:

1. Defining objectives clearly and in measurable terms
2. Checking against objectives to determine correct or incorrect responses
3. Helping learners to supply their own prompts, set measurable expectations for themselves, and obtain appropriate reinforcements
4. Arranging the learning environment and presenting stimuli to elicit appropriate responses
5. Providing for transfer
6. Reducing interference and forgetting by making topics distinctive, using meaningful associations, distributing practice, and relating topics to over-all conceptual frameworks

Illustrations of the ways in which supervisors can put these principles of learning into action in helping teachers with instructional problems follow.

Defining Specific Educational Objectives in Measurable Terms

The supervisor programs the steps toward objectives just as programmed learning provides a specific sequential series of learning steps with proper reinforcement and immediate feedback to the learner indicating his degree of success. Examples of the effectiveness of hinging all effort around central objectives and providing reinforcement are numerous. Studies conducted in the armed services have shown the importance of knowledge of specific purposes and reinforcement in the training of students. In a study using three groups, the students in one group were given only their total test scores; in another group they were provided with more detailed information about their achievement of test objectives; and in a third group they were provided continuous and complete reinforcement. The third group was shown "why they were wrong and why they were right," being given information which helped change behavior. As testing continued achievement for the third group became even more pronounced.

It is the responsibility of the supervisor, therefore, consciously to program the steps toward objectives. This implies that the supervisor will *actively* help the teacher formulate a rational and sharp definition of concepts to be taught. But more than this, he must make explicit what exactly is required to teach these concepts. In this connection, the importance of constancy in reinforcement of pupils' responses cannot be overstressed. Reinforcement is just as important in the teaching of pupils as it is in the teaching of staff members. "If the same response is consistently reinforced it will have greater stability than if sometimes one, sometimes another, response is reinforced under the same stimulus conditions. Variability in the behavior of the reinforcer implies that he is saying:

"I cannot tell you when the use of this term is applicable and when not." [7] For example, if a teacher of elementary school mathematics is not certain of the precise ways in which the dividend-divisor-quotient relationship can be defined and presented, then the teacher cannot be explicit. He cannot tell when the application should be reinforced, approved, and given immediate correction. The teacher in the elementary grades who clearly understands the many functions of zero (that zero can be a place holder, or that zero is not any, or that zero is a beginning point from which one moves in any direction, or that zero is a number and one of the ten primary digits) is in a posture to teach the specific concepts about zero and to reinforce pupils' responses. He can use related materials meaningfully since he is not working with mechanical prescriptions or with half-truths about the concept, such as "Whenever you use a zero remember it means nothing." He is better able to set pupils' pencils to paper.

In brief, basic understandings represent the foundations for reliable generalizations in any teaching-learning situation. A teacher's uncertainty in teaching may be due to his never having learned the particular concepts to be taught and the exact ways in which the development can be programmed. In the areas of highly specific or generic concepts, the supervisor sharply defines what is to be taught, determines the sequence, and helps plan the reinforcement and follow-up practice.

The better defined the class of responses which the teacher must recognize in himself before he can come up with a thumping reinforcement, the more nearly invariant the response becomes in the language, and the less likely he is to omit a reinforcement or to reinforce a wrong response.

The teacher can identify the appropriate conditions for reinforcement whenever he himself makes the response to be reinforced, or else makes a complex of identifying responses (definition) which remains constant from occasion to occasion.[8]

John Dewey once spoke of the need for "dramatic rehearsal" as a prelude to teaching, a rehearsal in which the teacher actually goes through the program planned for children. It is this dramatic rehearsal of concepts, principles, and responses that the supervisor and teacher should mutually engage in so that the teacher has embedded in his nervous system the basic ideas to be taught with appropriate language and proper reinforcement. Supervisors and teachers need to test one another in model teaching tasks, experimenting with different kinds of practice and

[7] George Mandler and William Kessen, *The Language of Psychology,* John Wiley & Sons, Inc., New York, 1959, pp. 62–63.

[8] *Ibid.,* p. 63.

follow-up activities, with evaluation pegged to the purposes of teaching. This approach helps avoid teaching in a mechanical way (e.g., "Always invert the divisor when you multiply") and focuses on the process of grasping the essential concept, sharply defining it, and teaching to elicit only the specific responses called for.

Using Varied Approaches to Implement Objectives

Operationally, there are numerous ways for the supervisor to set up a system of checking on the effectiveness of *his teaching* during the execution of any task with staff members. This is where process enters the picture. The supervisor can utilize the seminar-summary approach in which he brings together the results to date on a project. He may do this himself; he may use a small staff team; or he may use individual reporting procedures. However the seminar is conducted, its purpose is to assess progress toward goals. There is constant feedback from the participants by means of such questions as these: "To what extent are we achieving the objective as defined?" "Is this what we originally decided to try to accomplish?" "What are the next steps in light of what we have accomplished?" "What further tasks must we plan?" The supervisor carefully thinks out in advance the possible contingent steps to be taken so that his thought and language can give some direction to the actions of the group members. He avoids standardizing on the ignorance of the group in this process. In-service training, focused on some major task of the school, can be genuinely productive. Although large planning groups can suggest topics for research or raise questions, usually small teams of two or three, or even individuals, can best execute the project. Small research teams, of course, are accountable to the larger group and their findings open to examination. The results of team research can be fed back to the larger group for questions, further assignments, and the involvement of others in the tryout of certain proposals. It should be kept in mind that "only those directly involved need execute"; others can be critical evaluators and consumers. The law of parsimony applies here also. The supervisor who has as many projects as there are staff members would seem to have mounted the horse and galloped off in all directions. Staff seminars, demonstrations, role playing, reports, and other process techniques should be concentrated on only a few critical problems in any one school year. The leadership of the supervisor bulks large in determining through consultative effort only those important tasks which must be done instead of initiating as many studies as there are ideas. For example, supervisor X attends a meeting and hears what school system Y has done, returns to the provinces, and initiates the same project without regard to the specific goals of his particular school system. Or the board of education hears that the neighboring school system has thrown out its developmental reading program and has hired only remedial reading teachers, and then the heat is on. The supervisor who stands by principles may have a hard fight on his hands. To keep from being overwhelmed by such pressures, he must gather every possible bit of evidence to support his position.

Supervision by objectives and evaluation of "how well the specific ends are being achieved" lead to greater precision and productivity in educational practices. This view poses a special role for supervisors. No longer can they flit from one "off-the-cuff" workshop to another and from meeting to meeting, wait in the office "to be called to help," or be a "stimulator." They must get dirty with the hard core of specifics. They must know what is to be learned, provide or have access to technical help, assist others to learn, and know how to measure the results of effort.

Arranging the Environment to Produce Worthwhile Responses

Arranging the environment does not mean that the supervisor provides flower arrangements, coffee and doughnuts, and travel posters for the meeting room. (This is not to derogate the importance of such processes.) Arranging the "intellectual" environment means providing content on which staff members can nourish themselves as they work through problems. For example, a curriculum council of a school system planned a two-year project to revise the program of teaching geography in the junior high schools. A supervisor, with the help of a few teachers, was responsible for initiating and directing the study. The problem was to bring together and adapt present-day thinking about the scope of the field of geography covering those factors pertaining to the human habitat. In planning for the initial staff meeting the supervisor made extensive preparation, including specific data, content, ideas, and materials with which to start work. Utilizing the services of a specialist, the supervisor prepared a working paper for consideration by the study group. A list of current principles for the study of geography was prepared, not as doctrinaire statements, but as ideas for consideration, implementation, and validation. Included in the working paper were possible objectives, stated in highly specific terms and covering such areas as the orderly treatment of the physical elements of the human habitat, the ways in which man utilizes his physical environment, the distribution of the physical and cultural elements composing the human habitat, the interpretation of variety in the human habitat, and suggested standards against which changes can be measured. The working paper concluded with some hypotheses of a reasonable kind and suggested content for planning a curriculum. Every effort was expended to bring together the best thinking in the field and to outline those elements which could be applied in the educational system concerned.

This approach is quite different from one which involves collecting a number of courses of study from other school systems and compiling a geography curriculum without regard to any central theoretical framework. This supervisor began the study by assessing the basic understandings which underlie the field of geography, outlining the essential objectives, and proposing some ways in which the sequence might be developed. The supervisor took major responsibility for providing content, even though it may have been partly accomplished with the help of some one member of the study group. The point is that the providing of content was a key piece of motivation. Staff members became aware that there was real substance and an exciting learning task to which they could commit themselves, such as gathering additional information, making subsidiary studies, and programming content. The objective presentation of the specialist and the supervisor, uncritical of the existing program, and both eager to know the best thought in the field, assured some degree of confidence that the study could get under way at a higher level than "We tried that ten years ago and it did not work," or "We ought to have a geography program like school X does," or "Why don't we adopt the X school's geography syllabus?" The supervisor, through the strength of knowledge, was focusing on the basic understandings necessary to begin a curriculum revision, to challenge the study group to test out ideas, and to realize how much they and other teachers could expand their knowledge in the field.

The follow-up of such study might include: (1) additions and expansions in the original working paper and the tryout of various proposals in the classroom; (2) continuous feedback from participating teachers and dissemination of results periodically to others on the staff; (3) a calendar of operations prepared, with research studies described, and target dates set for completing certain tasks; and (4) evaluation instruments, needed tests, and other measuring instruments prepared early in the sequence of operations in order that all teachers participating in the tryout of content would know beforehand exactly what was to be measured, how, and in what degree. Thus, evaluation tools would be used to assess progress toward the stated goals and not to test after the fact. This use of measuring instruments makes them internal to the task and not afterthoughts.

Providing for Appropriate Pacing of Work

Differentiating the tasks carved out of a project or study so that each staff member accepts a task at a level he can successfully accomplish helps achievement of purposes. The supervisor seeks consensus on reasonable goals and welcomes self-selection on the part of the staff for assignments and setting of target dates for the completion of responsibilities. In consultation with study groups he sets up a calendar of events and holds firmly to the contract. The emergency meeting, or a statement, such as "We will just have to put in extra time on this," is avoided. A staff well-committed to the mission of a school system will usually determine the time and place for extra effort voluntarily. The supervisor may spend much time in small-group or individual consultation in order to pace work at a reasonable level. After a group has selected a problem and planned a work program, the individual members begin to move at varying rates. The supervisor assumes a consultative role to assist teachers with their particular responsibilities, having assessed the differential abilities among staff members and determined "who does what best and who likes to do what best."

Reducing Interference and Forgetting

The supervisor tries to make the various aspects of proposals so distinctive that everyone involved can see relationships. Tasks are defined and separated from other tasks by use of meaningful associations. The supervisor makes certain that he himself understands what he is about and that the proposed study is geared to the over-all program of the school. He assures transfer by using actual situations to try out ideas or proposals looking toward application. This may involve using case studies and classroom demonstrations and relating them to principles of teaching and theories of learning.

Helping Others to Become Their Own Best Teachers

In helping teachers learn how to learn, the supervisor assists staff members to supply their own frame of reference, set reasonable expectations for the accomplishment of tasks, and receive rapid reinforcement. The supervisor emphasizes the need for verifying principles or setting up a rationale for self-study so that the efforts of individuals can be placed in an over-all framework. Techniques can be emphasized after staff members have conceptualized the approaches they are to use. After a procedure is selected in accordance with reasonable levels of attainment, the supervisor takes the responsibility to see that the work is logically distributed over a period of time and that self-teaching and retention occur. There is a sharp difference between knowledge and understanding.[9] The supervisor who recognizes this difference in working with teachers

[9] Nathaniel Cantor, *The Learning Process for Managers,* Harper & Brothers, New York, 1958, p. 143.

realizes that he does not transfer facts to the learner, but helps the learner to translate the data, to make use of the facts, and to find meaning for himself. It requires insight on the supervisor's part to set the stage, provide content, and pose hypotheses so that the learning which occurs is a remaking of experience which guarantees a genuine difference in the behavior of the teacher. The teacher is led to define problems, to integrate past experience, to obtain new data, and to test his ideas in practice.

Recognizing the Association between Effective Learning and Commitment

The supervisor recognizes that effective learning is associated with commitment to specific and essential tasks and problem-solving activities. Learning may be initiated when one does not know the answers to a problem. The learner who has a problem usually will seek an answer. Learning is often accompanied by personal disturbance. Problems, however, do not always arise spontaneously, and the supervisor's responsibility is to help set problems in terms of mission and purposes. Problems are more likely to become visible in a climate where hypotheses are constantly being proposed. This atmosphere is a two-way street and the feedback which is provided encourages staff members to engage in problem-solving activities. However, it should be observed that the profitable types of feedback revolve around the testing of ideas and task orientation and not the ego-orientation of the supervisor. Blame fixing and recrimination as means of improving staff participation are not profitable techniques. The supervisor who resorts to negative measures when teachers do not resolve problems may be showing them "how wrong they were" but doing nothing to help them to see "what is the right thing to do." The supervisor who is a leader in bringing learning out of confusion asks such questions as "What is the problem we are trying to solve?" "How effective are we in solving the problem?" "What steps do we need to take next?"

Recognizing Resistance to Change

The supervisor recognizes that many persons resist new learnings which conflict with established ways of behavior.[10] There are few human beings who welcome confusion or unsolved problems. New ways of behavior are often difficult, especially when individuals are faced with the discomforts of myth destroying or changes in the *status quo*. It is often easier and certainly more comfortable to justify things as they

---

[10] *Ibid.,* p. 144.

are, to deny the need for change, to use ready-made prescriptions, or to fall back on personal anecdotes or testimonials. For example, "The X school system does not do it this way." "What is wrong with what we have been doing in reading?" "Mr. Supervisor, I tried that in my classes and it was not successful." "I took a college class last summer and Professor X was against any tinkering." A supervisor, therefore, must be aware of the mechanisms developed to defend oneself or an organization and maintain established ways of behavior. Among these mechanisms are rationalization, lying, projecting, and compulsive processes, such as talking about and around a topic.[11] Professional persons with a command of language can often talk themselves and others into or out of uncomfortable situations.[12] The supervisor who is aware of the effect these mechanisms have on the communication process may not always be able to meet the resistance to change, but can recognize the symptoms of poor communication, of the need to work around the biases of individuals. He learns to focus effort on tasks and to avoid blame or the fixing of guilt. Unquantified emotional language, such as "Our reading program is miserable and you have got to change it or we are in trouble with the board," is an example.

Most individuals experience feelings of guilt, shame, or lack of self-esteem when they have not met responsibility, or have avoided a decision, or have not faced up to solving critical problems. The supervisor who brings problems into the open, who is prepared to face facts and take the consequences rather than disguise, conceal, or distort wrong decisions, is more likely to obtain positive learning behavior among staff members. Just as the teacher-model affects the behavior of children, the supervisor who is consistent, objective, task-oriented, and technically competent is more likely to find the same behaviors reflected by others. This implies that the supervisor will provide the kinds of ideas for learning, for designing studies, for testing results, that will obviate the avoidance mechanisms, the feelings of insecurity that result from highly personalized approaches to problems.

Accepting Differences among Learners

Recognition of differences among learners is not new to classroom teaching. However, supervisors may stress this principle in working with children, but negate its application in their own work with adults. The supervisor is charged with setting a consistent climate where staff members can afford and dare to be individuals and can express opinions and

[11] *Ibid.*, p. 145.
[12] *Ibid.*

ideas, even if these views conflict with those of the supervisor or others. Recognition of differences among learners encourages creative thinking. There should be ". . . no fear of disapproval, no threat to self-esteem, no ugly competitiveness, no badgering sarcasm, no wisecracking but a deeply felt sense of mutual respect and common seeking for growth and development." [13] When the supervisor recognizes the differential abilities existing both in himself and in others—the difficulties and confusion experienced in learning situations, the resistance to change, the need to defend positions, and the desire to be right—he is better able to establish himself as a mature coworker and leader.

[13] *Ibid.*, p. 150.

TECHNICAL SKILLS IN SUPERVISION

THE human skills in supervision, discussed in previous chapters, and technical skills, the subject of this section, are interrelated in practice; distinctions between them should be considered arbitrary and only for purposes of discussion. Human or social skills are determined by knowledge of the make-up of individuals—their personalities, motives, and commitments to tasks—and the ability to act upon knowledge in appropriate ways in order to change behavior. In his role as a leader, the supervisor is able to implement ideas or to direct others successfully when others consider him capable of this role and he perceives himself in the same way. Technical skills make behavioral changes possible because these skills are based on specialized knowledge and scholarship. They supply the firm foundation on which to focus and determine the direction and implementation of various operations in complex situations. Supervisory skills, based on a body of knowledge, theories, or propositions, in addition to human understandings, are needed to handle the practical and technical problems of education in the laboratory of the modern school. It should be added that a necessary function of supervision is the continual study and development of new technical skills in order to discover better ways of defining purposes, predicting the outcome of proposals, managing situations, and assessing the consequences of actions.

No inclusive coverage of this topic has been attempted. The general requirements for thought and action in selected situations to be discussed include: (1) a proposal for teacher assessment, based on principles related to the teacher's tasks; (2) an analysis of some of the factors pertaining to educational research, with emphasis on the kinds of technical skills and the degrees of competency required of supervisors and teachers; and (3) a rationale for curriculum development, based on principles for determining objectives, guiding and assessing learning, and setting an organizational structure for effective curriculum.

10

ASSESSMENT OF TEACHER PERFORMANCE

EXTENSIVE research has been conducted on problems of judg-ing teacher performance.[1] Research investigators have sin-gled out various factors for analysis and described the complexity of the problems which make teacher assessment difficult, but definitive answers to the problems have not been formulated. The materials in this chapter provide (1) a brief overview of some of the problems which researchers have encountered in assessing teacher effectiveness; and (2) a proposal which might serve as a basis for helping supervisors develop a reasonable and testable assessment procedure.

SOME FINDINGS ON TEACHER EFFECTIVENESS [2]

Methods of judging teacher effectiveness are subject to several kinds of difficulties. First, the various methods which have been utilized yield results which do not correlate highly with each other; hence they do not measure the same aspects. Second, the methods which appear most valid are often the most difficult to administer. Third, and most important, the determination of teacher effectiveness depends to a large extent on the

[1] Harold E. Mitzel, "Teacher Effectiveness," *Encyclopedia of Educational Research,* 3d ed., The Macmillan Company, New York, 1960, pp. 1481–1485.

[2] From an unpublished paper by John C. Gowan, San Fernando Valley State College, Northridge, Calif.

criteria used. In essence, if different methods and different criteria are used in measuring the factors which contribute to teaching success, the results will inevitably differ. In various research studies attempts have been made to isolate factors in order to determine criteria which might provide the most objective measures of success in teaching. One such division would analyze research findings in terms of the criterion variable —that is, whether teachers are judged effective—on the basis of (1) general ability; (2) rating scales or devices; (3) emotional adjustment; (4) attitude toward the teaching profession; and (5) pupil gain or achievement.[3]

General Ability

This criterion is the oldest in point of research emphasis, but research based upon it alone has shown a marked decrease as a result of findings. Investigators have agreed that there is some relationship between intelligence and teaching ability, but that the relationship is far from perfect. Studies have reported correlations between these two measures ranging from zero to .45. In general, teaching appears to require a threshold level of intelligence, but once general ability is judged to be clearly above average, other factors appear to influence teaching efficiency. Since all measures of performance are more or less affected by intelligence, there is a tendency to overweight this factor as a source of variance in measuring teaching effectiveness.

Teacher-rating Factors

Historically, the use of rating indices followed measures of general mental ability as a method of estimating teacher competence. Such rating indices have been global in nature, covering such factors as personality, personal appearance, a wholesome philosophy of life, and lists of teaching skills, and have not differentiated among these general variables. That is, over-all ratings have been considered valid measures of teacher performance without regard to specifically defined criteria. A number of studies of rating indices have indicated that high ratings, especially those assessed by authority figures, do not necessarily mean superior teaching performance. Instead, high ratings appear to be an artifact determined, in many instances, by the personal and role relationship between rater and ratee. The halo effect in rating appears constantly and seems related to the teacher's position in a particular group. Principals' ratings, reported as scores on rating indices, have been shown to correlate signifi-

---

[3] A. G. Hellsfritsch, "A Factor Analysis of Teaching Abilities," *Journal of Experimental Education,* vol. 14, pp. 166–199, December, 1945.

cantly only with the socioeconomic status of teachers.[4] It might be said that authority figures such as principals or supervisors tend to rate in inverse order of social distance; that is, to confuse personal closeness or the teacher's position in the status hierarchy with teaching skill. Just as some people photograph well, others appear to rate well. The popular expression "he rates" perhaps denotes a factor measured by many rating devices.

In general, rating devices have received decreasing attention in research studies because of their obvious shortcomings. Ratings by peer figures and by pupils under proper circumstances appear to be somewhat better indicators of teacher effectiveness. And ratings by trained observers, when criteria have been defined, seem to secure even more meaningful results, since these persons are less likely to compile ratings colored by extraneous influences.[5] However, the pitfall in most research that uses the rating criterion is in overstating the importance of rankings, in not using statistical controls for reliability and validity, and in not supplementing the ratings by other measures of performance. Evidence does not favor the use of rating indices as inclusive measures of teaching effectiveness.

General Emotional Adjustment

The factor of emotional adjustment has been given prominence in studies of teacher effectiveness, and research has contributed to a better understanding of the importance of this factor.[6] The difficulty has been to develop adequate procedures for measurement. Competent teachers, in general, seem to possess more stable and mature traits of personality than the less able, and there are clusters of traits which distinguish competent teachers from others. The premise that emotional aspects of personality are important in teaching is hardly in dispute, for it would seem reasonable that emotionally disturbed teachers

[4] J. C. Gowan, "Prediction of Teaching Success, Rating of Authority Figures," *California Journal of Educational Research,* vol. 6, pp. 147–152, September, 1955.

[5] David G. Ryans, *Characteristics of Teachers: Their Description, Comparison and Appraisal,* American Council on Education, Washington, 1960, pp. 92–95 and 115–135.

[6] H. C. Gough and W. H. Pemberton, "Personality Characteristics Related to Success in Practice Teaching," *Journal of Applied Psychology,* vol. 36, pp. 307–310, October, 1952.

See also William H. Lucio and M. A. Wenger, *Prediction of Teacher Performance and Emotional Stability: A Psychophysiological Pilot Study of Female Student Teachers,* Final Report, U.S. Office of Education, Contract SAE 8311, University of California, Los Angeles, Calif., September, 1961, 91 pp.

would be less effective than emotionally sound ones. But once this point has been conceded and the psychotic or psychoneurotic teacher has been screened out, it becomes much more difficult to demonstrate that there is any particular pattern of mental health which is especially effective in teaching. It may be that there is a mental health threshold in teaching effectiveness, just as there may be a threshold in mental ability. Beyond this, effectiveness would depend on other factors. The precise relationship between good personal-relations behavior and teaching effectiveness has yet to be determined. It is known, however, that the two factors are associated and that integrative values in individuals are components of successful teaching. It would help to know the degree and the kind.

It has been pointed out, also, that it is not the amount of psychopathology which limits function. The crucial factor is the ability or disability of the personality to operate effectively in spite of any personal defects. It appears that methods of selection and retention of teachers based upon sound measures of personality assessment have some validity, and that in the future we may expect even better results from further research in this area. Meanwhile, there are ample theoretical and empirical reasons for continuing to screen out those who demonstrate the obvious tendencies toward emotional and psychological disturbance or imbalance likely to affect teaching effectiveness.

The Laudatory Attitude toward Teaching

This criterion of teacher behavior represents a positive attitude on the part of the teacher toward the teaching profession and, essentially, reveals his lack of tendencies to project blame.[7] Since this attitude originates within the teacher, it is expressed toward those whom he encounters. It is in this sense that the phrase "attitudes toward teaching" needs to be understood. Individuals who reflect this factor of teacher behavior possess the disposition or the temperament to look on the bright side, to see good in and seek out the best in others, and to consider the profession of teaching in light of its finest ideals and traditions. There is some evidence that teachers who possess this factor of personality help pupils more easily to realize their goals, because these teachers believe in their pupils, have more favorable attitudes toward them, and are more supportive in their behavior.[8] In general, the attitudes a teacher brings to the classroom may be an important part of the classroom climate. That many of the positive attitudes expressed by the superior teacher

[7] Hellsfritsch, *op. cit.*

[8] Edwin Wandt, "The Measurement and Analysis of Teachers' Attitudes," *California Journal of Educational Research,* vol. 3, pp. 10–13, January, 1952.

toward other persons and toward the teaching profession stem from superior environmental backgrounds is noted by Gowan: "A superior teacher is the social legacy of a good home." [9] There is evidence that education and psychology courses can "get below the surface" enough to influence attitudes of students toward a favorable outlook, at least during the period of pre-service training. Studies in the field of sensitivity training have revealed that directed changes in personal behavior are possible, and that these changes in attitudes may be related to the classroom behaviors of teachers and reflected in their pupils. The continued study of teaching attitudes during in-service teaching should be a fruitful avenue for research.

Pupil Gain or Achievement

This criterion is usually conceded to be one of the more quantified and effective measures of teacher performance. The results of pupils' learning, obtained under carefully planned and controlled conditions, are seemingly related closely to teaching performance. Research in automated teaching has contributed to the increased emphasis upon this factor, because the criterion for effective autoinstructional programs, i.e., programmed learning with its systematically arranged sequences, is the extent to which the learner achieves the explicit outcomes specified for the program. Increasing numbers of studies which have used measures of pupil gain have yielded promising results.[10]

Various problems seem to be connected with measures of pupil gain, none of which is insurmountable. In general, measures of pupil gain require that only one teacher direct the specific learning contacts or that the effects of several teachers be controlled in some manner. Although emphasis has generally been given to the measurement of subject-matter achievement before and after teaching in studies of pupil gain, it is reasonable to assume that application can be made to other aspects of learning as well. Areas sometimes thought to be intangible, such as pupils' self-understanding, social attitudes, and similar behaviors, are equally open to assessment if they are defined in discrete or measurable terms and

[9] J. C. Gowan, "A Summary of the Intensive Study of Twenty Highly Selected Women Elementary Teachers," *Journal of Experimental Education,* vol. 26, pp. 115–124, December, 1957.

[10] W. B. Brokover, "The Relation of Social Factors to Teaching Ability," *Journal of Experimental Education,* vol. 13, pp. 191–205, June, 1945.

Morris L. Cogan, "Theory and Design of a Study of Teacher-Pupil Interaction," *Harvard Educational Review,* vol. 26, pp. 315–342, Summer, 1956.

W. B. Webb and N. D. Bowers, "The Utilization of Student Learning as a Criterion of Instructor Effectiveness," *Journal of Educational Research,* vol. 51, pp. 17–23, September, 1957.

formulated as desired outcomes from instruction. Research results have indicated that pupil-gain criteria can be used to determine the outcomes of particular teaching acts rather precisely, since these criteria are focused on the essence of teaching—the achievement of pupils.

A PROPOSAL FOR ASSESSING TEACHER PERFORMANCE

In the past, the assessment of teacher performance has been dealt with in amorphous and diverse ways. Someone, in some fashion, remote or proximate to teaching, has been responsible for the evaluation of teacher performance. As a result, evaluations have been based upon every conceivable criterion, technique, and individual style imaginable. Because many assessment procedures have had little relation to teachers' essential tasks, the reasons for recurring criticisms by teachers and others are understandable. Research on problems of judging teacher performance has served to indicate the questionable value of some methods of assessment.

The assessment of teacher performance is an essential responsibility of the supervisor, not that of others less skilled or remote from the teaching process and organizational goals. To place this function in the hands of others weakens the supervisor's power to effect his major responsibilities toward improvement of teaching and curricula. Assessment procedures apply to all teachers regardless of length of service. No teacher is expected or allowed to consider the classroom his inner sanctum where he alone determines how and what to teach and assesses his own performance. New teachers, particularly, need to know that their expertness will be evaluated according to how effectively they perform in the classroom, and that they are not to be judged by how well they impress others with their social graces. Early concentration on teaching competence serves to focus the new teacher's attention on what he is hired to do, and the reinforcement of good performance sets his behavior in professional directions early. The supervisor wants the new teacher to be secure and happy, to be sure, but this is best done by helping him to be successful in his teaching.

Phases of the Assessment Procedure

The supervisor, in working out procedures for the assessment of teacher performance, starts with the goal of committing teachers to defined and measurable tasks and establishing the conditions by which the teacher can succeed. Accordingly, the supervisor places teachers in a situation where (1) teaching objectives are defined and there is every reasonable probability of achieving them; (2) every effort and resource is applied to help teachers succeed in accomplishing the defined objectives; and (3) the quality of performance is judged in terms of how well the defined and agreed-upon objectives are achieved. These three phases of the assessment procedure are presented in Figure 10-1.

Operationally, supervisor and teacher jointly define the objectives of instruction, specify the pertinent and necessary procedures required to accomplish these purposes, and determine in advance the assessment measures to be applied. *They mutually predict the consequences of their*

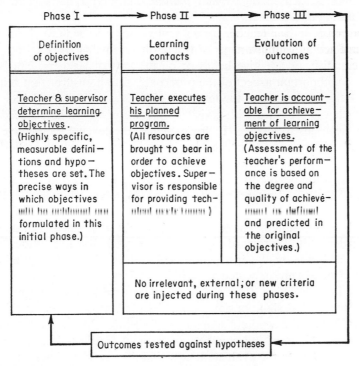

Figure 10-1. *A model for assessing teacher performance.*

hypotheses and work jointly to test their predictions. If the objectives are not achieved by the pupils, or only approximated, the reasons for lack of achievement are determined, the objectives and hypotheses are restated, and a new attack is made. This procedure not only avoids the use of irrelevant criteria for judging teacher performance but helps break the bonds of "alikeness." It reduces emphasis on uniform and sometimes mediocre standards of achievement. The teacher is directly responsible for the design and execution of the learning contacts to be used with pupils. His teaching is targeted at what needs to be done for a specific group of pupils, based on a long-term, carefully defined program designed to achieve major objectives and uninfluenced by transient or irrelevant demands. Subsequently, he is not evaluated on the basis of a brief observation, a demonstration lesson for a group of visitors, a special lesson requested by the principal to see "how well he teaches," or his behavior in staff meetings and social situations. When appropriate teacher behavior is defined as that which leads to the attainment of objectives, then many varieties of criteria can be employed. The assessment procedure is focused on *explicit planning, specific requirements to be met,* and *predicted outcomes.*

This proposal for teacher assessment presents a framework in which the expected accomplishments of the teacher, whether directed at cognitive, conative, or affective behavior on the part of learners, can be defined. An important aspect of the proposal is that it ensures that required aid for the attainment of the teacher's objectives will be available. Also, the teacher is provided with a visible measure of where he succeeded or where he needs to change. If, for example, the teacher's objective is to teach the four concepts concerning decimal integers which underlie all work with decimal fractions, then the assessment of his performance in this area is the degree to which he is effective in achieving the development of these understandings as defined. However, it must be clearly understood that a narrow view of this particular mathematical function is not being suggested. The teacher may well be concerned with developing certain attitudes toward mathematics as well. But if attitudes are to be included among the instructional objectives, they are explicitly defined. If pupils are expected to acquire understandings of mathematics for use in daily living, these goals are recognized and made operational in the teaching design. In any event, the evaluation of the teacher will be based upon the accomplishment of all defined objectives. A teacher's performance in teaching concepts of decimal fractions is not contaminated by adding to the evaluation equation the number of parent-teacher meetings he attended, the number of school committees on which he served, or the quality of his peer or pupil relations. The teacher's engagement with these latter tasks may be open to assessment, but only if they were defined as objectives to be achieved.

Values of practice are of a different order from particular instructional objectives requisite to teaching specific concepts or developing certain attitudes. In short, the teacher must not find himself in the position of having contracted to meet an objective only to discover that his actual assessment is based on added, different, or irrelevant criteria. In the procedure of evaluating by attainment of objectives, teachers can be effective allies in the assessment of performance, since they are and should be most intimately involved. Teachers do understand and welcome the use of rational assessment procedures when there is genuine desire on the part of all concerned to establish legitimate and systematic procedures for evaluation.

In summary, procedures for the assessment of teacher performance should be based on the following considerations:

1. Early agreement is reached between the supervisor and teacher on what is to be judged and on the relevant criteria, and performance is assessed in terms of the attainment of objectives which are realistic and actually attainable. The teacher is given every help to reach the goal. Consistent failure to achieve results is faced by supervisor and teacher, and in the case of new or probationary teachers affects recommendations for continuance on the job.

2. The assessment procedures are clearly defined, known, and adhered to by all. Communication of the "how" and "why" of teacher assessment lessens the threatening aspects of teacher evaluation, because only that which the teacher contracts to do is evaluated. No rating devices, inventories of attitudes, administrators' written characterizations, evaluation interviews, or other devices are injected into the evaluation process, if they were not originally included as a part of the assessment procedure.

3. The assessment of teaching performance is based on proximity; that is, those who are close to the setting of instructional objectives and their attainment should have this responsibility. Administrators who are remote from supervisory functions should delegate the responsibility to others.

4. The authority of expertness is agreed upon as a major consideration. Expertness calls for the ability to predict the consequences of particular acts upon the learning of pupils. It is incumbent upon those who possess the most expert knowledge of teaching to use this knowledge to set instructional outcomes, to select and arrange learning contacts, and to evaluate results. This responsibility is shared by teacher and supervisor. In the process both should grow in their professional competencies.

Inadequate Teaching Performance

Over the years various procedures have been used to meet the problem of inadequate teaching performance. These procedures have often been rule-of-thumb techniques to handle unpleasant problems. They have developed because those concerned sought an easy way out or because thought was not given to examining more precise and rational ways to meet the problem. Among such procedures have been those which (1) place the inadequate teacher where he will do the least harm; (2) transfer him to another school for someone else to supervise; (3)

move him up to an administrative position; (4) send him to a "salt mine" school in the hopes that he will resign; (5) traumatize, shock, or embarrass him in the hopes that he will perform better; or (6) wait for his retirement. None of these approaches fit in with the accountability of the supervisor and teacher to pupils and purposes of the school. They degrade a profession which should pride itself on high standards of human performance, service to others, and the view that human talent can be cultivated. How many of us would like to be passengers in commercial airlines if we felt that pilot selection was based on such questionable personnel procedures? If we accept the proposal which focuses on the task to be done and its evaluation, we can apply more objective and reasonable procedures to meet the problems of inadequate performance.

Supervisors and teachers must face the facts of inadequate performance and accept the consequences of their review. Prospective teachers should experience this kind of objective assessment during their collegiate training and expect it to continue after employment. The twofold nature of assessment is kept clearly in mind: (1) essentially, to help in the improvement of skills; but also (2) to evaluate the accomplishment of the requisite, agreed-upon purposes of the school. The careful review of accomplishment is the responsibility of the supervisor. Teachers who, during a reasonable period of time, in varying situations, and after careful review, cannot set valid instructional objectives and attain their set purposes should not continue teaching. To permit incompetent teachers to remain in schools seeking excellence is to nourish a virus in the midst of health. If what schools do with children has validity, what teachers do must be assessed in terms of what schools intend to accomplish.

The supervisor must give special attention to the improvement of the permanent or tenured teacher whose performance is inadequate or who has "normalized" his teaching. The supervisor's statesmanship is sometimes put to the most rigorous test in effecting desired changes. His success in working with such teachers may depend upon the model he presents—on the demonstration and exemplification of his expertness. Factors such as his skill in human relations and his ability to determine and assess objectives will be important in his actions to change behavior. Essentially, his purpose is to bring about changes in agreed-upon directions and not to punish or shock the teacher into submission. He must face the teacher with accountability to pupils, insist on performance in accordance with objectives, and, in this process, accept negative reactions without retaliation. Every possible resource should be employed to help the teacher make changes in the desired directions. In those rare instances where incontestable evidence has been accumulated to prove that a teacher is adversely affecting the learning of pupils, then this teacher must be removed from the classroom.

In positive terms, attempts to improve the competence of permanent teachers should almost never lead to a graveyard. It is not asking too much to expect the supervisor to find a way to improve competence through effective help—the kind of supervision which helps teachers to obtain new visions of teaching, to define better instructional objectives, to select appropriate learning contacts, and to determine the kind and quality of outcomes. Many teachers whose performance has lagged are simply "dying on the vine," and their inadequate teaching has resulted from years of technical neglect and from lack of opportunity or encouragement for utilizing current and valid information to help improve their teaching. The permanent teacher must be impacted with the kind of help that emphasizes knowledge of the requirements of his pupils, the ways to go about obtaining pupil achievement, and the ways to examine results of teaching.

The kinds of in-service help contained in general institutes, in-service classes, or even workshops which do not relate to the teacher's inadequacies are of little help to him. Human talent is wasted when a teacher mechanically participates in activities because he is required to do so even though the activities are removed from his particular needs. Only when such activities are carefully designed for the specific requirements of individual teachers is their existence justified. The supervisor, by working directly with individual teachers and directing efforts at particular problems, has the opportunity to achieve more substantial results. Careful organization of his time schedule and utilization of the expertness of others should make individual attention possible. The supervisor gets results by ignoring the idiosyncrasies of recalcitrant teachers and by "pouring into the vacuum" testable suggestions and content information. He supports the teacher in his efforts to improve his performance with more than words of inspiration or encouragement. In some cases, the more specific, systematic, and even directive the supervisor's proposals for change, the greater the opportunity to pinpoint problem areas.

That changes *can* be effected in the permanent teacher who has slipped backward or who has never been effective cannot be overemphasized. Changes may be slow in some instances or they may occur only in limited areas of performance. The competent supervisor, especially one who may be new on the job himself, takes the long view of the change process. He reinforces or rewards each change but persists in seeing that over-all performance continues to improve both in kind and in degree. As with a sick patient where the prognosis indicates an eventual cure, the supervisor patiently nurses an ailing teacher back to health. If both teacher and supervisor are convinced that each improvement in performance is one more step toward professional reinstatement, their mutual actions ought to be productive.

In implementing assessment operations both supervisors and teachers may ask themselves:

1. Do I know what is to be taught? Have I selected valid instructional objectives?

2. How can I best teach to achieve the instructional objectives? Have I determined the relationship between what is to be taught and the learning contacts which will lead to the learner's attainment of objectives?

3. Have I a plan for ordering the presentation of these contacts?

4. Have I established criterion measures which will indicate successful attainment of the objectives?

Do I possess the requisite skills to accomplish the above tasks? Do I clearly understand the basic concepts and methodology underlying what is to be taught? If my knowledge is limited with respect to a particular problem, what investigations must I undertake? What self-study by the teacher is necessary? What help is needed from the supervisor? What expert informants can I use to test out proposals before embarking upon teaching?

In implementing assessment operations, the supervisor may ask himself:

1. Have I helped the teacher to view supervision as a technical resource designed to help him achieve the objectives of the school?

2. Is there conscientious attention on the part of the teacher to support the objectives of the school?

3. Have the motives which caused the teacher to enter teaching and the motives which currently sustain him emerged in our person-to-person relations? If these motives were assessed negatively (e.g., a temporary career interest), has the teaching experience developed an awareness of professional responsibility on the part of the teacher?

4. Have I controlled my bias against those aspects of the teacher's personality which are at variance with my expectations but which do not relate to, or stand in the way of, competent teaching performance?

5. Has the teacher met the agreed-upon criteria for achievement in spite of what might seem to others undesirable personality traits or the application of unique or "different" classroom teaching procedures? In other words, do criterion measures show that the teacher's methods of instruction have resulted in positive educative experiences for pupils?

11

METHODS OF RESEARCH

THE DIMENSIONS OF EFFECTIVE RESEARCH

An essential characteristic of any profession is the possession of expertness by its members. Just as expertness in teaching calls for the ability to predict the consequences of particular acts upon the learning of pupils, so in supervision expertness is a reflection of the skills required to test the validity of various proposals. The supervisor is a hypotheses maker and tester, and expertness in educational research is one of his major responsibilities. He is not a neutral technician who merely offers proposals and lets others decide what to do. His accountability for accomplishing research action implies possession of professional knowledge and technical skills which will enable him to analyze and solve problems with insight and imagination.

The Growth of Educational Research

Although the term research has been used to describe varied educational activities, it can be defined broadly as a systematic method of inquiry directed toward the development of a science of behavior in education.[1] A brief review of the development of educational research will indicate some of the changes in purpose and emphasis which have occurred.

At the turn of the century and in the years following, laboratory research, in general, emphasized the selection of specific problems, con-

[1] Robert M. W. Travers, *An Introduction to Educational Research,* The Macmillan Company, New York, 1958, pp. 1–67.

centrated on the study of isolated variables, maintained controls of the experimental procedures, and recorded the results of findings as precisely as possible. Research investigations were concerned with psychological and physiological aspects of learning and behavior, ranging from eye movements in reading and perceptual factors in learning to the measurement of various human skills and aptitudes. During the early part of the century considerable effort was expended on studies of child growth and development, and because of this emphasis the label "Century of the Child," indicating the child-centered aspects of education, appeared.[2] Studies conducted initially in laboratories were later repeated in school settings and the findings used to change practices in the schools. Supervisors, teachers, principals, guidance specialists, and university staff members became involved in various research studies. Because many of these researchers had been trained in laboratory research methods, the quality of educational research improved. Areas of investigation stretched from controlled experimentation to operational and action research.

Early research on classic topics such as memorizing and learning had commonly been called psychological research, but as studies were more and more frequently conducted in schools or were shown to have implications for classroom teaching, the term educational research came into common use. Educational research has been shaped by a number of forces: (1) the burgeoning school population; (2) the results of research conducted by researchers in the armed services, particularly in World War II; (3) the demands for more and better education; (4) the development of courses in educational research in colleges and universities; and (5) the establishment of such organizations as the National Society for the Study of Education, the American Educational Research Association, and the American Psychological Association, among others.

The application of promising research findings in schools had a salutary effect on the growth of educational research and resulted in continued productivity of laboratory workers and workers in the field. Although educational research has been and will continue to be closely allied to psychological research, the need for more objective information about indigenous educational problems has formalized it as a distinct and necessary field of endeavor. Educational research problems have interested workers in the behavioral sciences, and these workers have contributed procedures and techniques of analyzing evidence from their own disciplines. Thus the field of educational research has increasingly attracted workers from other disciplines to deal with a

[2] Peter B. Neubauer, M.D., "The Century of the Child," *The Atlantic* (Monthly), vol. 208, pp. 84–87, July, 1961.

variety of problems directed at the improvement of the educational process.

All fields of human endeavor have depended upon and profited from research. The mission of educational research may be stated thus: to provide objective evidence to improve school learning; to controvert myths; to change beliefs and attitudes; and to help place the work of the school on firmer ground with the consumers of education. Conclusive evidence, based on research, is necessary to ensure that in meeting the pressures for more precise teaching of content in elementary and second-ary schools, proposed changes are not based on opinion, unexamined hypotheses, or proposals from power agencies outside the school. The controversies over school practices, ranging from such concerns as the most effective methods of learning to the specific qualities of teacher competence, may be partly traceable to lack of objective and scientific evidence about these factors. When relevant knowledge is absent, forces which are questionable may take over the decision-making function. Historically, research in other disciplines has expanded knowledge and used it as the basis for containing ignorance. Research in medicine, of course, is a dramatic example. Studies in the armed services also have attested to the importance of research findings as bases for the scientific assessment of human skills, the improvement of learning, and the more adequate use of human talent.[3] In school research, properly conceived and based upon well-defined theories of content, learning, and teaching, is a systematic way to develop justifiable learning programs. Supervisors and teachers have a responsibility to obtain objective evidence to justify existing and proposed programs and to communicate the results of their investigations to the public.

The Teacher and Research

The idea that the teacher should have an active role as a researcher has not always been accepted by either the administrative staff or even the teacher himself. However, there have been degrees of involvement, and knowledge of the various views may help the supervisor to assess his own assumptions.

1. One view of the teacher is that he is primarily a practitioner con-cerned with improving his teaching only as he is given the results of scientific inquiry. This view would see the teacher as relatively un-touched by basic constructs and comprehensive theories in his daily work. He attends institutes, reads what others have to say, and engages in a second-hand kind of participation. Since he deals only with practice

[3] Frederick B. Davis, *Utilizing Human Talent,* American Council on Education, Washington, 1947.

or with application in restricted situations, he is not required to make use of sustaining theoretical constructs nor to test his educational goals against a set of hypotheses. He is constrained by the system to be no more than an implementer. In brief, he is not to be concerned with the development and understanding of structures, systems, or theories which will undergird and explain his daily teaching. These tasks are to be left to the educational researcher outside the classroom.

2. Another view would see the teacher as a limited consumer of research findings. Here, the assumption is that the teacher is sympathetic, supportive, and well-disposed toward the researcher and his findings. This view casts the actors in two distinct roles: on one hand, the educational researcher who formulates theories, tests them, and arrives at generalizations; on the other hand, the teacher who tries to interpret as best he can the statements of the elite group.

3. Somewhere along this continuum is another view which places the teacher at a point where he participates in various kinds of research studies but is not provided much opportunity to become involved at the core of theory development or theory testing. The teacher is envisaged as a kind of well-meaning amateur who can tackle some of the peripheral "hardware" but is not to tamper with the critical components.

Each of these three views places a limit, in varying degrees, on the teacher's participation and involvement in research. For example, a teacher may be strongly supported by a principal or supervisor as long as he implements a beginning reading program as outlined in a course of study. If, however, the teacher raises serious questions about the premises on which the program is based (e.g., theories of readiness), he discovers that such questions are to be left to others supposedly better qualified to answer. Basic premises or fundamental questions of theory are not supposed to be within the purview of amateurs. This concept of the teacher as a researcher would allow him a limited view of the target of, say, an action study and give him some degree of participation in the formulation of hypotheses or questions. Segments of the over-all research are then parceled out so that the teacher may be involved in securing some small part of the data, administering tests, or compiling observational data. In general, the teacher is provided *limited access* to the total plan of the research, to the factors of the design, to the setting of hypotheses, to the conduct of the study, and to the formulation of conclusions.

Assumptions such as those just stated underlie a point of view which maintains a myth that teachers are not competent to engage in research, that they can be consumers only, and that their *imperative need to know* is not critical. Teachers as well as supervisors act within some defined or undefined framework, and to restrict the opportunity for the examination of problems from a systematic and scientific point of view, or to set up dichotomies between the practitioner and the theorist, the laboratory and the classroom, is questionable. Further, to contend that research conducted in any one school cannot yield implications useful to other school systems is to avoid or ignore an essential premise—that the results of research based on accepted or universal theories are testable and usable elsewhere. The classroom is the laboratory for learning, and it is here that theories are tested and the results of research disseminated to other classrooms.

If the view is accepted that the task of the school is to teach wisely and systematically those things which cannot be learned elsewhere or by chance, then teachers and supervisors must be more than enthusiastic providers of previously determined learning opportunities. They must take responsibility for new kinds of learning programs which will provide sound bases for improvement of school practice. Supervisors and teachers are accountable for the precise analysis of the content to be taught, the exact materials to be used, the program of presentation, and the effective assessment of learning. The accomplishment of these tasks cannot be effected by loosely conceived goals or personalized impressions of purposes. Careful delineation and determination of objectives are needed at all times, since these are critical essences of teaching and supervision. Advances in learning occur in an atmosphere in which all persons involved are challenged to innovate, to test the choice of subject matter, to analyze teaching procedures, and to assess results.

Forces Affecting Research

Historically, a number of influences have shaped curricula and teaching-learning processes in schools. Among them have been (1) the influence of tradition—behavior expressed by "We have always done it this way, and we think we have been successful"; (2) the social values of the nation or of a particular community which determine the emphasis to be placed on curricula directed at teaching the fundamental skills to the exclusion of other areas, or on a particular type of physical education program, such as Little League baseball, or a girls' baton-twirling team; (3) the available types of instructional materials, including textbooks or locally prepared instructional guides or teaching materials; (4) the educational ladder and grade system which has constrained the program of the schools to certain fixed limits; and (5) the teacher—his training, general cultural level, perceptions, and degree of research-mindedness. These elements have to some extent determined the kind and quality of research and the extent to which it has been focused on the problems of what and how to teach.[4]

Doctrinaire and generalized forces can no longer serve as bases for shaping the goals of schooling or for testing outcomes. The times are such that most intellectual disciplines, research agencies, corporate enterprises, and government bureaus are moving toward the testing and examination of fundamental propositions. Supervision as a system function cannot escape this trend. The numerous factors affecting pupils—curricula, teaching methods, learning theory, social and physical environment—must be subject to systematic study. However, recognition of this mandate does not negate the fact that there are forces and pressures operating continually and that cognizance must be given to them in assaying rationally the productive tacks to take in accomplishing research functions. These current forces and sources of decision making might be shown as follows:[5]

1. *Private opinion.* Experts who have a formula. Organizations holding particular positions. Private citizens who have developed unitary prescriptions.

2. *Public debate.* Manifested in discourse on radio and TV, in motion pictures, and in the press. Corporate and agency documents; citizens' groups.

3. *Personal experience.* Akin to the perceptions expressed by the participants in 1 and 2. Rests on tradition, personal views, training, observation; the practical man and his personal experience. Teachers who depend in some degree upon this source for their rationale.

4. *Demonstration.* Exemplified by standardization on existing practices; by pilot studies conducted by organizations, study groups, and others. Purpose of studies may be to prove instead of to test a hypothesis.

5. *Operational research.* Studying a procedure as it occurs in its natural setting. Action does not necessarily follow in the sense of modifying classroom practices.

6. *Applied research.* Action research in which techniques of research are applied to school problems, changes in current practices are introduced, and assessment is made of the effects of the changed practices.

[4] David H. Russell and J. Cecil Parker, "Using Research to Point the Way in Curriculum Change," *Educational Leadership,* vol. 12, pp. 269–276, February, 1955.

[5] Adapted from Roger W. Russell, "Research in Education: A Neglected Question," American Psychological Association, Division 15, *Newsletter,* no. 1, pp. 15–21, December, 1958.

7. *Basic research*. Experimental in nature, requiring the setting of special conditions to test carefully stated hypotheses.

In general, each of these sources provides information which affects education. Communications media are emphasized in the first two. Many teachers and supervisors rely on the third. Foundations, lay study groups, citizens' committees, and other similar organizations have supported the fourth. And the last three sources are based upon a logical method for scientific inquiry.[6] Although any of these sources may be involved in educational decisions, it should be recognized that the first four tend to yield prescriptions and limited answers to questions of educational import. The criticisms sometimes voiced about action-research projects are that a lot of diffused action occurs, but not too much of it is of a research quality. Inadequate research designs, poorly formulated hypotheses, and other shortcomings lead to such criticisms, judgments which can be leveled at any poorly planned research. Well-conceived action research if competently planned can be as productive as research of a strictly experimental type.

It is true that supervisors are accountable to the populations represented by all these forces, but this only serves to point up the need for action at a professional level. Providing firm evidence for the public is to ensure that support for educational programs will be based on sound findings. As stated by Russell "The general improvement of education results from the long-term, empirical study of problems using different kinds of research approaches. Such studies require continued support over a number of years and the involvement of many kinds of schools in different parts of the United States." [7] Seeking answers to pressing problems at an empirical and fact-finding level rather than at the level of tradition and practice alone is the responsibility of the school.

The Objects of Research Concern

In essence, the kinds of research tasks which supervisors and teachers should undertake are those which revolve around the systematic, long-range study of *what* (including how much) to teach (and to whom), and the determination of *how* (and when) to teach it most effectively. Research investigations which provide a basis for generalizations about causal relations between teaching and measured instructional outcomes are planned in terms of the objective sought. In no sense should it be interpreted that only one kind of research methodology is prescribed

[6] *Ibid.*, p. 15.
[7] *Ibid.*, p. 16.

for in-school research.[8] No one technique should be considered better than another; nor is it necessary that techniques be mutually replaceable. Each is chosen in terms of purposes. There is a place for all research problems and techniques which are built upon carefully stated hypotheses for predicting expected data and which hold promise for providing answers about the critical questions of teaching-learning in schools. In addition to new problems and new approaches to problems, replication of prior studies is an important technique for adding to knowledge.[9] The replication of studies in many different areas and school districts can yield knowledge in depth about persistent problems common to all. For example, many promising studies concerned with elementary school mathematics have not been replicated.

Research problems concerned with such matters as managerial examinations or status are not the research responsibility of the supervisor. Studies on plant construction, district population trends, comparative finance, organizational structure and operation, the number of teacher dropouts, the ways to float a bond issue, or general status investigations of any type are the responsibility of others in the administrative system. The supervisor who commits himself and a staff to these types of studies is abrogating his central responsibilities for helping the teacher. There is evidence that too much emphasis may be given to problems of an administrative nature and not enough to what and how to teach.[10]

CHARACTERISTICS AND CRITERIA
OF EDUCATIONAL RESEARCH

It is the purpose of this section to outline some of the fundamental considerations in the conduct of educational research. In defining educational research, Ryans has pointed out that it ". . . stresses an inductive or empirical approach to the understanding of education facts and principles. It reasons from observed facts, experience, rather than tradition, intuition, or dogma." [11] Educational research is not informal, loosely planned experimentation, nor is it rationalization—the seeking of selected testimony or data to confirm or defend some educational practice. Proving a point of view rather than testing hypotheses is to be avoided.

[8] Ronald G. Jones, "Research, Intuition, and Analysis," *Phi Delta Kappan,* vol. 42, pp. 263–265, March, 1961.

[9] Ellis Batten Page, "Educational Research: Replicable or Generalizable?" *Phi Delta Kappan,* vol. 39, pp. 302–304, March, 1958.

[10] David G. Ryans, "Are Educational Research Offices Conducting Research?" *Journal of Educational Research,* vol. 51, pp. 173–183, November, 1957.

[11] David G. Ryans, "The Preparation of Educational Research Workers," *Journal of Educational Research,* vol. 49, pp. 195–202, November, 1955.

Quasi-educational researchers sometimes set out to prove that a particular practice is effective and manipulate data within some loosely designed investigation in order to obtain desired results.

The specific characteristics of educational research have been defined by Ryans as follows:[12]

Educational research refers to the careful and thorough-going investigation of educational phenomena (observable facts or events) leading to the discovery of verifiable facts, principles, and relationships which are fundamental to the systematic explanation of these phenomena. It implies the orderly seeking of educational facts and their systematic connections by means of, first, selective observation of educational phenomena and, second, valid reasoning, applied to the data obtained through observation.

Ryans describes the generic fields of research, considered as an ordered frame of reference, as follows:[13]

They range from school administration to child growth and development, from history of education to the psychology of learning, from curriculum to guidance. Although the key concerns of the researcher (having to do with sampling, reliability, validity, and significance of findings) are similar from area to area and approach to approach, the methods for obtaining data and the techniques for interpreting them vary considerably from field to field.

In historical research in education the interest is to determine relevant and significant features of the past (with the hope of better understanding the present and suggesting guides for the future). In descriptive research the interest is in describing designated characteristics of an existing population (or in describing relationships between certain characteristics of a population, or in testing some hypothesis about some characteristic of a population) undertaken to accomplish classification, to suggest trends, to reveal "needs," or to make comparisons. In experimental research the interest is in the description of the effect of some "treatment" or "treatments" upon some characteristics of a population, or in the testing of some hypothesis about this effect.

In descriptive research and in experimental research statistical techniques loom particularly important, both in the design and the analysis stages of the investigation, as the researcher seeks to control relevant variables, to summarize the data, and to make the estimates of error that are basic to the determination of whether or not observed differences in data are differences due to grouping or treatment, on the one hand, or to sampling error or error introduced by the influence of extraneous factors, on the other. In historical research statistical techniques are of minor importance, but logical analysis and the logical comparison of data in determining their reliability, validity,

[12] *Ibid.,* p. 195.
[13] *Ibid.,* pp. 196–197.

and significance require a variety of related but somewhat different skills and techniques.

The professional worker who plans and conducts educational research of good quality has three basic responsibilities, according to Ryans:[14]

1. To raise pertinent questions—to ask, "Why?" "Which?" "What if?" "For whom?" "How much?"

2. To arrange observations (design investigations) that will provide testable answers to the questions.

3. To provide estimates of, or information about, the validity and reliability of the answers, i.e., the extent to which systematic and random error enter into the answers.

Those criteria which should be considered essential for any properly conceived research investigation, as adapted from Ryan's report, follow:[15]

1. A clear-cut definition of the population or sources to be studied, including precise descriptions of the relevant characteristics of the population that will be sampled, experimented with, described, compared, or analyzed.

2. A description or estimate concerning pertinent aspects of the particular population to be studied.

3. Estimates concerning the reliability of the sample data and the methods or instruments used for obtaining those data.

4. Evidence concerning the validity of the data obtained, including (a) control of relevant variables or factors; (b) avoidance of bias in sampling, or, at least description of uncontrolled bias; (c) validity of instruments used to obtain data; and (d) the appropriateness of the statistical or other procedures used to tabulate, summarize, compare, and analyze the data.

Outline for a Research Proposal

In general, all aspects of a research design must be so clearly and precisely described that the study may be repeated by other competent researchers. Factors to consider in planning a research investigation will be found in the following outline:

RESEARCH OUTLINE

1. Statement of the problem and its setting
    a. Importance or significance to the field of education
2. Related research

[14] *Ibid.,* p. 196.
[15] *Ibid.*

    a. Evidence of comprehensive knowledge of research allied to the problem
3. Basic hypotheses to be tested and/or questions to be answered
4. Dependent variable (criterion behavior)
5. Population description
    a. Universe population
    b. Sample population
6. Sampling technique to be utilized
    a. How the sample is to be derived
7. Description of the general procedure
    a. Ex post facto, projected, descriptive, genetic
8. Specific procedures
    a. Before-after, experimental and control groups, time sampling, polling, or others
9. Relevant variables to be controlled
    a. Sex, socioeconomic status, study habits, in-class learning
10. Control technique
    a. Precision control (pairing)
    b. Frequency-distribution control (matched means and variabilities)
    c. Randomization
    d. Analysis of covariance
    e. Training of observers or raters
11. Statistical tests of significance of results
    a. Chi square, *t* tests (means, correlation), *F* tests (analysis of variance and covariance)
12. Equipment
    a. Autoinstructional devices, laboratory equipment, tests, rating instruments, scales
13. Instruments
    a. How tests, questionnaires, interviews, or other instruments used to measure the dependent variable are to be developed
    b. How validity and reliability are to be determined
    c. Knowledge about the validity and applicability of any commercially prepared tests to be used in the study
14. Facilities
    a. Personnel required; qualifications for the task
    b. Subjects to be used—number, age, grade, schools
    c. Time required and duration of the study—in-school, out-of-school, length of sessions, number of sessions, spacing of sessions
    d. Space required
    e. Assistance of other personnel

Determining Standards and Responsibilities

As noted earlier, the objects of research concern can be fairly well defined. However, it is important for supervisors to have clearly in mind standards by which to judge whether or not a particular research proposal can be initiated and carried to a satisfactory conclusion. In thinking through a proposed research project, the following list of questions might be given consideration:

1. Is the project well designed? Has it been subjected to examination by a number of expert judges?

2. Are the persons who will conduct the research technically qualified? Will they need assistance?

3. Can a high degree of objectivity be maintained? Will the study use hypotheses to predict data? Is the study in a sensitive area where other forces constrain the accomplishment of genuine research? Is the target of the research to prove a thesis or to test one?

4. Are there provisions for additional observations (replication)?

5. Have value terms been excluded from the proposed design?

6. Are the variables well defined?

7. Can the research be accomplished in the existing situation? Can controlled observations be carried out in the area?

8. Can behavior in the area be measured?

9. Can the research be conducted with reasonable demands on the time of other personnel? Is the research a part of the long-term program of the school district, or is it a short-term study which nevertheless will make a contribution?

10. Can facilities be provided without unreasonable inconvenience or disruption of regular programs?

Although involvement and commitment on the part of all staff members are important, it is reasonable and effective practice to encourage the formation of small research planning teams consisting of two or three representatives from the staff, trained in research if possible, interested in the major objectives of the school system, and willing to take general responsibility for research planning. Such representative teams can develop *with* and *for* the staff various aspects of research studies: (1) establishing criteria for the assessment of research proposals; (2) obtaining consultant help as required; (3) setting up a slate of projects with priorities for action; (4) planning training sessions; and (5) helping to manage systematically the various research efforts. A research planning team can be particularly effective in helping to plan and develop standards for long-term studies.

In larger school districts where there is a central research office, research planning teams can operate in a subdistrict or among groups of schools. There must be autonomy for these teams within the organizational system and within the framework of major objectives. Research teams lose effectiveness at the operational level if they are constrained by a central office to conduct only certain kinds of research, e.g., administrative research, or if they are to act merely as rubber stamps for the proposals of central supervisory officers. Their purpose is to serve as an indigenous operating unit, with delegated responsibility for determining and finding solutions to questions with and for the teaching staff in local situations. The central office staff in a large school system may determine general broad objectives, suggest research topics for investigation at the classroom level, provide consultant help and in-service training, and encourage local research teams to take responsibility for specific research tasks.

A research planning team (or teams) can be invaluable to the supervisor in implementing objectives. The use of such units, no matter how large or small the school system may be, is consistent with the concept that the supervisor multiplies himself through others to the end that as many persons as possible are involved in testing hypotheses. Research will get done but poorly if the supervisor keeps the task to himself, or encourages research only by the occasional wandering graduate student, commercial researcher, or eager individual teacher. In the long run useful research will be accomplished by involvement of more and more technically competent staff members whose research concerns are closely related to their daily tasks.

TOPICS AND QUESTIONS FOR RESEARCH INQUIRY

The whole range of problems in education to which research can be directed is vast and complex. However, every school system must examine the urgent questions requiring answers and devise a set of priorities for long-term attack on its problems. The importance of research inquiry in these three areas would seem to be evident: (1) the learner and the learning process; (2) the improvement of instruction; and (3) social factors in learning.

The Learner and the Learning Process

All school programs are based upon some sort of assumption about the nature of the learner and the learning process. That there is a balanced program of research which examines the problems of learners in degree and kind is not so certain. Study of problems of the learner and the learning process may be approached in a variety of ways, some of which are represented in the following questions:

1. How adequately is the school examining assumptions and testing results of the learning dimensions among, for example, (*a*) the mentally retarded; (*b*) the mentally superior; (*c*) the especially talented; (*d*) the emotionally maladjusted; (*e*) the physically crippled; (*f*) the sensorially handicapped?

2. How is knowledge of learning theory applied to classroom situations which may include many or all of the types of learners just mentioned?

3. Which are the essential characteristics of a teaching program which makes the most of pupils' divergent abilities and aptitudes?

4. How can the rate for developing superior abilities among gifted pupils be increased to a maximum?

How can objective focus be directed best on the purposes of learning for these pupils, the quality of their achievement, and their continued progress, rather than on arguments about acceleration versus enrichment?

5. In what ways are studies of the development of thinking in problem solving, thinking in concept formation, or thinking in the various content fields being examined?

What effects do attitudes of the pupil toward the content—and the teacher—have on learning?

Are there particular situations which differ in degree and kind from others in the same school and, therefore, require analysis of the attitude-content factor?

6. What are the differential effects of various teacher-models upon the learning and productivity of pupils?

The Improvement of Instruction

Many of the methods used in schools appear to be largely the result of tradition; but they have by no means been shown to be the most effective. Research aimed at improving the instructional process increasingly must view this process as a technology or set of technologies based on the findings of the sciences of human behavior. Such a view of instruction leads to some of the following questions:

1. How can teaching materials be organized systematically into programmed sequences for learning which the pupil can understand step by step?

What is the place of standardized tests in such an approach to instruction?

Does an adequately designed teaching program call for new types of evaluation or alterations in existing assessments of learning and the learner?

2. What evidence can be obtained regarding the validity of textbooks, films, and other materials for improving learning?

3. What particular content, at any level of schooling, can be introduced earlier or at different times than now currently programmed?

4. How can the effectiveness of the ungraded system of instruction be tested as contrasted with fixed standards of grade progress?

What are the measurable effects of each organization on the achievement of pupils presently and later?

5. Precisely what knowledge should pupils acquire at different levels of development in order to ensure transfer value to new and recurring situations both in school and after leaving school?

6. How can the contingencies of societal changes and the emergent demands of new knowledge be met so that content and instructional procedures will be changed rapidly enough to develop the capabilities required in the next five years—or the next ten years?

What internal changes are occurring in content, e.g., new emphasis on second language teaching as a vehicle for international understanding, new structures for the organization of mathematics, the application of linguistic principles to native language instruction, or the obsolescence of traditionally favored content?

Social Factors in Learning

While research continues on what to teach and how to teach effectively, there are also increasing demands to know more about the effects of forces in the social matrix on learning. Questions illustrating the problems in this area might include the following:

1. What belief-attitude patterns of pupils are to be changed—by whom—in what value direction—for what ends? Who is responsible for what?

2. What forces in modern society motivate pupils?

What impacts of society constrain the mission of the schools? What forces facilitate the mission?

3. To what extent are gifted students achieving their potential power and in what vocational careers?

What are the fundamental reasons why pupils of outstanding ability do not continue their education?

4. What are the forces in the family structure that affect the motivation and achievement of pupils?

5. What is the responsibility of the parent in developing learning attitudes?

How does this responsibility relate to the teachers' functions?

What avenues of unexplored information in this complex are possible of investigation?

6. What are the perceptions of the teacher, the administrator, and the parent which constrain, determine, or direct their actions in the school as an organizational system?

Basic information rather than superficial surveys or opinions must be sought for these and similar questions. More and more relevant material is available in educational and psychological research journals, in government and agency studies, and from the laboratories of universities and the classrooms of schools. In the long run, those responsible for the supervisory function can make important contributions to the complex problems in education by *substantiating* or *refuting* propositions presented in previous research investigations.

RESEARCH AS A METHOD OF LEARNING

Improving Technical Competence

The supervisor must keep in mind constantly the vision that the results of educational research can provide a primary source of data for the implementation of objectives. If the supervisor does not develop research skills, his efforts to set and test educational objectives may result only in accomplishing useful, but not critically important, tasks. The ability to conduct research and to help staff members in research requires a spirit of inquiry, knowledge of content, and skills in the research process. The supervisor who lacks training in the design and execution of research investigations is *simply going to have to obtain such training.* A supervisor cannot be effective if he lives on his capital, or talks about research, but does not himself know the what and how of it. Training in educational research at some point in past time is not enough; the expansion of knowledge and the imperative need to obtain answers to new and critical questions require continued study throughout the professional career of every individual. Technical learning does not end with the granting of a degree or a certificate to supervise.

Further, the technical knowledge of research methodology cannot be obtained by an auditing or absorptive process, such as attending occasional conferences, listening to inspirational lectures, reading professional journals, or consuming the results of research accomplished by others. Valuable as these activities may be for keeping abreast of current issues and problems, the supervisor must participate actively and directly in research processes, basing his actions upon sound, up-to-date technical knowledge. To become an expert leader in the research function, the supervisor must have engaged in scholarly study, undergone some form of systematic instruction, and learned to apply his knowledge in research operations. He tries to develop the kind of technical skill which will permit him to work at a rational, intellectual level rather than to depend upon tradition, personal intuition, cults, or the untested proposals of every bystander at the scene.

Supervisors who lack the requisite background in educational research might consider either or both of these steps: (1) engaging in advanced study of educational research at an institution of higher learning; (2) setting up a program of in-service seminars and obtaining an expert instructor to work with the staff. Advanced study means the systematic study of research theory with related laboratory experience. Taking short-term courses in how to interpret research studies, or participating in a series of lectures on current trends in research, is not sufficient. Two general areas of coverage are recommended as a minimum: (1) basic courses in the fundamentals of research which treat the application of scientific method to problems in education, consider problems in the design of experiments, analyze instruments and techniques for gathering data, and examine the ways to analyze and interpret data; and (2) specialized courses in educational or psychological statistics which treat the ways of quantifying data and applying tests of significance, and focus on the skills necessary to present the results of studies in quantitative and scholarly form. The work in this latter area should include elementary statistical procedures and sampling error theory through analysis of variance and covariance.

It is not uncommon to hear derogatory statements about statistical theory in education from both professional workers and laymen. Such views may be a part of the growing pains of a new discipline; they may reflect ignorance, represent general anti-intellectual attitudes, or express the feelings of the practical man who relies upon his own experience and intuition to deal with the problems of probability. The visible evidence of the value and practical use of statistical theory and methods to treat the data from experiments is overwhelmingly against such views.[16]

Advanced work in the field of tests and measurements and courses on the technical aspects of the scientific writing of research studies would provide invaluable training. However, the supervisor whose undergraduate or graduate work has not provided him with a background in research methodology may find it necessary to take work in the psychology

[16] Warren Weaver, "The Disparagement of Statistical Evidence," *Science,* vol. 132, pp. 1859, Dec. 23, 1960.

of learning, experimental psychology, and sociology, and refresher work in mathematics before embarking upon the detailed study of research theory. The educational training basic to competence in various kinds of research assignments, including planning of programs of self-improvement or staff improvement, may be found in Ryans' work on the preparation of research workers.[17]

In setting up a program of in-service seminars with a qualified instructor to work with the staff, the same areas of content suggested for advanced study could serve as a basis for study. The supervisor, while a participant-learner along with other staff members, would be responsible for providing data and problems directly from the schools themselves as content for the study of research methodology. With such help from the supervisor and the staff, a skillful instructor can build the theoretical content around realistic and close-to-home problems. The study of the methodology of educational research is thus a profitable and realistic experience.

In-service seminars should be long-term, continuing for a year or longer and meeting regularly, and should be recognized by the administrative staff of the schools as a legitimate activity on the part of the participants. The staff members who participate in long-term seminars should be interested volunteers or selected individuals who will be able to multiply their skills by helping others. As they attain insight and skill through training in seminars, they can be utilized to train others within schools or within a school system. The supervisor thus develops a cadre of trained persons who can help others to learn—and learn, be it said, in an organized fashion. It should be understood that seminars conducted during the school year become the major mission of an in-service program with few, if any, other tasks interjected, at least for those who are devoting major effort to these seminars. The complaints of teachers that they jump from one institute to another workshop without accomplishing any one task in depth should be sufficient reason for caution. Worthy in-service education hinges on a parsimonious selection of endeavors directly related to the teacher's job, so that he has long-term involvement and the satisfaction of completing one task and completing it well.

If it is not feasible to conduct seminars during the school year, supervisors should consider planning a summer seminar in the school district under the direction of a trained consultant, e.g., a university or college instructor. In the kind of seminar which has an outside instructor in charge, supervisors and teachers may spend a period of several weeks on a project with regular university credit for the work. The school

---

[17] Ryans, *op, cit.,* pp. 199–202.

district applies the course work toward so-called "hurdle credit" on the promotional scale; some of the participants use the credit toward higher degrees; others take the program simply for self-improvement. Where this kind of program has been tried, evaluations have shown it to yield high dividends in terms of improved teaching. Staff members engage in the study of basic content, use data from their own school system as bases for study and application, work closely with other staff members, relate their learnings to live problems, and develop a commitment to a task which has real meaning for them. Fringe benefits include the opportunity to live at home, to use facilities provided by the school system, and to obtain some visible status within the organizational system.

The supervisor who has the proper vision of educational research develops his own skills by participating in seminars directed by experts, so that he, in turn, can plan and conduct study seminars for others. By teaching others, by recreating his understanding of research procedures, he becomes even more proficient himself, contributing vis-à-vis to the learning of the staff. These kinds of activities are his responsible way of multiplying himself.

Will such in-service learning on the part of the supervisor and staff result in every member's becoming a technical specialist in research? Obviously the answer is "no"; but out of a staff which undergoes such exposure will come differentiated interests and skills. There will be those who display a high degree of insight and research skill, take major responsibility for continuing research efforts, and provide leadership for the less skilled. There will be others who are interested in and know the nomenclature or the broad dimensions of research methodology, and have strong biases toward the research approach. All who participate will have a more catholic appreciation of the complexities inherent in designing research, determining the validity of data, testing results, and developing generalizations from findings. At first some teachers may find the concepts new and difficult, but through constant encouragement and consultative help from supervisors and other staff members, they become dedicated to more systematic ways of studying the teaching process. Sometimes a "sleeper effect," not observable until long after the initiation of a program of study, emerges, and teachers appear to take fire. The supervisor may have aroused this interest by reinforcing the initial exposure and continuously involving those who have not yet become highly skilled. Certainly, training in how to apply methods of research to educational problems cannot be a one-shot deal. There must be follow-up restudy, application, and continual assessment. The whole process of committing a staff to the research vision becomes a kind of wholesome contamination, followed by hearty reinforcement which leads, on the one hand, to improved technical skills and, on the other hand, to warm attitudes toward the systematic, scientific approach to problems.

The Climate for Effective Research

While it may be true that the intelligence, interest, and background of individuals may determine the limits of their technical performance, it is also true that if they are given training in research skills and the opportunity to participate in research investigations, they are more likely to capitalize on their abilities. There are various ways in which a supervisor may set an atmosphere for research, encourage self-confidence, and secure more widespread participation in research endeavors by individual staff members.

1. It has been noted that one of the central problems in a democracy is the necessity to obtain from each individual participation in matters affecting his own destiny. Teachers, after all, are professionally trained workers and responsible citizens. Teachers want to do a good job of teaching. They are eager and willing to discover better ways to do the tasks to which they have committed themselves. The supervisor who creates an atmosphere for the free exchange of hypotheses, encourages the desire to seek answers to questions, no matter how these results may offend tradition, and stimulates divergent creative thinking cannot help but improve staff competence.

2. Teachers should be encouraged to think broadly, to see all facets of a problem, and to be open-minded. The supervisor makes every effort to be aware of and to control his own biases. Mistakes along the way are treated as a means to seek other leads, not as failures or shortcomings.

3. Better researchers develop when teachers are encouraged to understand principles through the study of theories so that they move from abstract concepts to concrete applications. Too often in the study of problems supervisors start with existing practice or with examples rather than with an investigation of the theoretical basis or the rationale which undergirds a particular practice. This may be defined as the "how to do it" approach rather than the "why" approach. Starting from experience or practice only may lead to studies which manipulate data but do not answer questions, since these studies were not cast in a theoretical framework to begin with.

4. Encourage the incubation of ideas. Allow time, and then more time. Ideas should not be rushed. By pushing ahead one may get across the tropical marshlands rapidly, but a slower journey would permit seeing some of the lilies which grow among the reeds. So, it is well to involve staff members in investigating every avenue before finalizing a

research proposal. Take time, in some instances several months, to survey the known sources of data and to consult other supervisors and staff members who may have conducted research in the particular field of interest.

5. Encourage personalized research ideas. That is, give individuals every opportunity to work out ideas on their own—alone if desired, but at any rate at a personal level of commitment. Every research study does not necessarily call for a director and workers. What is desired is a group of interested people with ideas and the freedom to work them out, sometimes with others and at other times by themselves. Sometimes the individual is able to achieve results which slip the grasp of groups of experts or committees.

6. Tackle the idea front as if it were new and fair game. Avoid the attitude that all ideas have been used up, or that most major problems have already been investigated; for example, "After all, Dr. XYZ investigated children's concepts in arithmetic and the answers are all in." Encourage the replication of studies, the expansion of ideas, the reassessment of old ideas, keeping in mind that such explorations are to be related to major purposes. They are new pathways along the main road, and may lead to a rewarding surprise.

7. Encourage the long-term pursuit of problems. The problem which is solved for one particular purpose during any one school year may not yield generalizations applicable to a similar problem in the next year. The fact that conclusions have immediate use does not necessarily mean that they are fundamentally good or have long-term application. Isolate major, critical tasks for long-term study whenever called for. Individual teachers should have complete freedom to spend several years on the study of a problem if the purpose and design of the particular investigation so warrant. There are few objects of research concern that can be neatly packaged year by year or topic by topic. Setting forth a theme or area of research for the year, and then passing on to another, illustrates what seems questionable targeting of research action at the organizational level. This kind of professional flitting about is not in keeping with the criteria of competent research and can no longer be afforded. Create the attitude that hypotheses can be examined in almost infinite fashion. When one phase of a project is completed, reexamine the results to see what further research possibilities can be squeezed from the data and what further study is indicated. Avoid the project approach to research problems; for example: "When we complete this project we can go on to another."

8. Distinguish between purely administrative studies and studies which test hypotheses for the purpose of prediction or validation. Both

types of studies have their place, but the supervisor's major concern is with those investigations which are characterized by theory, assessment, and experimentation and which lead to possible answers to problems of behavior and learning.

9. Learn to treat other individuals as equally desirable participants in a mutual research endeavor. Reinforce positive attitudes toward research by rewarding others with overt recognition of their accomplishments as research workers. Treating teachers as if they were interested students of research is to suggest the possibility that they will try to be such persons. The supervisor who accepts others as intellectually curious persons who also wish to find answers to questions is creating a climate in which a staff can move toward productive research action.

If the supervisor plans research activities in terms of a consistent set of hypotheses about how educational goals are to be achieved, e.g., changes in behavior, he becomes a model for others. Like the competent teacher, he should see himself as a skillful cultivator who consistently demonstrates how a well-disciplined mind operates on the objects of research concern. He helps others to determine when conclusions are invalid, inconclusive, or incomplete and when they are firm and honest. He takes time occasionally for introspection to ensure that he does not become so engrossed or involved in *his* mission that he forgets that the busy teacher must find time to prepare daily lesson plans and think about teaching in the classroom each day. The supervisor's objective and considerate behavior is his assumption of responsibility, his evidence of accountability to those who support him. Success in the accomplishment of research tasks with others and for others validates the supervisor's ultimate worth to any school system.

12

A RATIONALE FOR DEVELOPMENT OF CURRICULUM

The school cannot teach all things. A central task of the supervisor is to help others select wisely among (1) possible instructional objectives and (2) the various things that can be done to ensure that pupils develop the habits, attitudes, skills, and knowledge called for in these objectives. This chapter contains a rationale for developing a vision of what to teach and how to teach. To this end, the chapter focuses first on the characteristics of well-stated instructional objectives and the measurement of the learner's attainment. Second, it relates instructional objectives to the school as a social institution with special functions to perform. Third, the chapter deals with social conditions, subject matter, and certain factors concerning the learner which must be taken into account in ascertaining appropriate objectives. Last, attention is given to the principles which offer the greatest promise for guiding both the selection of contacts or learning opportunities, such as textbooks, films, questions, and activities, and the organizational structure by which objectives can be met.

STATING INSTRUCTIONAL OBJECTIVES

One cannot choose from among objectives until they are made explicit or concrete, i.e., until one can perceive how attainment of the objective will change the behavior (understanding, competence, or performance) of the learner. Let us examine a few instructional objectives to illustrate the importance of stating objectives so that they serve to specify both the behavioral changes sought in learners and the knowledge or situation to which the behavior is to apply.

1. The learner has the ability to translate relationships expressed in symbolic form, including illustrations, maps, tables, diagrams, graphs, and mathematical formulas, into verbal form, and vice versa.

2. The learner has the ability to differentiate value judgments from predictions of consequences.

3. The learner can identify the basic elements (balance, unity, rhythm, etc.) in guiding a work of art.

4. The learner can explain and predict the occurrence of physical phenomena in terms of the concept of energy.

5. The learner can analyze new words quickly, can pronounce them and guess their meaning, using phonetic and context clues.

6. The learner faces a normal range of tensional problems in everyday life without temper displays, crying, or other extreme overt reaction and without persisting internal strains.

7. The learner can state and identify in current events examples of those premises of American liberty which relate to basic political beliefs, i.e., public officials are responsible to the people, the church and state should be separate, etc.

8. The learner creates or makes new mathematical discoveries and generalizations.

9. The learner illustrates principles of responsibility by obeying rules established by the group, working independently during study periods, and coming to class on time with necessary work materials.

It should be remembered that we are now considering these statements of objectives in connection with a discussion of appropriate form for an objective rather than for the purpose of deciding whether the objective is desirable for particular individuals and in keeping with the responsibility of the school. The formulation of an instructional objective is partly dependent upon whether it is to function as an objective for an entire program in the school, a particular course, or a part of a course. An objective such as number 1 above represents a wider and longer range of instruction—the kind of objective that might guide instructional planning at a total school level. Note, however, that broad and cumulative as this objective is, it is not nearly as general as commonly stated social objectives, such as "citizenship," "self-preservation," or "critical thinking." To qualify as an instructional objective rather than an educational or social aim, the objective must be explicit enough to suggest appropriate learning materials, assignments, or methods. A statement such as number 5, on the other hand, represents an objective which could operate in a more limited period of time and in particular class-rooms, pinpointing the content—phonetic and context clues—to be introduced.

The teacher must have available a statement which specifies the particular principle, concept, skill, value, or other knowledge that is to be taught. Certainly, this does not mean that the teacher must seek to attain objectives in a prescribed daily order. On the contrary, he must be prepared to vary his objectives and instructional procedures in light of developments in the classroom. Also, both the level of behavior sought and the content selected will differ for individual learners in those teaching situations where it is not expected that all pupils will achieve objectives to an equal degree and at the same time.

Three distinctions are to be seen regarding any statement of instructional objectives. First, the objective should always be stated in terms of the expectations held for the pupil. The focus is upon the learner, not the teacher. Second, the behavior sought in the learner is specified. As the sampling of objectives presented above shows, there is a verb form which indicates a level of performance, i.e., "illustrates," "can explain and predict." This level of expected attainment is graduated in some order of difficulty and importance. That is, the phrase "the learner can state and identify" indicates a lower level of behavior than the phrase "the learner predicts" or "the learner creates." Other behaviors are found in such verbs as "compares," "contrasts," "interprets," "explains," and "analyzes." The third essential in stating instructional objectives is that they must define either the area of subject matter or content (skill, concept, principle, value) which the learner is to use or the nature of the situation in which the behavior is to function. As seen in objectives 3 and 4 above, "balance," "unity," "rhythm," and "the concept of energy" are illustrations of terms which point the way to the subject matter to be introduced. Until an objective is made operational, it will not guide the teacher's course of action. Operationality is present when the statement describes the expected performance, permitting one to observe whether or not the learner has attained it.

CRITERION MEASURES OF PERFORMANCE

An excellent procedure for establishing the operationality of an objective is to specify the criterion performance which will reveal that the learner has attained the objective sought. The criterion test usually includes the particular responses the teacher would like to see in the learner's repertoire when he completes the instructional program. For academic material, this behavior can sometimes be expressed in the learner's responses to a test covering the entire course. A test of this kind should be comprehensive, sampling both the different levels of behavior sought (i.e., recall to create) and the range of content taught. If the teacher has stated in his objective that he wants the learner to be able to recognize a given principle when the learner comes across it and to apply the principle to a new situation or problem, the criterion test should provide an opportunity for the learner to demonstrate this ability. Too often, teachers state objectives which call for high-level behavior like *prediction* but sample in final examinations only those behaviors which demand *recall*. There is likely to be less negative criticism for "teaching to the test" when the test adequately reflects the objectives selected and when it samples the full range of behavior desired. Teacher and pupils should have the opportunity of knowing the kinds of items they are to respond to. If, for instance, the objective states that learners should be able to apply a formula relating the area to the length and width of a rectangle, a number of problems like the following one might serve as part of the criterion test: "The length of a rectangular lot exceeds its breadth by 20 yards. If each dimension is increased by 20 yards, the area of the lot will be doubled. Find the shorter dimension of the original lot." This problem would represent one sample of behavior. Other problems of the same class of behavior, but different examples from those used in instruction, should also be included in the criterion test.

The selection or construction of criterion measures must be determined from the objectives of the course and take into account both the behavior and the content that students are expected to achieve. A technique involving the preparation of a matrix is an excellent way to ensure that measures are developed which adequately reflect all objectives. The illustration in Figure 12-1 features such a matrix.

It is seen in Figure 12-1 that thought is given to the total domain to be tested, including behavior (abilities) and content (subject matter). Only those squares of the chart which represent the particular objectives sought need be marked. If, for example, a student were expected to be able to use graphic presentations of data in connection with measurement and diffraction of light, the appropriate square would be marked and specific tasks or test questions would then be set up to reveal the student's attainment of this objective. Items comprising the criterion measures (questions, problems, etc.) are selected until the objectives are specified in the matrix. Parenthetically, this matrix not only directs the planning required for measurement, but also serves as a guide to the plan-

SUBJECT MATTER	Ability to demonstrate qualitative understanding of fundamentals	Ability to apply knowledge to unfamiliar situation	Ability to analyze problems, situations mathematically	Ability to use graphical presentation of data	Ability to identify problems in a new situation	Ability to formulate a simple scientific model	Ability to make logical predictions based on a model	Ability to make relevant observations	Ability to suggest new lines of investigation based on observation	Ability to draw valid conclusions from observations and data	Totals
Time											
Space											
Motion											
Mass											
Matter											
Measurement											
Behavior of light											
Geometric optics											
Wave motion											
Interference and diffraction of light											
Force											
Momentum											
Conservation of momentum											
Kinetic and potential energy											
Heat and molecular motion											
Conservation of energy											
Magnetic fields											
Photons and matter waves											
Quantum systems											
Totals											

Figure 12-1. *Secondary school physics course comprehensive achievement test design.* (*From F. L. Ferris, "Testing for Physics Achievement,"* American Journal of Physics, *vol. 28., pp. 269–278, March,* 1960.)

ning of contacts or learning opportunities necessary to attainment of objectives. If, for instance, the learner is expected to be able to use graphs which present data regarding the interference and diffraction of light, he will have to have an opportunity to practice using graphs, including perhaps the skills of extrapolation, interpretation, and translation from one symbolic form to another, as well as experience with the theories of light.

The selection and preparation of criterion measures require one to consider the initial repertoire of the learner's competence and the actual possibility of attaining the objective as well as the kinds of learning contacts necessary for the task. Such considerations early in the planning stage often have a sobering effect upon one's tendency to state idealistic but unattainable ends. On the other hand, if the learner does not perform as expected, the findings serve as a stimulus to the teacher's problem solving which, in turn, modifies future objectives and instructional procedures.

The supervisor realizes, of course, that teachers should be major participants in the selection of any tests used in a classroom and should be given help in the interpretation of results. As the supervisor works with others in the development of criterion measures, he is expected to follow the principles of measurement and evaluation. Central among these principles are those which stress the importance of (1) assessing the behavior of the learner over various intervals of time; (2) noting concomitant and unexpected outcomes; (3) using reliable and valid instruments; and (4) properly interpreting and using the results.

Importance of Extended Measurement and Evaluation

In his study of the relative efficacy of pupil discovery versus teacher-dominated instruction, Ray[1] found that pupils taught by the two methods did not differ significantly in their ability to meet certain criterion performances *when the criterion measures were administered immediately after instruction.* However, when criterion measures were given *six weeks after instruction,* pupils taught by the discovery method were significantly superior in their ability to recall material initially learned and to apply the material to new and related situations.

Ray's account illustrates an important reason for comparing differences between scores made by individuals initially and at other later periods, i.e., identification of instructional effects which would not be noted in single attempts at measurement. While this finding is a direct contribution to the area of improved technical procedures of assessment,

[1] Willis E. Ray, "Pupil Discovery vs. Direct Instruction," *Journal of Experimental Education,* vol. 29, no. 3, pp. 271–280, March, 1961.

at least two other reasons can be given for undertaking frequent measurement. Both reasons relate to Abraham Lincoln's statement: "If we could first know where we are and whither we are tending, we could better judge what to do and how to do it." First, the evidence collected enables the teacher to appraise the learner's lacks and competencies, thereby guiding the teacher in the selection of more appropriate objectives and requisite learning opportunities. Second, it provides information needed to determine the effectiveness or ineffectiveness of instructional practice.

Extended evaluation over time is seen in those practices associated with follow-up of learners after they have left the teaching situation or the school. The purpose of follow-up studies is not only to get cumulative evidence and to note the permanence or impermanence of learning, but to determine (1) if the learner is able to apply the learning in new situations (transfer) and (2) if the instructional objective actually is related to the social or educational end it is supposed to serve. By assessing long-term consequences, we have been able, for instance, to weaken the myth that the study of particular subject matter will be of value in subsequent scholastic success, in participation in political affairs, or that it will add to one's mental power. Long-term measurement has shown that the *methods* employed and learned in particular subjects of study *may* bring an increase in mental power and contribute to future superior academic and civic behavior,[2] but coverage of the formal subject matter itself will not.

The principle of comprehension in evaluation is of importance when one conceives the supervisor and teacher as hypotheses makers. In testing a hypothesis, one not only collects evidence of the behavior expected but also takes into account unexpected consequences. A teacher may be very successful in getting first-grade pupils to pronounce words or to read from left to right, but his method may also be associated with the children's signs of extreme anxiety and hostility (i.e., wetting, thumb sucking, and tearing of clothes). In testing a hypothesis, one seeks evidence of undesirable outcomes as well as outcomes signifying attainment of instructional objectives.

Instruments in Evaluation

Instruments for use in evaluation are the means by which one obtains information on the progress of the learner and the effectiveness of instruction. Quantitative and qualitative data, objective measures, subjec-

[2] Percival M. Symonds, "What Education Has to Learn from Psychology, VII, Transfer and Formal Discipline," *Teachers College Record*, vol. 61, no. 1, pp. 30–45, October, 1959.

tive impressions, tests, observations, anecdotal records, case studies, sociometric methods—all may serve as instruments for deciding whether or not instructional objectives have been attained. Standardized instruments for assessing pupil performance (information, proficiency, and attitudes) in a variety of areas are presently available. It is possible, for instance, to procure standardized tests which measure the specialized behavior associated with thinking, maturity, and social relations. The appropriateness of these tests depends upon (1) the validity and reliability of the test and (2) the aspects of instructional objectives important to the particular class.

The supervisor will find the latest edition of the *Mental Measurements Yearbook*[3] one of his best sources for review of standardized instruments. This publication gives descriptive and judgmental information regarding particular tests, indicating, for instance, the extent to which a test will provide evidence of the behavior desired. Although the high quality of many of these published instruments warrants their use, they are not alone likely to fulfill classroom requirements. The individual teacher is expected to employ instruments which fit his particular teaching situation. One way to do this is to adapt a published test by dropping out irrelevant material and questions which are inappropriate for the class in which the test is to be used. Usually, it also will be necessary to develop supplementary instruments.

Because numerous textbooks on educational measurement and evaluation have been prepared specifically to help classroom teachers construct their own instruments, only brief mention of the procedures for construction of an instrument will be made here. One essential is the devising of situations which will give the learner a chance to reveal whether or not he has acquired the behavior desired. Key decisions must be made regarding how to record the learner's responses, how to judge the appropriateness of a response, how many and what kinds of responses will be necessary in order to see if the learner has really acquired the behavior sought. It is also important to consider ways (1) to get agreement from others that the behavior has in fact occurred; (2) to distinguish between those who have acquired greater or less mastery of the learning sought; and (3) to analyze the particular strengths and deficiencies of the respondents.

The Measurement Program

A number of advantages can follow the wise interpretation and use of criterion measures: direction and motivation in learning; diagnosis and

---

[3] Oscar K. Buros (ed.), *The Fifth Mental Measurements Yearbook,* The Gryphon Press, Highland Park, N.J., 1959.

guidance of the individual pupil; improvement in instructional procedures; and better selection and placement of objectives and content. As
a key person in developing better understanding and use of criterion
measures, the supervisor will find it helpful to have an organized measurement program. Such a program would permit coordinated and continuous planning among test specialists, administrators, guidance personnel, and teachers. It would be desirable to have a professionally
trained director of testing available for helping participants interpret and
use test results and understand technical matters involving norms, scores,
errors of measurement, and the like.

One characteristic of such a program, now seldom realized in practice,
is that the testing program would not be separated from curriculum planning and all tests would contribute to instructional outcomes. The program would probably include these activities:

1. Development of the purposes of the testing program
2. Definition of the teacher's part in testing
3. Provision for (*a*) the instruction of teachers in the interpretation
and use of test results (undertaken along with the actual administration
of school-wide tests and featuring specific ways in which these results
can be used in the classroom) and (*b*) the construction of instruments
by teachers themselves
4. Selection and regular school-wide use of a limited number of tests
as well as special tests to meet individual needs

FUNCTIONS OF THE SCHOOL AND INSTRUCTIONAL OBJECTIVES

Although the school has its special functions which differentiate it
from other institutions, it may perform subsidiary tasks which supplement or contribute to the primary ones. Priorities in today's school are
not the same as those of yesterday or tomorrow. The school is not an
end in itself, but a means of serving the changing demands of society.
Much of the conflict over instructional objectives derives from efforts of
some pressure groups to extend the functions of the school, while others
seek the restriction of functions to tasks which are not likely to be performed by any other agency.

As indicated previously, the search for the school's own distinctive
function and character has been intensified of late in the direction of
those things that the school can provide best:[3a]

[3a] Ralph W. Tyler, "The Education of Teachers: A Major Responsibility of Colleges and Universities," *Educational Record,* vol. 39, pp. 255–6, July, 1958.

1. Learning that requires organization of experience and distribution of practice over considerable periods of time

2. Learning in which the central factors are not obvious to one observing the phenomenon, and where basic principles, concepts, and meanings must be brought especially to the attention of the learner

3. Learning . . . where the experiences cannot be provided directly

4. Learning which requires experiences of higher quality than are commonly available in the environment of students

5. Learning where examination and interpretation of experiences are essential; where it is not enough simply to have had more contact with, but where periodically there is need for reflection upon, and examination of, experience and an effort to interpret it to have it become more meaningful

The foregoing criteria for the selection of objectives are in keeping with the often quoted characterization of the school as a place (1) where existing social life can be simplified, (2) where the environment can be deliberately manipulated; and (3) where one can receive the best and deepest moral training by proper relations with others in a unity of work and thought. Ideally, schools can be so organized that pupils intensively pursue a selected number of studies without the distraction of competing demands. In short, teaching pupils how to acquire and use subject matter which must be singled out for differentiation and related to a larger system of facts and theories is an especially appropriate task for the school. More than other institutions, the school can economically arrange those conditions which are necessary to the learning of difficult ideas, ideas which require prerequisite experiences and the deliberate noting of cause-and-effect relationships. By placing a child in selected situations which are likely to give rise to understandings not likely to occur by chance, the schools render a unique service.

In this sense, "It is the business of the school to see that the child does not grow naturally." Instead of preventing a child from going beyond the obvious everyday world, the school can give him a new freedom. In addition, the school can help combat growth in natural but undesirable directions. Instead of encouraging numerous and conflicting possibilities of growth, the school is selective with respect to outcomes it seeks for learners. The professional backgrounds of the teachers and the fact of compulsory attendance help to determine the school's acceptance of particular functions. In general, teachers are prepared to share with children specific processes and notions drawn from the organized disciplines of the arts and sciences. The expertness of teachers is not derived from the personal and emotional values of the home, the revealed knowledge of the church, the skills of business and industry, or the particular practices of a local community. Because all children are required to attend, the school is uniquely fitted for the important task of supplementing the values of primary groups by making clear the premises of the larger social order. The child's provincial values derived from his home, church, and other local associations must be amplified if we are to attain a climate which permits diversity. The continuance of a pluralistic society (one in which diversity of thought and practice is itself a value) requires acceptance of certain "ground rules" for all. For instance, the teachings that the minority has the right to become the majority and that one should guarantee the freedom of another to worship in the manner of his own choosing are especially proper for the school.

It should be clear that there is a philosophical position regarding a good society, man, or school underlying each function of the school. The philosophical position of Dewey with respect to the school, for example, is shown in his preferred outcome for the learner:

> Clearly, they [teachers] will have to cultivate the habit of suspended judgment, of skepticism, of desire for evidence, of appeal to observation rather than sentiment, discussion rather than bias, inquiry rather than conventional idealizations. When this happens schools will be dangerous outposts of a human civilization. But they will also begin to be supremely interesting places.[4]

We can also take note of the assumptions implied in four commonly stated functions of the school:[5]

1. *Integration.* The furtherance of those skills, knowledge, and attitudes necessary to preserve the common culture and to promote the general welfare. To a large extent, public education for all came into existence in response to the need for preserving society. We maintain our schools as a means of protecting the state from the consequences of an ignorant and incompetent electorate. The belief that because of what the schools teach, the community can be a better place in which to live has led to the selection of those objectives which are necessary for all who are to exercise practical intelligence, i.e., the skills and understandings which enable all citizens to assess the consequences of social policies and institutional arrangements. An excellent description of the ways to discharge this function and develop special methods associated with practical intelligence is given by Smith, Stanley, and Shores.[6] Ob-

[4] John Dewey, *Characters and Events,* Joseph Ratner (ed.), vol. 2, Holt, Rinehart and Winston, Inc., New York, 1929.

[5] William B. Featherstone, *A Functional Curriculum for Youth,* American Book Company, New York, 1950.

[6] B. Othanel Smith, William O. Stanley, and J. Harlan Shores, *Fundamentals of Curriculum Development,* World Book Company, Yonkers, N.Y., 1950.

jectives in keeping with integration are, of course, stacked in favor of the particular system of value our society happens to possess, i.e., democratic sentiments.

2. *Supplementation.* Individuality is the key term in understanding this function. Objectives undertaken within it deal with lacks or unusual potentials found in the individual learner. Does he have a socially observable speech or physical defect? Then let us select behavioral objectives by which he can overcome his deficiency. Does he have an unusual talent which could enhance the welfare of others if developed? Then let us individualize the instructional objectives for its cultivation. It is important to note that while objectives supporting a supplementary function are usually centered in the individual, they are not for the purpose of furthering *individualism,* i.e., his own private interests. Rather, the development of an individual's talents is undertaken together with helping him recognize his responsibility for using these talents in behalf of the welfare of others, *individuality.* Although this supplementary function of the school assumes that it is good to stress individuality but not individualism, supplementary objectives which are remedial in nature are predicated on the ideal that all should have an equal starting place in life. Parenthetically, it should be said that if a society seriously expects to give all an equal starting point, it must control environmental factors such as food and affection during the most formative period of life, i.e., prenatal to age five.

3. *Exploration.* There are many objectives reflecting the desire that the learner be aware of a wide range of opportunities which exist both in and out of school. Unless the learner acquires outcomes associated with the introduction to a variety of content fields and activities, he may make educational (recreational, vocational, instructional, etc.) choices which are not in keeping with his talents. The trend in the school, however, is to limit exploration to those areas which the teacher believes to be "growth producing," i.e., activities which enable one to enter more fully into his environment, as opposed to those which are immediately pleasurable but do not change behavior.

4. *Specialization.* Specialization, the attainment of high-level academic or vocational proficiency, has usually come late in school life, if at all. In view of the increased clamor for excellence in particular fields and the desire for economy in the use of school time, it is expected that teachers will state objectives calling for the learner's ability to perform in accordance with the standards of, say, the mathematician, historian, or master stenographer.

5. *Hidden Functions.* Daily teachers face pressures from those who would have the school serve private ends. Attempts to capture the

school for special interests are increasing. An example of an unstated objective illustrating a latent function would be: she (the learner in the class in homemaking) will not be satisfied as a homemaker without the latest product—refrigerator, stove, or other material possession. This latent objective is, of course, pointed toward the development of consumer demand.

A supervisor performs a valuable service when he makes latent functions explicit so that they can be considered alternatives and their consequences seen in terms of their effect upon recognized and expressed functions of the school. In considering whether an unstated objective should be accepted, supervisors should ask, "How will it help the learner choose among possible actions, perceive new relationships, and be more sensitive to factors which hinder attainment of the goals valued by our society?

SOCIAL CONDITIONS: A PRIMARY SOURCE IN ASCERTAINING APPROPRIATE OBJECTIVES

Critics have always protested the way objectives of the schools have lagged behind the actualities of life in society. For many, the content of the curriculum should be oriented to the demands of the present or to a speculated future. Often their efforts have been successful. During the war years, the vocational skills necessary to production of materials for defense received emphasis. In times of depression and change toward collective goals, outcomes were in terms of the learner's ability to participate in group deliberation and persuasion. Currently, demands for those who can attack problems with abstract models are influencing the selection of expected learnings at both elementary and secondary school levels. Instead of emphasizing concrete applications of mathematics, for instance, possession of a view of the structure of mathematics is given precedence. The development of mathematical concepts is receiving more attention than the skills of operations.

Commencing in 1918 and continuing until the present, "activity analysis" has been a means of determining curriculum objectives.[7] One way of making such an analysis is to look at the community with respect to its health, leisure time, ethics, home membership, citizenship, and other categories important to a changing social order. Teachers are then asked to see what objectives would help fill these needs. This approach is appropriate when the content of the school is not relevant to the realities of life and when other agencies are not available for meeting new de-

[7] Franklin Bobbitt, *The Curriculum,* Houghton Mifflin Company, Boston, 1918, p. 42.

mands. Today, however, the responsibility of many aspects of problems like leisure time and health is shared among many other institutions, and the school is increasingly confining its obligations to the intellectual aspects of these problems—to those tasks which the school can discharge because it possesses the required means.

Studies are also made of the ways people fulfill their roles as citizens and employees. Data from these studies are used to suggest what should be taught. Limitations of this approach are seen when one recalls that current roles may be outdated by the time pupils are expected to fulfill them. Basing objectives on the limited roles of those in a particular community is miseducative in a society where pupils do not live out their lives in the same or similar community. Further, there is the philosophical position that practices current in a community should not set the standard. The teacher as a vicar should encourage pupils to fulfill ideals rather than follow existing practices. If, for instance, pupils from one side of the tracks have always gone into immediate employment rather than advanced schooling, it might be better for the school to foster objectives aimed at upsetting the predicted trend. This could be justified on the premise that it is the school's job to open doors rather than to preserve the *status quo*.

Although community analysis is a poor single source of data for objectives, it is most valuable in revealing learning opportunities. Analyses of community situations suggest ways pupils might apply the theoretical systems which the school is teaching. While the community is an excellent laboratory for instruction, the activity itself must be second to the outcomes sought from instruction. It is not so important, for example, that pupils succeed in bringing about better traffic conditions as a result of their survey and petitions. It is important that the survey result in the pupils' being able to define, explain, and illustrate the real nature of power as well as the skills for effecting social change.

Social scientists have suggested some measuring rods of the good culture which may be helpful to the supervisor as he seeks implications for instructional objectives from social conditions.

1. How will attainment of the objective further subgroup communication? Will it relieve individuals with different interests from the waste of negative struggle, conferring upon them the positive understanding and common experience necessary for the climate which permits individuality? Does it lead to acceptance of the American canons of tolerance and does it call for illustrating the procedures for conduct of life in a multivalue society?

2. Will the objective help the learner reach aspirations rather than

merely foster aspirations without providing means? The dangling of tantalizing prizes, such as the power of understanding, status position, wealth, grades, while closing off pathways to attainment is the way to create rebels and cynics. Enabling objectives must accompany those of a long-range nature. Consistency between the two is a necessity. Ends and means should agree with each other. There is, for example, little likelihood that learners will attain the skills of critical thinking for use in social situations when schools forbid treatment of controversial issues.

3. How will the objective help the learner effect a smooth transition from childhood to adulthood? Although ability to deal with developmental tasks, like coming to terms with one's body, relating to members of the opposite sex, and achieving economic independence, has been recommended as an important outcome for learners, schools have not been quick to build a curriculum upon such a basis. Consideration of this guideline by the social scientists might mean fewer instances of students being restricted in their opportunities to discharge responsibility of adulthood until graduation day and then being abruptly expected to perform as adults.

4. How will the objective help the learner adjust to the tempo of change? The teacher, who has faced more change in his lifetime than the changes faced by several generations of his forebears, recognizes the importance of this criterion for personal and social adjustment. Too often, objectives have helped the learner learn about the known, a known which later turns out to be less certain than it was supposed to be. Therefore, it is currently fashionable to say that in a world of change, teachers should select objectives by which the learner evidences ability to use a method of discovery. This method involves attitudes such as the habit of suspended judgment and recognition of the *probability* of truth and the tentative nature of explanation. It also includes the technique of inquiry in which the learner (1) uses formal patterns or mental structures in new situations and (2) invents new patterns or models for dealing with existing difficulties.

Seldom have supervisors considered other alternative kinds of objectives to meet the problems brought by maladjustment of persons to change in the material bases of the society: (1) objectives which will enable the learner and others eventually to slow down the technical pursuits responsible for the predicament arising from a conflict between material conditions and lagging values and (2) objectives which instead of emphasizing the *answers* to perennial questions help the learner find stability in change by recognizing universals in *questions* dealing with such ultimates as vocation, life, and death.

SUBJECT MATTER: A SECOND ESSENTIAL ELEMENT
IN ASCERTAINING AN OBJECTIVE

Definition

Subject matter and content are interchangeable terms. They stand for
the thoughts and behaviors which are carried from generation to generation. The meanings of words and symbols, statements of principles,
rules of conduct, as well as skills, constitute subject matter. Events and
objects are not subject matter, but their interpretations are. So, too, are
the cultural modes of thought or the processes by which the interpretations are formed. It is the business of the supervisor to select from among
vast cultural resources subject matter which is consistent with the role
of the school and to make this subject matter meaningful to the learner,
i.e., help him find it "a tool to do something with."

Subject Matter Drawn from Personal Experience

In selecting subject matter, the supervisor may draw from folklore,
common sense, or wisdom derived from his own experience. It is likely,
however, that this kind of information will reflect tradition and lack a
built-in method of self-criticism. The danger of obsolescence is especially
acute under such circumstances.

Subject Matter Derived from the Specialist

The supervisor may, on the other hand, go to the master of a discipline and ask, "What subject matter in your field will help the learner
choose among possible actions? Take more of his environment into
account? Perceive new relationships?" There are at least two ways the
scholar may respond. First, he may review his discipline, including the
outcomes from recent research, and indicate the contributions or conclusions the discipline offers to the education of all citizens. The physical
geographer, for instance, might answer, "Earth movements of rotation
and revolution are basic to understanding climate and time; rotation of
the earth on its axis is a measure of time and causes night and day; sea-
sons are caused by a combination of revolutions, inclinations, and paral-
lelism of the axis." The political scientist might say, "In organizing government, it is essential to endow rulers with power and make provision
for holding them responsible for its use." It is not anticipated, of course,
that generalizations like these from the disciplines will be taught per se,
but that they will become the content aspect of objectives, offering direction to instruction. From these generalizations, subgeneralizations, concepts, and factual data will be incorporated into a sequence of learning

opportunities designed to make the terms meaningful to the student.

Second, the scholar within a discipline may feel that any "canned" notions given to the learner are limited and that these facts cannot be treated as self-existing "givens." In science especially, the scholar may say, "Place more emphasis upon method or upon a systematic way of viewing situations." After all, it is method, including a set of processes, standards of performance, and ways of analyzing and testing solutions, which constitutes a discipline. The power of a discipline to increase the mental ability of the learner lies in its method rather than in its substantive aspects or formal content. Following this advice, the supervisor will then select from the discipline a kind of subject matter which relates to the way one trained in a field tries to subjugate or accept nature—what the specialist observes, the way he frames his questions, the concepts he draws upon for, say, adoration, explanation, or prediction, and, especially, the way he decides whether his performance and conclusions are sound. In transmitting this kind of knowledge to the pupil, the teacher, in turn, must afford an opportunity for the learner to challenge the truth of existing rules and laws and to engage in inquiry, formulating hypotheses about phenomena which the learner has handled, seen, heard, and puzzled over. The learner will help define the alternatives and examine views in light of supporting evidence which he himself collects. But in testing his hypotheses, he will be armed with the belief that there is a relationship or regularity to be found, for attitude, too, is an ingredient of a discipline.

Let it be remembered, however, that method requires knowledge of the principles and conclusions as well as awareness of the structures by which these principles are organized (formal content). Formulation of a hypothesis to solve a problem will, for instance, require understanding of certain vocabulary or key principles with which to conceptualize the problem and to plan an attack upon it. In other words, method as content is not sufficient; formal content is also necessary: "We think topics and subjects, not thoughts." [8]

Considerations before Confronting the Specialist

Before turning to the scholar for advice about the selection of content, the supervisor has to be clear about his own expectations of how the subject matter is to serve the learner. First, the supervisor may be interested in furthering communication between the specialist and the public. He may, for instance, expect that learners will be able to understand the

[8] John Dewey, *Philosophy and Civilization,* G. P. Putnam's Sons, New York, 1931, p. 261.

writings of the specialist which appear as general articles in magazines and books to be read by those who are outside the scholar's community of discourse. He might desire learners to be familiar enough with a discipline to support the efforts of the specialist in the field because they (1) recognize the discipline's value as a human activity, (2) can define its domain of interest and authority, and (3) are able to compare its rules for asserting "truth" with the canons of other disciplines.

Although it is unlikely that the supervisor will expect learners to be experts in a field as a result of common schooling, he may want to equip them with the thinking patterns of several disciplines, so that they can raise questions important in their everyday life and be able to get at the answers.

Second, if the supervisor believes that learners should be equipped with the power to add to knowledge in a field, he should make this known to the specialist. It may be desirable that learners be able to discover new facts and relate them to a discipline's particular scheme for classifying and ordering events, facts, laws, or theories. If so, it will be necessary to go beyond the selection of conclusions and include the grounds upon which these conclusions rest and the reason they were selected as relevant in the first place.

The New Subject-Matter Approach

There is much evidence that teachers at all levels are being urged to help learners acquire an understanding of the way specialists of a discipline make knowledge, i.e., that learners understand, for example, how a physicist makes physics and a poet makes poetry. Foshay's "modest proposal" for the improvement of instruction carries an illustration of this new approach:[9]

Let us consider an illustration of how the approach works, in the field of history. It is eleven o'clock in the morning. The date is March 13, 1961, and the teacher has proceeded in American History to the immediate post-Civil War period. I want to suggest what he would do. He would begin—if he had not already done so—by remembering what history is. History is a disciplined way of confronting the past. It deals with periods, within a chronology. It seeks consistencies within these periods, and generalizations about them. The historian constantly deals with ambiguities—with the haunting knowledge that the events he studies can never be known directly—only the records that happen to remain of these events. The historian feels his responsibility to deal with the record accurately, fully, and in a way that honestly reflects

[9] Arthur W. Foshay, "A Modest Proposal," *Educational Leadership,* vol. 18, no. 8, pp. 511–512, May, 1961.

the point of view he has chosen to adopt. He knows his discipline as being in part an art, in part a science; he acknowledges that aesthetic judgment plays a significant part in his decisions as historian. History, he knows, does not exist apart from the historian's interpretation of it.

Our teacher, I say, remembers these things. Now, what does he do about the post-Civil War period? If he wishes to pursue the ideal of intellectual excellence that is represented by an attempt to study the disciplines directly, he carries the children to a confrontation of the historian's problem. He asks of the children, that is, in the Progressive tradition, that they be producers of knowledge, not mere passive consumers of it. He raises with them the question, therefore, "What kinds of events after Lincoln would be most worth knowing?" (Does this seem too advanced? You should see how children handle it!) "Now," he goes on, "how can we discover what these events were?" (We can read, ask, search, tell one another.) "What do historians say they were?" (Not one historian—several, for not all historians choose to deal with the same events, and the sooner we understand this, the more liberated we are from a naive view of our past and of the historian's place in understanding it.) "What are the principal ways the period has been interpreted by the historians?" "Do you, as a student, think of other ways?" "What information do you think the historians might include that they appear to have omitted?" "Why do you suppose they omitted this information? Because they couldn't find it? Because it didn't fit with their interpretation?"

This is how a teacher might conceive of his work in teaching history, if he meant to pursue the idea that the discipline of history might be confronted directly.

Priorities among Disciplines

The notion that certain studies more than others are best adapted to developing the intellectual and spiritual powers of the individual dies hard. Yet, a particular discipline does not of itself make a man wise nor permit him to exercise good judgment in areas outside the specific field. There is no assurance that because a physical scientist has acquired the thought processes for appropriate behavior in his own peculiar field, he will contribute to the solutions of problems which are, say, essentially political or religious in nature. No subject matter is inherently intellectual or spiritual. As Dewey says, "Any subject, from Greek to cooking, and from drawing to mathematics, is intellectual, if intellectual at all, not in its fixed inner structure, but in its function—in its power to start and direct significant inquiry and reflection." [10]

[10] John Dewey, *How We Think,* D. C. Heath and Company, Boston, 1933, pp. 46–47.

The Supervisor and the Fields of Knowledge

We have said that the supervisor will find organized subject matter one of the most important sources of objectives. As a repository of knowledge, the disciplines offer arrangements of schemes and processes with which to solve practical problems and extend knowledge. It is also assumed that the supervisor who possesses *knowledge about* the logically organized subjects will be better able to maintain balance in the curriculum because he recognizes the virtues of each. Further, the supervisor with universal wisdom, "pansophy," should be able to communicate with those teaching in particular fields, for he will be familiar with their orientation. How, then, does a supervisor attain such a vision of knowledge? In the seventeenth century, Comenius gave an answer: "If we know the fundamental conceptions and the modes of their differentiation, we shall know all things." [11] Modern educational philosophers like Phenix[12] and Broudy[13] have continued to show how it is possible for the supervisor to gain knowledge about knowledge by which he can identify the key concepts, facts, and principles of a number of disciplines and master these ideas to the point that he can use them to explain the basic continuities and contrasts among subject-matter fields.

The supervisor will find it helpful to analyze disciplines in terms of elements like the following:

1. *The sources used in different fields for the discovery and validation of knowledge.* The supervisor will, for instance, be certain to notice that mathematics may be derived and validated by reason. He will recognize that valid conclusions in mathematics are rigorously drawn from basic assumptions, assumptions which themselves have no absolute validity and do not necessarily need to be confirmed in the everyday world. Because he can see that a logically consistent system of mathematics is timeless and not subject to improvement, the supervisor will recognize that the demand for "new content" in mathematics is in response to social conditions rather than errors in earlier mathematical thought. On the other hand, the supervisor will see how science requires *the direct appeal to nature* through experiment and objective observation of predicted consequences in order to obtain its truths. He will also find that unlike mathematics, the new scientific truth is not taken as

[11] M. W. Keatinge (trans.), *The Great Didactic of John Amos Comenius,* Adam and Charles Black, London, 1896, p. 34.

[12] Philip H. Phenix, "Key Concepts and the Crisis in Learning," *Teachers College Record,* vol. 58, no. 3, p. 137, December, 1956.

[13] Harry S. Broudy, *Building a Philosophy of Education,* Prentice-Hall, Inc., Englewood Cliffs, N.J., 1954.

final but as hypothetical. As he looks into the humanities, i.e., art, literature, religion, the supervisor will notice the importance of the person's
own *subjectivity* and *intuition* in the making of esthetic judgments and
find that *revelation* is necessary in attaining knowledge from the divine.

2. *The kinds of objects, data, and systems of organization of importance to a discipline.* The importance of particular entities to a field
suggests a basis for ordering the curriculum. Events in history, places in
geography, molecules in chemistry are examples of entities associated
with certain fields. The supervisor who knows the scheme by which
these parts of a structure are arranged for efficient storage, application,
and extension should be better able to help teachers arrange conditions
by which the entities take their place in a larger system, thereby taking on
greater value and meaning. Examples are seen in the two fields, history and grammar. In history, the schemes are aimed at interpretation
and therefore attempt to relate events around such topics as (1) political
forces and movement, (2) wars, (3) conflict among social beliefs, (4)
institutions, or (5) individual persons. Grammar as a system for noting,
classifying, and explaining distinctions in the pattern of language gives
increased significance to words by relating them to such factors as form,
order, and meaning.

In making his philosophical analysis of subject matter, the supervisor
will seek the theoretical statements or concepts which are necessary for
formulating questions in inquiry. As schools move from the transmission
of general information and prescriptions which are static in time toward
the teaching of statements which attempt to explain and predict, there
will be fewer objectives, and the aspects of content included in these objectives will be the central concepts of the discipline. Cases in point are
the modern school programs in (1) mathematics, whose cornerstones are
the concepts of set, function, and logical thinking and (2) physical science, which features the powerful ideas of time, distance, motion, measurement, and atomic structure of matter.

A concluding illustration will point out the desirability of the supervisor's frequent examination of a field in light of the philosophical position which is to receive emphasis in the school and the importance of
selecting a limited number of inclusive objectives. Let us take as an example the dimensions of literature. Teachers have reflected many of the
different ways of conceptualizing literature. Some have seen it as a mechanical matter of form, a fine art, or an imaginative interpretation of
human experience. To some learners, it has been a source of amusement,
curious information, or answers to the momentous riddle of personal
identification. At one time, teachers regarded it as a science in which
the language and process of literary criticism, history, and versification

were essential entities. Paralleling this emphasis pupils were assumed to have learned to appreciate literature when they demonstrated their saturation with information about specific authors, literary periods, and types of literature. At another time, the various forms of literary expression were used as handmaidens to factual sociological, psychological, and historical studies as well as personal problem-solving activities. As such, literary selections were expected to contribute to the objectives by stimulating an emotional feeling toward the situations under study. Currently, there are signs that the schools are regarding literature as a vehicle for helping pupils feel and reflect upon what it means to be a human being. In other words, the religious dimension in literature is becoming paramount. Literature is being used to raise crucial questions about the meaning of life and death, the nature and destiny of the human person and society, as well as the basis for our values. This point of view is not new; it has underlain age-old guidelines for selecting literary content: (1) that which has been most important to those who have been most influential in developing civilization; (2) that which raises ideas of permanent and universal concern, like friendship, family, conquest of self and nature.

To the extent that the religious dimension becomes central and schools have responsibility for knowledge about literature, teachers themselves will find it helpful to possess a unifying principle derived from a philosophical view of knowledge. One such principle is that the value of literature is not in conveying a new piece of information but in directing the whole focus of one's imagination toward a particular aspect of life in which new possibilities are created. Accordingly, literary statements are not seen as statements of fact but as springboards for the individual in drawing his inspiration and reaching a unique conclusion. The great sentences of literature "are not definite; they are left vague; that makes them all the more tremendous." [14] In keeping with this idea, the learner will understand that when he reads literature, he will not gain factual knowledge because the content is not exactly true, but that he might acquire a passionate longing to know the meanings to which literary expressions point.

THE LEARNER AS A SOURCE
OF INSTRUCTIONAL OBJECTIVES

Inspection of a pupil's cumulative folder could reveal (1) anecdotal accounts which imply his need for approval, (2) analysis of test results

---

[14] Gilbert Murray, "Literature as Revelation," *Tradition and Progress,* George Allen & Unwin, Ltd., London, 1922, p. 131.

which show gaps in fundamental skills and understandings, and (3) descriptions of living conditions which are detrimental to his health and his attitude toward school. Observations and interviews with the pupil may reveal interests which warrant encouragement and deliberate development. If the school controls or can gain control of the variables which will fulfill the objectives suggested by such study of the learner, it probably should do so. Certainly it should—if these objectives can be undertaken without detriment to other pupils and other priorities among instructional responsibilities. Special guidance services and arrangement for discharging supplementary, exploratory, and other functions testify to the school's good faith in attempting to (1) change those behavior patterns of the learner which keep him from sharing in the values of society and (2) enable him to make new contributions, new inventions, and to stake out new paths in keeping with his right to individuality. In order for desirable practices in behalf of the individual learner to continue, we must reward supervisors who (1) establish the means by which pertinent data about the learner can become available and (2) make it possible for teachers to implement objectives derived from analysis of these data.

It is a cardinal tenet of those responsible for vision in the development of instructional objectives that the learner be considered as an end in his own right—his welfare to be considered as well as the demands of society and subject matter. This premise differs from the belief that social or subject-matter ends should first be established and the learner studied primarily for the purpose of finding the best way for manipulating him and the classroom situation to the predetermined ends. Conversely, instructional objectives in behalf of the learner must also be formulated with regard to society, subject matter, and the role of the school.

Supervisors and teachers at times talk past each other because of the term *needs*. When some speak of the "needs of the learner," they refer to psychological and physiological needs, i.e., need for affection, need for activity, etc. Others use these same terms in the sense that the learner had better match up to a normative standard of behavior if he expects to progress both in and out of school.

There are implications for teaching from a vast number of studies which generalize both kinds of needs. Much more is known about personality, emotional problems of learners, and the demands of the social context upon learners than we have been able to act upon. However, just because these needs exist does not mean the teacher should respond. The supervisor should help teachers to separate from scientific studies those implications for instructional objectives which are relevant to the school. It is probably desirable for a teacher, for instance, to know the reasons underlying many of the personal difficulties which a learner faces. But the teacher is not a therapist and must deal with the learner in a manner consistent with schooling rather than, say, psychopathology. Usually, the psychological and sociological factors affecting the learner have been taken into account, so far as the teacher is concerned, as means to the attainment of prior instructional objectives rather than as ends peripheral to the teacher's area of expertness. Knowledge of child growth and development will, of course, be useful both in arranging environments consistent with instructional goals and in reducing the number of sociopsychological problems aggravated by miseducative instructional methods.

Objectives Not Valid if They Cannot Be Reached

Source materials on the learning process are available to help the supervisor decide whether a particular outcome is likely to be attained by learners with given characteristics. It is surprising to note, however, the number of objectives which are inconsistent with experimental evidence. Teachers continue to propose unrealistic changes in attitude, cognitive processes, "creativity," and physical growth in disregard of the findings about the variables which must be controlled if these changes are to occur. It is equally true that many falsely assume that given objectives can be attained only by learners who exceed a particular chronological or mental age. On the basis of research findings, for example, many schools changed the placement of the teaching of algebraic structure from the ninth to the tenth grade. This shift was undertaken without sufficient attention to the question whether the younger pupils might have effectively acquired the desired outcomes earlier if the method had been revised. In an article on "What Is Coming in Elementary Mathematics," Rosenbloom[15] reports how altered instruction makes possible the successful teaching of formal logic, laws of number system, number theory, and the like to both bright and retarded children in the elementary school. Current experiments involving different conditions of learning are causing supervisors to take another look at what is possible and economical to teach. Economical considerations include the amount of effort required to reach the objective, undesirable by-products, the likelihood of the learner's retaining what is taught, the immediate usefulness of the objectives to the learner, and the importance of the learning as a prerequisite to subsequent experiences. Fortunately, there seems to be a shift in procedures for making decisions about what *can* be taught. De-

[15] Paul C. Rosenbloom, "What Is Coming in Elementary Mathematics," *Educational Leadership,* vol. 18, no. 2, pp. 96–100, November, 1960.

cisions derived from procedures resting on opinion are giving way to those which entail controlled experimentation, specifying detailed conditions of the inquiry and relevant characteristics of the learners involved.

CRITERIA FOR SELECTION OF DESIRABLE CONDITIONS FOR ATTAINMENT OF OBJECTIVES

Content and behavior as objectives are only of worth when they become manifest in the lives of individual pupils. A linkage must be forged between the objective and the learner. Examples of linkage points or contacts are questions, stories, assignments, discussions, projects, field trips, maps, films, readings, demonstrations—all the numerous activities, objects, processes, or learning opportunities of the classroom which constitute attempts to help the learner attain instructional objectives. Success in teaching depends, in a large part, upon the wisdom shown in selecting the contacts. It also depends upon the manner in which these contacts are ordered. At the present time we have barely begun to understand the basis for selecting and arranging good contacts. We have, however, a number of leads derived from experimental studies of learning and the principles of teaching given by masters of the art throughout history.

In reviewing the following criteria for successful interaction between objectives and pupils, the reader is cautioned that these principles may change.

1. *Select contacts which are likely to bring forth a particular response from the learner.* We believe that one learns the responses he makes. One does not teach by talking or, at least, the pupil does not learn merely because the teacher expresses himself. Unless he reacts to the teacher's presentation, the pupil is not learning. Learning takes place not so much because of what the teacher says or does, but because of what the pupil can be led to want, notice, think, and do. Therefore, the teacher must be clear about the kind and quality of responses the contact should elicit and the way of initiating these responses. Although many responses can be of a covert, rather than overt nature, the latter is preferred because it gives the teacher an indication of the effectiveness of the contact, allowing him to confirm the appropriateness of the response and suggesting next steps. Although there is room for argument as to whether one should ever be allowed to make errors in learning, the general principle is that the learner should meet contacts which will not lead him astray.

Before initiating any action in the classroom, the teacher might ask questions such as these: What skills and understandings are prerequisite to the response I am seeking? Is the learner familiar with the terms and

illustrations necessary for appreciating the contacts I propose to introduce? What are his likely predispositions to them? What has the learner
found satisfying in the past that he can use to effect his identification
with the new instructional values to be presented? What activities,
events, objects, problems are of importance in the learner's present life
and also relevant to the content and behavior sought? Is it possible to
bring, for instance, a greater intensity to the instructional situation by
associating it with, say, the values of the learner's peer group or family?
What would be likely to further his desirable emotional attitudes toward
the task? Can a contact be presented which will cause the learner to see
that his present behavior is inadequate for attaining something he wants?
How can his perplexity be increased without increasing his personal level
of emotional stress that hinders learning?

2. *Select contacts which give the learner opportunity to practice using
the behavior and subject matter of the objective.* Again, assuming that
a pupil learns what he does, it becomes essential that the outcomes
sought should be part of the instructional process. If an objective of a
teacher calls for the ability to compare and contrast interpretations of
history, the learner must be given a chance to engage in this behavior at
some point. A contact by which pupils are led to compare Beard's interpretation of the Constitution with Schlesinger's would be an illustration
of this principle.

3. *Contacts must be satisfying to the learner.* Most psychologists believe that one is likely to continue to make those responses for which he
has been rewarded or reinforced. The old adage, "Nothing succeeds like
success," holds true in the use of instructional contacts. Children have
miseducative experiences when they reach their threshold of frustration
and withdraw from association with the instructional opportunities and
the outcomes to which these contacts lead. Tolerance for frustration can
be increased. But one of the best ways to help a learner develop tenacity
in the face of obstacles is to give him much success in the early stages of
his learning.

Most teachers will accept the desirability of rewarding contacts but
they have some difficulty in deciding what constitutes reward to the
particular learner. Tangible tokens—grades, comments on papers, and
orally saying "right"—may be rewarding to some, especially if the
learner can exchange these tokens for the approval and affection of
others—parents, peers, and teacher. The satisfaction of "fitting the
puzzle together" will be enough for many learners, and the power which
comes from the ability to use in new situations that which has been
taught carries its own reward for most learners. Ideally, the learner will

come to reinforce his own behavior and judge what he is doing if he first acquires the conscience and ability to judge.

4. *Present contacts so that they will evoke the relevant response.* We have mentioned the importance of the learner's being successful. How, then, can we ensure success? The answer seems to be in guiding the learner's responses by helping him make correct responses and see the point of his lessons. In addition to letting him know the standards of desired behavior, he must be given prompts and cues, examples and illustrations in which the teacher calls attention to similarities and differences. As learning proceeds, however, the learner must be weaned from the liberal aid provided at the start so that he can make the correct response without help. This means that soon after the learner has learned the response, he should be presented with situations in which the response is appropriate but cues to how to respond are few.

5. *Contacts must lead to the relating of ideas.* We have said that schools are responsible for helping pupils establish relations between things and ideas in the environment—not merely concerned with events or things in themselves. Initial contacts are likely to represent specific situations or activities with which the learner has had some previous acquaintance. But it is not enough merely to reiterate his present status of knowledge. He might, therefore, be helped to see the familiar event in a new way. In any case, there is no successful teaching unless the learner is learning a new response. Also, the teacher must do more than arrange novel, vivid, and exciting contacts. With the possible exception of those "consummations" associated with the best of art and instances of unforgettable human relations which are sufficient unto themselves, activity within the school is a means rather than an end. Events, facts, activities, and the like, which are correlated with other events, facts, and activities by a common system or scheme of interpretation affect rational conduct. To this end, pupils first should be given the opportunity to work with numerous and varied tangible contacts. Next, they should be helped to abstract the common element and find an appropriate verbal concept or generalization for classifying or explaining the contact. Finally, they should have many opportunities for testing the usefulness of this abstraction in interpreting, explaining, and predicting other different concrete events and situations. By encouraging the learners to seek contacts which illustrate the principles taught, the teacher may help them develop a sensitivity to new applications of theoretical knowledge.

AN ORGANIZATIONAL FRAMEWORK

We believe that before any instruction can be effective there needs to be a plan for ordering contacts so that they culminate in the objectives sought. Two sources for guiding the supervisor in developing such a plan are (1) a rationale for attacking problems in developing curriculum and planning instruction[16] and (2) the results of experimentation in the ordering of contacts as reported by those working with programmed learning.[17]

Sequence and Integration

Essentially any plan for instructional organization must give attention to the problems of sequence and integration. Sequence is the provision for a cumulative development of an important skill, concept, or value. A teacher must provide for sequence in his classroom planning; a school system must also arrange for the recurrence of important elements and for the extension in meanings as the learner advances through the program. The California State Central Committee on Social Studies, for instance, has selected a number of key terms, such as interdependence, which are to be strands of emphasis throughout the social studies program, kindergarten through grade fourteen. Activities in the kindergarten, which usually center about the child's immediate environment of home, school, and neighborhood, lead to the generalization that interdependence involves interacting positions and roles for various members of the local community (i.e., mother, milkman, grocer). Subsequent contacts in later periods build upon this notion, extending it in depth and breadth until at the junior college level the student is expected to use the term as a tool for the critical analysis of forces affecting society, such as the effect of competing ideologies on the relations among nations and the interaction of forces influencing social change. Another example of sequence might be shown when a teacher arranges his contacts so that a child both reviews his skills of reading and extends them as he progresses from recognition of configurations to context clues, phonetic analysis, and syllabification.

The problem of integration is primarily one of overcoming the charge that schools tend to compartmentalize knowledge into subjects so that

[16] Ralph W. Tyler, *Basic Principles of Curriculum and Instruction,* University of Chicago Press, Chicago, 1950.

[17] A. A. Lumsdaine and Robert Glaser (eds.), *Teaching Machines and Programmed Learning—A Source Book,* National Education Association, Washington, 1960.

the learner cannot see the interrelation of his learnings nor use them in new situations (transfer). The combining of subjects into broad fields, the establishment of problem-solving courses, and the development of instructional units which center upon the logic of a task rather than the logic of a subject mark attempts to answer this criticism. Each of these practices is a shift from the faithful elaboration of a discipline to the breaking down of subject-matter lines. An illustration would be a practice where a teacher helps learners draw upon eight subjects in solving a "social studies" problem and students are both helped to see the connection between the concepts of the historian, sociologist, economist, and others, and encouraged to apply in other situations the key concepts from the various disciplines. Integration sometimes occurs when a school staff jointly plans how the mathematics taught in one classroom can be used in science, shop, and other classes. The argument for integration rests upon the assumptions that the learner can better form a general concept or skill when it is presented in numerous and varied situations, that this increased perceptual structure will enable him to shift key ideas into new patterns, and that the satisfaction of being able to use his knowledge in pursuit of goals other than those inherent in the subject itself is a powerful reinforcement.

Principles for Deciding upon the Placement of Contacts

Granted that certain key elements (that is, skills, attitudes, or concepts relevant to the objectives) are to be extended over a period of time and that suitable contacts are available to serve as the medium for bringing forth derived responses to these elements, how should the contacts be ordered? In answering this question, several principles may be followed. The relative *degree of difficulty* of the content is a customary principle for arrangement. Schools have typically placed the teaching of life science, chemistry, and physics in this respective order on the basis of an assumed level of difficulty. Only recently has the *principle of dependency* been offered as an alternative basis for decision. That is, understanding of life science is dependent upon prior understanding of the nature of chemistry. Accordingly, this view would suggest that schools should first offer physics, then chemistry, and last, life science.

Perhaps certain principles may be more appropriate for particular ends. The *chronological basis* for organizing the teaching of history may have some special merit for those specializing in the field, just as the use of *problems* as categories for organization may be most effective in developing the skills of practical intelligence. The belief that a learner should move from an acquaintance first with *things* then problems, and lastly systems of thought has prevailed in most schools. Like so many other beliefs, this one is being challenged by those who would offer contacts in each of these areas almost simultaneously. Programs are now being arranged, for instance, where contacts for pupils in the primary grades allow experience with (1) the *concrete* use of numbers such as in counting objects, (2) the *intuitive* use of mathematics, such as the idea that a number is not resident in a particular thing, and (3) experiences which involve something of the *laws of the number system* itself, as when the child generalizes the cumulative law as a result of his being helped to discern interacting relationships between numbers.

The psychological assumption that the younger the child is, the less capable he is of logical reasoning along any line continues to dominate most organizational arrangements. Prevailing practice in the arts, for instance, is that the elementary school child should meet contacts in the manner of spontaneous play and expression without much exposure to formal content. On the other hand, because the secondary school student is assumed to be undergoing a period of self-criticism and is, therefore, eager to learn techniques for improvement, some systematic study of the arts can be introduced, while advanced abstract studies are left to the college level.

Conflict over Organization

There are many unresolved questions as to how best to organize for instruction. We should expect to see the use of autoinstructional devices as research tools for determining the factual evidence regarding the most effective principles for organizing subject matter for teaching individuals of a given maturity. However, differences over what should be taught will require other methods for resolving this problem. There are those who argue that the school should organize for integration so that learners are able to solve moral and practical problems of a personal and social nature. Others advocate an organization which tends toward specialization because the proponents value the differentiation found in a particular knowledge as important in itself. Because there are definite advantages to both kinds of organization, the supervisor tries to find a more inclusive position than that held by either the disciplinarian or the functionalist. Bellack has envisioned a program which provides for both practical and theoretical aspects of the learner's development. His plan would involve basic instruction in the three major fields of study—humanities, social sciences, natural sciences—together with a coordinating seminar in which pupils deal with the problem "in the round" and special effort is made to show the intimate relationship between the systematized fields of study as materials from these fields are brought to bear upon a topic.[18] Broudy has a similar view of the curriculum organization, illustrating how the habits of acquiring organized knowledge can be related to the habits and skills for using knowledge in matters of significance to the individual and the social order.[19]

SUMMARY OF METHODOLOGY FOR ATTAINING PERSPECTIVE IN CURRICULUM

We have tried in this chapter to present a framework for conceptualizing the task of curriculum construction and to suggest procedures for effecting the synthesis of knowledge required in deciding what and how to teach. As a curriculum specialist, the supervisor must have a perspective, an inclusive awareness of aspects which are essential in developing a "good" curriculum. The critical aspects we have suggested are summarized in an outline to follow. The reader is reminded, however, that because curriculum construction is itself a dynamic process, it is not possible to capture its true nature in static analysis. Nor can one specify the full effects that interaction of the various aspects have upon each other in particular situations.

A PERSPECTIVE OF CURRICULUM

I. Ascertaining instructional objectives
   A. Supervisor must draw upon knowledge from
      1. The individual learner
         a. That which is revealed by gaps in the learner's understandings, skills, attitudes
         b. The special interests and purposes of the learner which should be cultivated
      2. The subject-matter specialist
         a. Powerful ideas which have wide applicability
         b. Ideas which are not likely to be acquired without formal instruction
      3. Studies of social conditions
         a. Data indicating present and likely future developments (technological, economic, political, religious, and other) which must be taken into account if instruction is to be relevant to the world in which the student lives

[18] Arno A. Bellack, "Selection and Organization of Curriculum Content: An Analysis," *What Shall the High Schools Teach?* 1956 Yearbook, Association for Supervision and Curriculum Development, Washington, 1956, pp. 97–126.
[19] Broudy, *op. cit.*

Note: The evidence from *each of these sources* must be considered in deciding what to teach. If data from any one of the sources are given emphasis to the exclusion of the others, the supervisor will have a distorted perspective of the curriculum, and the curriculum he develops will be warped.

   B. Supervisor must appraise proposed objective suggested by data from the above sources

     1. Likelihood of the objective being attained by particular learners

     Evidence from teaching experience and the behavioral sciences, indicating

      a. Probabilities of learners' acquisition, retention, degree of difficulty in learning, and other related factors

      b. Factors which must be controlled if the objective is to be reached, i.e., cultural influences which prevent desired behavior from occurring

     2. Consistency of objective with normative beliefs of the culture

      a. Values we prize, i.e., objective should not deprive learner of his right to opportunity for development of individuality

      b. Philosophical assumptions about the good man and world, i.e., objective must not imply that learners are incapable of reason and cannot acquire capacity to govern themselves wisely

II. Selecting learning contacts

   A. Supervisor draws implications from data regarding conditions of learning reported by

     1. Behavioral sciences

     Principles of teaching like these: learner must have opportunity to practice the behavior desired and the contact must be rewarding to the learner

     2. Classroom experiments and research in programmed learning

      a. Kinds of outcomes which can be economically brought about by mass media, lecture

      b. Rules for programming, including the importance of avoiding error in learner's response, number and placement of prompts, and others being formulated by experimenters

III. Selecting a pattern of organization

   A. Supervisor develops a plan for ordering contacts. There is a conscious organization for correlating and rationalizing the experiences acquired

1. Providing increasing depth and width of understanding implied in the behavior and content of the objective
   a. Selection of organizational structures for programs, core, activity, subject-matter organization, and their respective inherent approaches to organization, i.e., problem solving, interests of pupils, and a disciplinary scheme for relating facts and principles
2. Providing for sequence and integration as well as opportunities for both acquisition and application of knowledge
   a. Selection of elements for continuous reiteration and extension (threads of continuity), i.e., key concepts, skills, and important principles
   b. Selection of principles by which contacts are to be ordered, i.e., dependency, difficulty, logic, chronology

IV. Evaluation
   A. Supervisor plans for collecting evidence at frequent points in the instructional process. Uses of evaluation are specified; for example, improvement of instruction, guidance of learner, determination of new objectives
      1. Relation between measuring, evaluating, hypothesis testing, and learning is made explicit
         a. The plan states who will participate in the evaluation and how the results are to be used
         b. Valid and reliable criterion measures are made available

A SELECTED BIBLIOGRAPHY

American Educational Research Association: "The Methodology of Educational Research," *Review of Educational Research,* vol. 30, no. 5, The Association, Washington, December, 1960.

Annual Review of Psychology, vols. 1 to 12, 1950–1961, Annual Reviews, Inc., Palo Alto, Calif.

Argyris, Chris: *Personality and Organization,* Harper & Brothers, New York, 1957.

Association for Supervision and Curriculum Development: *Learning More about Learning,* Alexander Frazier (ed.), The Association, Washington, 1959.

————: *Research for Curriculum Improvement,* The Association, Washington, 1957.

————: *What Shall the High Schools Teach?* 1956 Yearbook, The Association, Washington, 1956.

Blau, Peter M.: *The Dynamics of Bureaucracy,* University of Chicago Press, Chicago, 1955.

Coladarci, Arthur P. (ed.): *Educational Psychology: A Book of Readings,* The Dryden Press, Inc., New York, 1955.

Corey, Stephen M.: *Action Research to Improve School Practices,* Bureau of Publications, Teachers College, Columbia University, New York, 1953.

Dewey, John: *Experience and Education,* The Macmillan Company, New York, 1938.

Finney, D. J.: *An Introduction to the Theory of Experimental Design,* University of Chicago Press, Chicago, 1960.

Fisher, Margaret: *Leadership and Intelligence,* Bureau of Publications, Teachers College, Columbia University, New York, 1954.

275

Guilford, J. P.: *Personality,* McGraw-Hill Book Company, Inc., New York, 1959.

————: *Psychometric Methods,* 2d ed., McGraw-Hill Book Company, Inc., New York, 1954.

Herrick, Virgil E., and Ralph Tyler (eds.): *Toward Improved Curriculum Theory,* Supplementary Educational Monograph no. 71, University of Chicago Press, Chicago, 1950.

Hilgard, Ernest R.: *Theories of Learning,* 2d ed., Appleton-Century-Crofts, Inc., New York, 1956.

Hunnicutt, E. W., and William J. Iverson: *Research in the Three R's,* Harper & Brothers, New York, 1958.

Lieberman, Myron: *Education as a Profession,* Prentice-Hall, Inc., Englewood Cliffs, N.J., 1956.

March, James G., and Herbert A. Simon: *Organizations,* John Wiley & Sons, Inc., New York, 1958.

Morsh, Joseph E., and Eleanor W. Wilder: *Identifying the Effective Instructor: A Review of the Quantitative Studies, 1900–1952,* Lackland Air Force Base, Air Force Personnel and Training Research Center, San Antonio, Tex., October, 1954.

National Society for the Study of Education: *In-service Education for Teachers, Supervisors, and Administrators,* The Fifty-sixth Yearbook, part I, University of Chicago Press, Chicago, 1957.

Phenix, Philip H.: *Philosophy of Education,* Henry Holt and Company, Inc., New York, 1958.

Ryans, David G.: *Characteristics of Teachers: Their Description, Comparison, and Appraisal.* American Council on Education, Washington, 1960.

Selznick, Philip: *Leadership in Administration,* Row, Peterson & Company, Evanston, Ill., 1957.

Smith, B. Othanel, William O. Stanley, and J. Harlan Shores: *Fundamentals of Curriculum Development,* World Book Company, Yonkers, N.Y., 1950.

Simon, Herbert A.: *Administrative Behavior: A Study of Decision-making Processes in Administrative Organization,* The Macmillan Company, New York, 1958.

Symonds, Percival M.: *What Education Has to Learn from Psychology,* Bureau of Publications, Teachers College, Columbia University, New York, 1958.

Thelen, Herbert A.: *Dynamics of Groups at Work,* University of Chicago Press, Chicago, 1954.

Travers, Robert M. W.: *An Introduction to Educational Research,* The Macmillan Company, New York, 1959.

Tyler, Ralph W., *Basic Principles of Curriculum and Instruction,* University of Chicago Press, Chicago, 1950.

INDEX

277